A Centuryof Evangelization (1921 - 2021):

American La Salettes in Madagascar

By

Bp. Donald Pelletier, M.S.
&
and Fr. Jack Nuelle, M.S.

Imprimi Potest:

Very Rev. Fr. William Kaliyadan, M.S., Provincial Superior, Missionaries of Our Lady of La Salette, Province of Mary, Mother of the Americas, 915 Maple Avenue, Hartford, CT 06016-2330, USA

Copyright © 175th Anniversary of the La Salette Apparition, September 19, 2021 by Missionaries of Our Lady of La Salette, Province of Mary, Mother of the Americas, 915 Maple Avenue, Hartford, CT 06016-2330, USA. All rights reserved. No part of this book may be reproduced, stored in a retrieval system, or transmitted, in any form or by any means, electronic, mechanical, photocopying, recording or otherwise, without the written permission of La Salette Communications Center, 947 Park Street, Attleboro, MA 02703.

This and other La Salette titles in digital form are available at www.lasalette.org and www. amazon.com.

Scripture texts in this work are taken from the New American Bible with Revised New Testament and Revised Psalms © 1991,1986,1970 Confraternity of Christian Doctrine, Washington, D.C. and are used by permission of the copyright owner. All Rights Reserved. No part of the New American Bible may be reproduced in any form without permission in writing from the copyright owner.

Printed in the United States of America

Editor: Fr. Ron Gagne, M.S.

Book Design & General Formatting: Jack Battersby and Fr. Ron Gagne, M.S.

ISBN: 978-1-946956-45-3

Contents

Preface – Beyond Lemurs and Baobab Trees   1

Introduction   7

Part One — The First La Salette Mission in Madagascar   10

The Vakinankaratra Region   10

Chapter 1 — The First Wave of Pioneering American La Salettes Arrive in Antsirabe   14

Chapter 2 — Fr. Alphonse Coté, M.S., The First to Give His Life   18

Part Two — A Separate Mission on the West Coast   **20**

Chapter 3 — Fr. William Breault, M.S., A Visionary on Mission   21

Chapter 4 — Morondava, A Mission-Building Experience   25

Chapter 5 — Mission Activity Flourishes   30

Chapter 6 – Belo Sur Tsiribihina, A New Mission Endeavor to the North   33

Chapter 7 — Manja, a Further Mission Initiative to the South   38

Chapter 8 – Brother Stephen Levickas, An Unforgettable Missionary Brother   40

Chapter 9 – A New Phase of Mission Activity: Catholic Schools   42

Chapter 10 – The Mission Spirit Grows Strong   47

Chapter 11 – Exodus of (Most) American La Salettes from Morondava   49

Chapter 12 – Fr. Thomas Mansfield, M.S., Remaining in a Garden Watered by Tears   51

Part Three — Apostolic Prefecture (1938-1955)   54

Chapter 13 — Fr. Arthur Le Blanc, M.S., Who Lived the Longest and Won Every Heart   57

Chapter 14 – Fr. Cecil McDonald, M.S., the Master Builder   70

Chapter 15 – Fr. Paul Girouard, M.S., First American Bishop of Morondava   78

Chapter 16 – Faithfully Filling the Gap   89

Part Four – St. Louis Province, 1958-1988   **93**

Chapter 17 – An Overview of the Political History of the Country   96

Chapter 18 – All Missionaries Left Part of Themselves in Madagascar   100

Chapter 19 – Second Wave of Trailblazers, Frs. John Repchick and Joe Silva   105

Chapter 20 – A Closer Look at Fr. John Repchick, M.S.   108

Chapter 21 – Fr. Joe Silva, M.S., God's Use of Creativity   113

Chapter 22 – The Second Wave Continues to Grow   117

Chapter 23 – The Arrival of Fr. Donald Pelletier, M.S.   119

Chapter 24 – Fr. Roland Bernier, M.S., A Deep-Hearted Desire to be a Missionary   122

Chapter 25 – Fr. Henry (Sam) McKay, M.S. Little to Say but Well Said   125

Chapter 26 – From Brother Steve to Brother Larry   127

Chapter 27 – Fr. James Jacobson, M.S., First Mission Procurator   131

Chapter 28 – Fr. Arthur Lueckenotto, M.S., A Man of Solid Dedication   133

Chapter 29 – Fr. Normand Mailloux, M.S., A Visionary   139

Chapter 30 – Valued Missionary Brothers   143

Chapter 31 – Anxieties in Times of Revolution   144

Chapter 32 – Fr. Peter Kohler, M.S., A Missionary Anywhere in the World   146

Chapter 33 – Brother Mark Gallant, M.S., A Multi-Gifted Brother   149

Chapter 34 – Fr. Gerald (Gerry) Biron, M.S. and Fr. Ernest Corriveau, M.S., Missionaries with a World Outlook   151

Chapter 35 – "Déjà Vu" Politics, On a Local Level   154

Chapter 36 – More Personal Experiences   155

Chapter 37 – Lay Catechists, Men and Women   161

Witnessing to God   161

Chapter 38 – The Beautiful Gate   163

Chapter 39 – Fr. Arthur Lueckenotto, M.S., The Perfectionist   166

Chapter 40 – Fr. Joe Shea's Leadership Role   170

Chapter 41 – Fr. John (Jack) Nuelle, M.S., A Friend and Life-Long Missionary   174

Chapter 42 – Nearing Fulfillment of a Mission Mandate   184

Chapter 43 – Fr. Jeremy Morais, M.S., Undaunted Champion of the Poor   186

Chapter 44 – Bishop Donald Pelletier, the Second American Bishop of Morondava   193

Chapter 45 – A Memorable Visit and Relics of a Saint   197

Chapter 46 – Missionaries Pay a Personal Price   198

Chapter 47 – Sent on Mission and Now Passing on the Torch   200

Preface – Beyond Lemurs and Baobab Trees

A dancing "Tsifaka" lemur and a majestic Baobob Tree; photos: Neil Strickland and Bernard Gagnon

Our intent in writing the following pages is not to set forward a complete, official history of La Salette Catholic Mission presence in Morondava, Madagascar. Rather the following pages are simply our memories, along with some preliminary research of the American La Salette Missionaries – of both United States and Canadian citizenship – who labored for many years with much zeal, dedication, and generosity in the Menabe Region of Madagascar. Since these pages contain our memories of persons, places, and times, we are not able to follow a strict chronological sequence. We ask your indulgence when repetitions occur. They have the advantage of allowing you to get better acquainted with specific names which would otherwise be so strange to you.

God willing, a complete history will someday be written wherein the French, Polish, Italian, and Malagasy La Salette Missionaries, ministering side-by-side with lay catechists, will be given proper recognition for their important and powerful contribution in the evangelization of this area. Beginning in 1936, women religious also contributed greatly to evangelization in the fields of education and medicine.

A history of evangelization of the Morondava mission also needs to highlight the vital importance of the laity. They were the first to bring the Good News of Salvation to the area and, in the absence of ordained ministers, to establish small but vibrant Christian communities. Their faith-filled lives authentically witnessed to the essential mission of the laity in the Church. Their strength was the strength of Faith. Their mission was that given by Christ Jesus in the Gospels, a mission embellished and solidified by their dedication to the mandate given by Our Lady of La Salette at the conclusion of her Apparition on September 19, 1846: *"Well, my children, you will make this message known to all my people."*

Our Ministry Spanning a Century

On the 100th anniversary of that Apparition or Our Blessed Mother at La Salette, France, and in recognition of the missionary efforts of the American La Salettes, the Rt. Reverend Thomas J. McDonnell, National Director of The Society for the Propagation of the Faith in New York penned these lines:

> Under the patronage of our Blessed Lady their heroic missionary endeavors have been extended to Africa, South America, distant Madagascar and Burma, and have brought in a rich harvest of souls through the extension of God's Kingdom on earth. To these missionaries, Our Lady of La Salette has been their inspiration as well as their protectress and their mother.

The French Army had invaded the island of Madagascar in December 1894, declared it a colony in 1896, and unified the country under a single colonial government in 1898. With this pacification it became possible for Catholics from the high plateau regions of Antsirabe, Antananarivo, and Fianarantsoa to migrate towards the vast, fertile plains of the West Coast. Having no desire to worship with the Protestants, these lay Catholics readily established their own churches. They did not wait for the presence of priests but organized their communities like the primitive communities of Jerusalem, gathering in homes.

No doubt a complete history of the First evangelization of the West Coast of Madagascar needs to be written. It is an extraordinary story that continues to this day. Telling the complete story will, however, need much more time and research than we have to give. The following pages are meant to be an introduction exclusively limited to the presence of the American La Salettes who worked in the Menabe Region of Madagascar.

As we write these words, it becomes more and more evident that the presence of American La Salette Missionaries is coming to an end. It began on the central High Plateau region in 1921 when two young American La Salettes arrived to strengthen the efforts of the original French La Salette Fathers and Brothers. It continued in a spectacular manner in the Menabe Region in 1928 when other American Missionaries came to help establish residency on the West Coast of Madagascar. It is all the more urgent than ever to leave a memorial of those 100 years of American La Salette presence, specifically of the 93 years on the West Coast – 1928 to 2021. Hopefully someday, when someone writes a complete history of the Catholic Church on the West Coast of Madagascar, these memories will be helpful.

(from left, front) Early La Salette Frs. Arthur Le Blanc, William Breault; (back) Fr. Cecil McDonald and La Salette Oblate Bro. Steve Levickas

(from left) Frs. John Nuelle (co-author), Jeremy Morais, Bishop Donald Pelletier (co-author), and Art Lueckenotto

When I, Donald, arrived in Morondava in 1958 I was graced to live and work with a few of the founders: Bishop Paul Girouard (1898-1964), Fathers Arthur J. Le Blanc (1899-1990) and Cecil McDonald (1897-1972).

And when I, Jack, arrived eight years later, Le Blanc and McDonald were still actively ministering to their beloved people. Today, how we regret that we did not record the experiences of those missionaries! Many diverse religious congregations of men have worked in Madagascar, coming from various countries such as France, the United States, Italy, Holland, Belgium, Switzerland, India, and Brazil; but we, the American La Salette Missionaries, were the lone rangers, striking out and blazing new trails in a quest for souls on the West Coast.

Map of Madagascar

Madagascar is mostly known as the "Great Red Island" due to the permanently reddish tint of its bare earth.

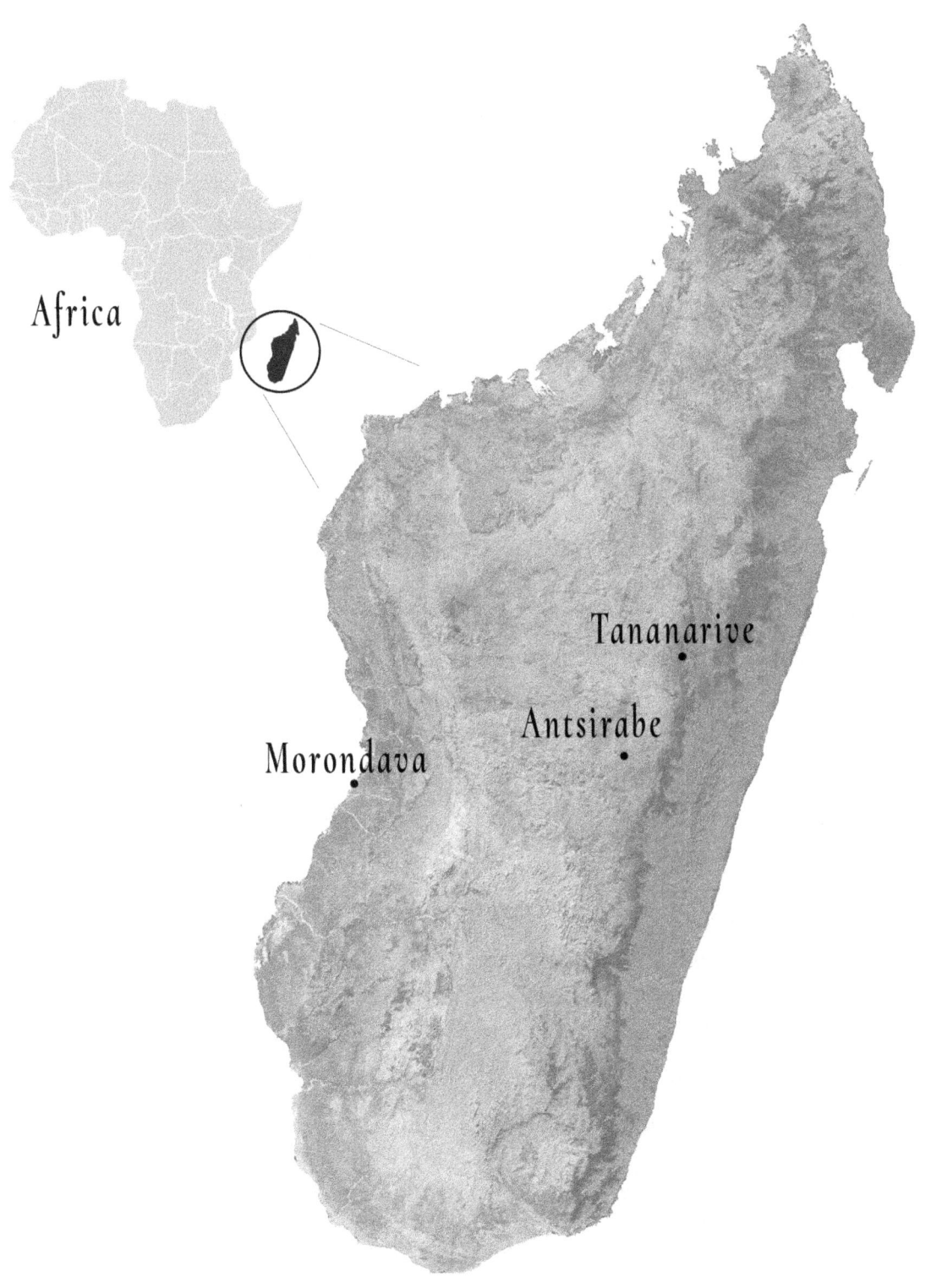

Milestones in the History of the Evangelization of the West Coast Mission —Congregation of the Missionaries of Our Lady of La Salette

1921-1937 — Hartford, Connecticut, U.S.A.

1937-1955 — French Province

1955-1958 — General Administration in Rome

1958-1988 — St. Louis, Missouri Province

1988-1991 — Region of Morondava

1991- today —Province of Madagascar

The Area of Morondava on the West Coast of Madagascar confided to the American La Salettes Ecclesiastical Status of Morondava:

1928-1938 — a Separate Mission

1938-1955 — an Apostolic Prefecture:

   1938-1947 — Joseph Futy, M.S.

   1947-1954 — Etienne Garon, M.S.

1955-to present — as a Diocese:

   1955-1964 — Paul Girouard MS

   1964-1998 — Bernard Ratsimamotoana, M.S.

   1998-2010 — Donald Pelletier, M.S.

2010 – to present — Marie Fabien Raharilamboniaina, O.C.D.
Seeds That Fell in Fertile Soil—
La Salette Missionaries Buried in Madagascar

Alphonse Coté — 1923

Thomas Mansfield — 1937

Paul Girouard — 1964

Cecil McDonald — 1972

Arthur Le Blanc — 1990

American La Salettes of the First Wave Who Later Returned to Minister in the United States:

William Breault, October 1933

Steve Levickas and John Newman, July 1936

Cecil McDonald, Jan 1937 (would then return in 1939)

John Brady and Aloysius Spielman, May 26 1937

Herald Clossey, January 1938

American La Salettes Who Ministered in Various Areas of Madagascar:

1) In Antsirabe (1921 – 1970)

William Breault — 1921-1928

Alphonse Coté — 1921-1923

Aloysius Spielman — 1923-1931

Paul Girouard — 1928-1934

Gerard Langlois — 1965-1970

Gerard Biron — 1965-1970

2) In Morondava (1928 to the present)

First Wave of Americans

William Breault — 1928-1934

Cecil McDonald — 1928-1972

Arthur Le Blanc — 1928-1992

Stephen Levickas — 1928-1936

Aloysius Spielman — 1931-1937

Paul Girouard — 1934-1964

John Henry Newman — 1929-1936

Harold Clossey — 1932-1938

Thomas Mansfield — 1932-1937

John Brady — 1933-1937

Gerard Langlois — 1949-1970

John Berube— 1954-1989

Second Wave of Americans

John Repchick —1956-1984

Joseph Silva— 1956-1982

Henry McKay — 1957-1961

James Hogan — 1957-1958

Roland Bernier — 1958-1978

Joseph Shea — 1958-2007

Donald Pelletier — 1958-20**

Lawrence Deschenes — 1959-1972

James Jacobson — 1960-1965

Arthur Lueckenotto — 1964-2016

Normand Mailloux — 1966-1980

Mark Koenig — 1966-1981

John Nuelle — 1966-1996

Peter Kohler — 1971-1976

Mark Gallant — 1971-1986

Gerald Biron — 1983-1985

Ernest Corriveau — 1983-1984

Jeremy Morais — 1987-20**

3) In Antananarivo (American La Salettes Who worked with Catholic Relief Services, 1961-1966)

John Berube

Jean Denis Roy

Jean Louis Pelissier

Introduction

When one speaks of Morondava or mentions the Menabe Kingdom on the West Coast of Madagascar, one immediately thinks of the many species of friendly, playful lemurs who find their habitat in the dense dry forest of the West Coast; forest with countless, precious species of trees from mahogany to ebony but dominated by impressive, majestic baobab trees. Tourists by the thousands come every year from all over the world to admire and gaze in meditative silence at the grandeur of these massive baobab trees. At sunset, as the last rays of sunshine through their outstretched, umbrella-like branches, these trees take on various shades of purple and grey that leave one speechless.

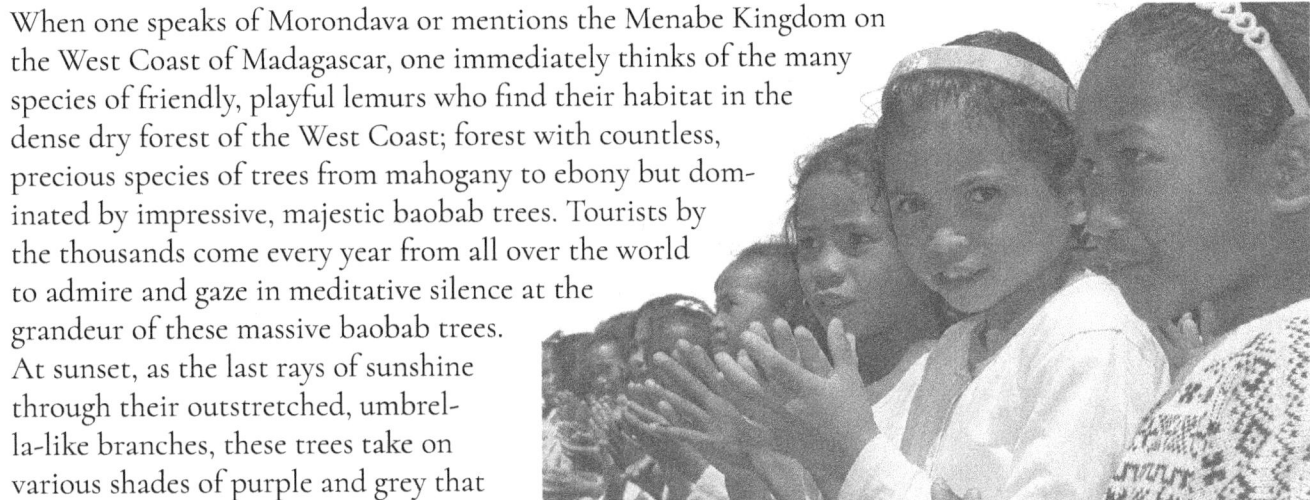

Merina girls of highland Madagascar; photo: Hery Zo Rakotondramanana

Morondava also boasts of miles of pristine beaches, where white sand merges with oncoming tides, filtering into thousands of square miles of mangrove swamps rich with birds and muddy crabs that are a delicacy of the country. Unfortunately, the Chinese have discovered this gift of nature and are presently over-exploiting our fertile and beautiful mangrove swamps. All of this seems to fade when we sit by the beach and allow ourselves to be mystified by some of the most beautiful sunsets in the world. However, sunsets, mangrove swamps, beaches, baobab trees and lemurs could easily distract us from the human reality – the people who live, work, and play on the western coast of Madagascar.

This unknown, distant area of the Great Red Island, as Madagascar is sometimes called, was the mission field that, in 1928, the Propagation of the Faith in Rome confided to the La Salette Missionaries based in Hartford, Connecticut. Three priests and one brother were initially chosen to establish a residence on that western coast, and to bring the light of the Gospel to this faraway land. In May 1928, Fathers William Breault (1894-1974), Cecil McDonald (1897-1972), Arthur Le Blanc (1899-1990) and Brother Stephen Levickas (1889-1965) were the first Catholic missionaries to establish a permanent residence in Morondava.

There is, however, a need to say a few words or at least name those who visited, ventured, explored or prepared a way for this permanent Catholic Mission of Morondava. Shortly after the discovery of Madagascar (1500) by the Portuguese, it seems that a son of Saint Dominic, Father Jao of San Toma, was the first Catholic priest to visit the northern part of the West Coast of Madagascar. Thirty years later two Jesuits, Louis Mariano and Antoine Azevedo, ventured there in view of opening a mission. It never materialized. We would have to wait two centuries (1849) before two French Jesuit Missionaries, Fathers Webber and Neyraguet, would begin exploring the Tsiribihina and Manambolo river areas. Father Neyraguet left a most interesting journal of their adventures, perils, and sufferings, even though their exploratory venture did not succeed in establishing a mission.

The first registered Catholic Baptism occurred in 1890 in Betolapia by Father Chesnay. In 1910, Father Castan, C.M., made a stop-over for a few days in Morondava on his way to France. In 1911 La Salette Fathers François Dantin and Edouard Rostaing visited Miandrivazo in the Betsiriry Valley of the central highlands of Madagascar. In 1914 a military chaplain, Father Moyne Berton, spent six months in Morondava with minimal possibilities for pastoral ministry.

Madagascar at sunset

We can justly affirm that the first missionary priest who came to Morondava with the intent of establishing a mission was Father Fernand Lesecq, S.J., in 1919. After three months of ministry – baptisms, confessions, communions, and marriages – he returned to the High Plateau, but with definite plans to remain in Morondava. He even bought land for the foundation. His Bishop, however, had different plans and kept him in Fianarantsoa.

Another Jesuit priest, Fr. Regis Royon, ventured all the way north to Maintirano. He was the first priest ever to visit that northern town. Much to his amazement, he discovered that already there were six Catholic chapels established in the region by lay people; Maintirano, Antsalova, Tsiandro, Ankavandra, Soaloka, and Ankondromena all had Catholic churches that had never seen a Catholic priest.

During the next nine years, there were two groups coming, at various times, to the area of Morondava – La Salette Missionaries (Breault, Michel, Torre) came from Antsirabe, while Jesuit Missionaries (Trachez, Picavet, Lesecq) came from Ambositra. All those sporadic missionary journeys may seem in human eyes to be unrelated excursions; but viewed in the eyes of faith, they contributed to the permanent foundation in 1928 of the Catholic Mission in the Menabe region of the West Coast.

Lutherans Establish Themselves in Morondava

It must be noted that, where Catholics hesitated and failed to establish a permanent mission, the Norwegian Lutherans succeeded. They founded the first Christian community in the Morondava region. That was in 1876 in an area that is now known as Bethel. Despite persecution and opposition from the Sakalava kings, they managed to remain there, and opened schools and churches. It was a time when Sakalavas ruled the area and migration from other areas had not begun. It is to the credit of these dedicated and faith-filled missionaries that they evangelized and established vibrant Christian communities. They deserve much credit because, with their faith, insight, and courage, they were the first to open the doors of Christianity in the Menabe Kingdom.

When Catholic Missionaries arrived 52 years later, a very friendly and true brotherhood existed between the two missions. As we concentrated our efforts and directed our ministry to the Catholic immigrants from Antsirabe and Ambositra, the Lutherans always had a very vital impact on the Sakalava who are the native people of Menabe.

Over the next ninety years, many others would follow in those pioneer footsteps. While a few of those American missionaries who served in Morondava are still living in the United States, today only two remain in Madagascar. With coordinated efforts, we write the last pages of an impressive and exciting history.

The Seed is Bearing Much Fruit

For many years only two Religious Congregations – the La Salette Missionaries (M.S.) and the Missionary Sisters of the Immaculate Conception (M.I.C.) – ministered to the people of the area now known as the Diocese of Morondava. However today, in 2020, there were twenty-five Religious Congregations of women and ten Religious Congregations of men who minister here, along with a handful of diocesan priests.

Presently, the Cistercian monks from Fianarantsoa are looking into the possibilities of establishing a Trappist monastery in Antsoha, Miandrivazo where they have already acquired twenty acres of land. The seed, firmly planted by zealous La Salette Missionaries beginning in 1928, continues to grow and bear much fruit. There are presently 24 diocesan seminarians in theology and philosophy.

Catholic Relief Services Enters the Picture

From humble beginnings, a total of thirty-one American La Salette Missionaries actively served on that western coast; four were brothers and twenty-seven were priests. Together with John Berube, another two American La Salette Missionaries (Brother Jean Denis Roy and Father Jean Louis Pelissier) were instrumental in introducing to Madagascar in 1963 the Catholic Relief Services (C.R.S.), a relief program of the American Bishops.

Three Malagasy men join hands in front of giant trunk of a Baobob Tree

They worked exclusively on the High Plateau, but the outreach of their programs touched the lives of numerous Christians and non-Christians throughout the island – including the area of Morondava. Today CRS is the best organized and most competent charitable organization in Madagascar with regional and local offices that serve the poor.

Our missionaries also introduced The Christian Foundation for Children and Adults or C.F.C.A. [now known as "Unbound"], a sponsoring organization that helped thousands of Malagasy children obtain an education.

Part One —
The First La Salette Mission in Madagascar

The Vakinankaratra Region

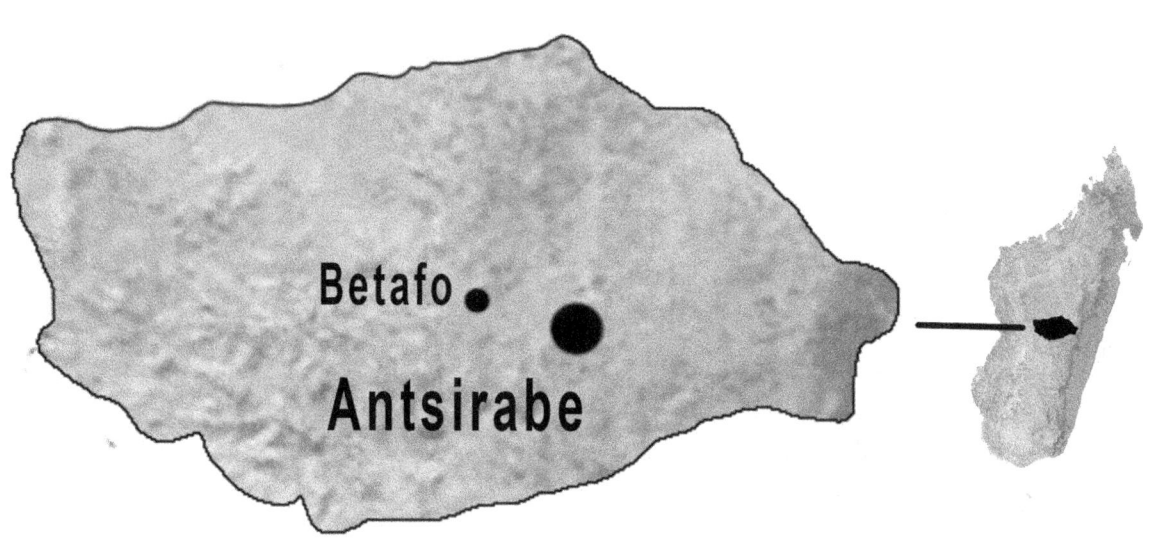

On May 26, 1898 the Missionaries of La Salette in France received a mandate from the Propagation of the Faith in Rome to strengthen the missionary efforts begun by the Jesuits in the Central Vicariate of the island. Their mission was located in the area known as Vakinankaratra. La Salette Missionaries from France would join three other missionary groups ministering in Madagascar: flanking to the immediate North and South within the Central Vicariate were missionaries from the Society of Jesus (Jesuits/S.J.); to the far South (Southern Vicariate) were the missionaries from the Congregation of the Missions (Vincentians/C.M.), and to the far North (Northern Vicariate) were missionaries from the Congregation of the Holy Spirit (Spiritans/S.S.Sp.).

The La Salettes arrived in August 1899, and were given the area of Vakinankaratra where they would work under the jurisdiction of the Bishop of Antananarivo or Tananarive. Their principal residence was in the city of Betafo – which would later be moved to Antsirabe, some fifteen miles away. Four La Salettes – three priests (Fathers François Dantin, Joseph Rutty and Célestin Gachet) and one brother (Brother Auguste Clerc Renaud) – were sent to found this mission. For a few months they worked alongside Jesuit missionaries who had already done wonderful work there for a few years. Slowly a specific La Salette stamp was put on their evangelization, formation of catechists, education of youth and overall Christian culture.

In 1910, the La Salette mission of Vakinankaratra would gain some initial independence when Father Dantin was named Vicar General of this section of the Central Vicariate. In 1912 the Vakinankaratra mission became an Independent Mission territory ("Missio sui juris" or "Independent Mission"). A year later, on May 15, 1913, it became the Apostolic Prefecture of Betafo, with Father Dantin as Apostolic Prefect.

World War I Begins and the First La Salette Bishop

World War I brought hard times for France. In fact, many La Salette Fathers, Brothers, Scholastics and Novices were inducted into the French army – and those who were in Madagascar remained there as soldiers for the duration of World War I. For those not inducted, evangelization and education remained the focus of ministry. Just before the end of the War, on August 24, 1918, Betafo was elevated to the rank of Apostolic Vicariate and Father Dantin became the first La Salette Bishop. Following the administrative move of the French Colonial administration from Betafo to Antsirabe, it was decided on January 10, 1921 to move the ecclesial seat of the new Vicariate to Antsirabe also. Antsirabe became a diocese in 1955.

It was into this background that the first American La Salettes were inserted when they came to the High Plateau to serve alongside their French confreres.

These American pioneers were Fathers William Breault and Alphonse Coté (1892-1923). They arrived in April 1921. With the sudden death of Father Coté two years later, Father Aloysius Spielman (1892-1948) came from the United States to replace him. It was from the Betafo/Antsirabe mission on the High Plateau that, in 1928, the mission to Morondava would be launched.

Few know that the door to La Salette missionary activity on the West Coast of Madagascar was opened

(from left) La Salette Frs. William Breault and Alphonse Coté

with an exploratory missionary journey from Betafo in 1911. Their destination was Miandrivazo, a town in the Betsiriry valley of the Menabe Region, situated at the escarpment of the Bongolava mountain range. After that first adventure to Miandrivazo it would take another seventeen years before the La Salette Missionaries would be authorized to establish a mission on the West Coast of Madagascar, but with the city of Morondava as its central post.

To understand why this time-gap occurred, it would be helpful to read the report of that 1911 expedition as cited in the *Bulletin des œuvres Missionnaires de la Salette* of November 1911. The Apostolic Vicar of Antananarivo, Bishop Cazet, had strongly encouraged the La Salette Missionaries ministering in Betafo on the High Plateau to visit Miandrivazo, a Sakalava town on the western plains. No Catholic priest had ever ventured there.

(from left) Frs. Léon Mousset, Etienne Garon, Bro. Eugène, Msgr. François Dantin, and Raphael Lanfranconi on June 6, 1927

Concerning this first visit, Father Dantin wrote:

> Your Excellency, we returned yesterday after our voyage to Sakalavie. It lasted all of 15 days: five days to go, five days to return, and a five-day presence in Miandrivazo.
>
> Despite the very bad condition of the trails, we encountered no mishaps. Those whom God calls and sends are well protected. We were cordially welcomed by the Hova Christians (natives from the High Plateau) living there. The Sakalavas came to watch our ceremonies with much curiosity, as they understand nothing of our religion. All were of one accord in their desire that we establish a mission among them. Miandrivazo, capital of that area, is about two hundred kilometers (125 miles) west of Betafo.
>
> It is in the vast plain of the Betsiriry Valley, on the shores where the Mahajilo River begins to be navigable. The town has a population of about 1,100, two thirds of whom are Sakalava. Many large villages, not far from Miandrivazo, are entirely Sakalava. We visited one, where we entered every house one by one. Our reception was as warm and cordial as in the High Plateau.
>
> Are the Sakalava's open to evangelization? We would want to hope so. Two very serious obstacles would be polygamy and pagan idols. The true Sakalava is totally covered with amulets from foot to head; they have them in their hair, on their forehead, in their nose, ears, neck, arms etc. Wearing them is their great pride. The matrimonial covenant is so brittle that a minor dispute will abolish it forever. The number of wives a man can take is determined by his wealth. Fortunately, most are poor. The children go the government schools where constant government pressure is needed for them to attend classes.
>
> The Sakalava is proud, boastful, a robber of cattle (but not of smaller objects), lazy, a drunkard, etc. Nevertheless, he is less prone to vice and more honest than the Hova. Many underlined their willingness to be grateful, something not found among the Hova population. In Miandrivazo heat is excessive and there are many mosquitoes: two factors that make life very difficult. Finding good workers is not easy and construction becomes very expensive. If the Lord where to

send two laborers to work in His vineyard, I believe there would be a wonderful harvest in the Betsiriry plain and the entire Tsiribihina valley all the way to the ocean.

The report was sent to Bishop Cazet, the Apostolic Vicar of Tananarive. The author of the article was hopeful that the La Salette Fathers would soon reach out to this region. Unfortunately, the wait would be long. It was not until 1922, when Antsirabe was an Apostolic Vicariate in its own right, that a second visit would be made by Fathers Clément Michel and William Breault, and the wait would extend further into 1928 before three priests and one brother would finally be allowed to establish a Mission in Morondava.

The Hospitality of the French La Salettes

The panoramic vista of the Tsiribihina valley

Before the American La Salettes would open their own mission on the West Coast, it was very providential that some of them would spend time in Betafo and Antsirabe with our French La Salette Missionaries who had begun working there in 1899. All of the American fathers who worked or spent some time in Antsirabe totally enjoyed living and ministering with our French fathers and felt very much like one family.

It was, however, not readily evident that the Americans, who valued their independence, would adapt to ministering in a mission dominated administratively, ecclesiastically, linguistically, and culturally, by a French colony. Certainly, it was an indispensable requirement that all missionaries learn the local language and be well initiated into understanding the Malagasy culture. Although they would work closely with our French missionaries, they dreamed, almost from the beginning, of a mission that would be their own.

We must also understand that, even though the La Salettes are considered a missionary congregation, there was little or nothing in their formation process – be it European or American – that specifically prepared them to work as missionaries in a foreign, non-Christian country. Yet it was precisely through the experience of working in Antsirabe alongside our French fathers that both Breault and Spielman would become so well equipped to undertake later the first sustained evangelization of the West Coast of Madagascar.

Chapter 1 —
The First Wave of Pioneering American La Salettes Arrive in Antsirabe

(from left) La Salette Frs. Thomas Newman, Aloysius Spielman, William Breault and Cecil McDonald

Twelve American Priests and one Brother were sent to Madagascar during the first wave which extended from 1921 to 1956.

1921: William Breault and Alphonse Coté

1923: Aloysius Spielman

1928: Arthur Le Blanc, Cecil McDonald, Paul Girouard, and Steve Levickas

1929: John Henry Newman

1932: Thomas Mansfield, Harold Clossey, and John Brady

1949: Gerard Langlois

1956: John Berube

We cannot think of the American La Salettes in Madagascar without remembering those three founders: Breault, Coté, and Spielman. They deserve much credit. In Antsirabe, they not only learned well the local language but then worked well with our French Fathers. Articles in the *Bulletin* speak well of their generous zeal and apostolic spirit. Father Hostachy in his book: *Une belle Mission à Madagascar* (pg. 227) wrote:

Fathers Breault and Spielman were two more workers greatly desired by Bishop Dantin, two elite workers who, after their training on the High Plateau, would become the founders of the Sakalava Mission.

When the first Americans departed for the foreign missions their destination was Antsirabe; they were sent to work with our French Fathers in a French colony. It was only after their arrival that the vision of a new mission on the West Coast began to take form. There were no missionaries on the vast central part of the West Coast of the island even though all the Ecclesiastical Vicariates had an area extending to the West Coast; priority was given, however, to the more densely populated High Plateau.

It will be good for us to remember what Father Walter Greene wrote on the occasion of this first departure of La Salette Missionaries from the United States.

(from left) Frs. Spielman and Breault

> On January 26th 1921, the College (in Hartford) was the scene of a stirring event in the formal leave taking of Rev. Fathers William Breault and Joseph Coté. Their plans for the long journey to Madagascar were complete, and everyone felt that one of the greatest days in the history of the College had come, for while its threshold had been crossed many and many a time by youths whom it had schooled in the elements of the priestly missionary career, and who had gone forth year after year to higher seats of learning to prepare for ordination: and by ordained apostles on short journeys for parish work and home missions: *its portals were now to swing wide for the glad exit of two young priests on their way to a most distant and uncivilized corner of God's earth to bring there the message of new hope in Christ's Gospel ...* They are the first American born members of the Congregation of La Salette to volunteer and be accepted for the work. This fact explains the enthusiasm to which the entire College was roused over their departure. (emphasis added)

The door that opened on that cold January day would see countless other La Salettes leave for Madagascar, Asia, Latin America and Europe. Departure ceremonies are always emotional, heart breaking events, but the 1921 departure held in the Hartford chapel had a very special memorable significance. With only twenty-nine years of existence in America, the young La Salette community in Hartford was reaching out to a distant unknown land. At that time, departures for the mission fields were definitive; this would ultimately prove true for Fathers Alphonse Coté (1892-1923) and Thomas Mansfield (1907-1937) who would never return. Our Lady's Missionary has a complete and beautiful issue relating details, homilies, speeches given at this occasion. Once again Mary's children were answering her call to *make it known to all (her) people*.

Fathers Alphonse Coté and William Breault left New York City by ship on Saturday, January 29, 1921 and later from Marseilles, France on March 22nd. They arrived in Madagascar on April 21st and finally set foot in Antsirabe on April 28th – a journey of ninety full days!

The year 1921 was to be a bumper year for the La Salette mission in Antsirabe. Five young priests arrived that year; three of them would eventually be pillars of the Morondava mission. Two of the French fathers who arrived that year – Etienne Garon and Raphael Lanfranconi – would also later serve in

Morondava for many years and eventually die there. Of those two zealous American La Salettes in 1921, Alphonse Coté would be the first to die on April 8, 1923 after a little less than two years of ministry. Breault would minister in Antsirabe, then go on to help found the Morondava mission. He served in Madagascar for 12 years, and would leave the Morondava mission definitely in October of 1933.

The First Three Pioneers from North America

Father Aloysius Spielman (1892-1948), who arrived from America in Madagascar in December of 1923 to replace Father Coté, worked in Antsirabe for ten years before descending to Morondava. Together with many other American La Salettes, he would eventually be called to leave in 1937 serving for fourteen years without a holyday in the United States. These three men – Breault, Coté, and Spielman – were the first pioneer Americans to come to Madagascar and thus deserve special consideration.

It is not easy for us to grasp the full extent of missionary departures in 1921. Today, with jet planes circling the planet, distances can be covered within a few hours. But in 1921, ocean travel was long, perilous, and fatiguing. If crossing the Atlantic by ship was quite comfortable, mostly enjoyable, and frequently a remarkable occasion to meet very interesting people, the journey from Marseilles to Madagascar through the Mediterranean Sea, the Suez Canal, the Red Sea, and the Indian Ocean presented, on the other hand, add the persistent heat of the equator.

Young Fr. Breault before leaving for Madagascar

Called to a New Country, like Abraham of old

Vision of the Lord directing Abraham to count the stars, woodcut by Julius Schnorr von Carolsfeld (1794-1872)

Intermingled with those comforts, joys, hardships, and worries was the understanding that a mission departure was a life-long engagement – truly an "Abraham" experience. The voyage, which would last at least two months, made one realize that the distance travelled by land and sea represented a separation of more than just miles and oceans. It closed many doors on past realities – family, friends, customs, language – while opening doors to undreamed-of adventures in faith, opportunities to love, and hope-filled possibilities of making Jesus' reconciling message known.

Missionaries going to Africa or Asia in the early twentieth century knew that they would be exposed to risks due not only to hostile populations but also to insect-infected areas that could cause deadly fevers. Of the thirty missionaries that St. Vincent de Paul sent to

Madagascar in the 17th century all but two succumbed to fever, and the mission had to be closed after only twenty-five years. Many of the first London Missionary Society members to work in Madagascar buried their wives and children after a few months.

If you visit the Lutheran Cemetery in Morondava you will see tombs of children and young pastors who died a few years after their arrival. Humanly speaking it is very sad and truly difficult to understand the untimely death of a young healthy missionary but in the light of the Gospel, we know the seed must die if it is to bear much fruit.

All for the Love of God

It is not surprising, therefore, that at the very outset of our American Mission to Madagascar, God would ask us to sacrifice one of our young men. Father Coté was destined to give the ultimate witness of his life for the people of Madagascar. It was a grace that would bring much life to the young church and prepare the foundation of the Morondava Mission. Many young American missionaries would be inspired by Fathers Coté and Mansfield's total sacrifice and follow in their footsteps serving in Madagascar and other countries. We have always felt honored to be following in the footsteps of such giants; felt privileged to visit and pray at their tombs.

As the Catholic Church flourished in the Highlands or High Plateau, the West Coast of Madagascar, to the contrary, was all but forgotten. Priority was given to this friendlier climate and a more densely populated area. It had been planned that the Ecclesiastical Vicariates, whose administrative centers were situated on the High Plateau, would extend their activities from the fertile rice fields of the highlands to the arid sands of the West Coast. This never became a reality.

Fr. Aloysius Spielman, M.S., carrying water with local children

As narrated above, in 1911 Father Dantin – Superior of the mission and soon to be made Perfect Apostolic of Antsirabe, and a Bishop – made a 150-mile exploratory visit to Miandrivazo. This entailed five days by filanjana – a chair carried by four men – to descend the mountains, five days in Miandrivazo, and five days for the return trip.

His report was not all that positive or impelling. On the one hand Dantin realized the necessity of a new mission on the West Coast, but did not have the men needed. On the other hand, he was not willing to abandon the Vakinankaratra territory of Betafo/Antsirabe in order to undertake the evangelization of Morondava. Add to this the devastation felt in Europe during the first World War, whose effects were felt even in Madagascar. Miandrivazo and the West Coast would have to wait until 1922 for a second visit of a Catholic priest.

When Bishop Dantin asked Father Breault to make a trip to Morondava in 1922 in view of exploring the territory, how Father Coté would have wanted to join him! Father Coté's fragile health, with constant bouts of fever, would not allow him to participate in such a long and arduous journey. When our two Americans, together with three French fathers, arrived in Antsirabe in 1921, they were given the opportunity to study the Malagasy language. All became very fluent. While these five young priests were studying the language, little did they suspect three of them would also labor in Morondava, and that both Father Lanfranconi and Bishop Garon would also die in that West Coast mission.

Chapter 2 —
Fr. Alphonse Coté, M.S., The First to Give His Life

Fr. Coté on horseback, making the rounds of villages in the bush

Though Father Coté could not undertake long journeys to the West Coast, he worked tirelessly in and around Antsirabe. Despite his poor health he would be out, come rain or shine, journeying miles on foot or filanjana or horseback, over mountains, through valleys and dales, and crossing flood swollen rivers, visiting the Christian communities, teaching and bringing the Sacraments. He, like St. Paul, found himself swimming in a cold river when his dugout canoe tipped over. Had he taken into consideration the debilitating nature of his frequent attacks of malaria, he could have stayed at home and rested. But his great missionary spirit would not allow him to rest.

This is most likely the reason he succumbed at such a young age. Aware of Father Coté's frequent attacks of malaria, doctors were not overly concerned when, in early April 1923, he came down with another fever. It too would pass, they thought. But not this time; in less than 48 hours he breathed his last.

Father Coté's missionary life was short. He had been a priest for only nine years, and in Madagascar for only two years. But he had won the hearts of everyone with his sense of humor, simplicity, and cheerfulness. Upon his arrival, while studying the Malagasy language, he was already giving music lessons and in charge of the Cathedral Choir. His influence reached far. Had Father Coté lived longer, he might have been able to introduce American baseball in Antsirabe.

After only a few outings he had already won over some very enthusiastic young men to the joys of playing baseball. Trying to impress the young people by his juggling skills of keeping three balls in the air at one time. He quickly had to move to juggling four balls because the young men began to better his performance!

Father Coté had a very promising future as a missionary and Bishop Dantin had great hopes for him. But God had other plans. It was a very sad day in Antsirabe when, on April 8th, news broke out that Father Coté had been called back to our heavenly Father. Father Coté was buried in the community plot in Betafo and, in 1999, his remains were transferred inside the church of Betafo. The first American La Salette to die in the missions showed outstanding human, Christian, and apostolic qualities. With missionaries like Father Coté leading

Fr. Coté's body was first buried in the La Salette cemetery in Betafo

the way, we can now understand why the American mission has had not only a long but also a very rich and interesting history in Madagascar.

In 1999 Fr. Coté's body was transferred into the church in Betafo

Part Two — A Separate Mission on the West Coast

The Vakinankaratta region of central Madagascar was the original mission territory confided to the French La Salette Missionaries in 1898. Its major cities are Betafo and Antsirabe.

The Menabe region on the west coast was the original mission territory confided to American La Salette Missionaries in 1928. Its major cities are Morondava, Belo sur Tsiribihina and Miandrivazo.

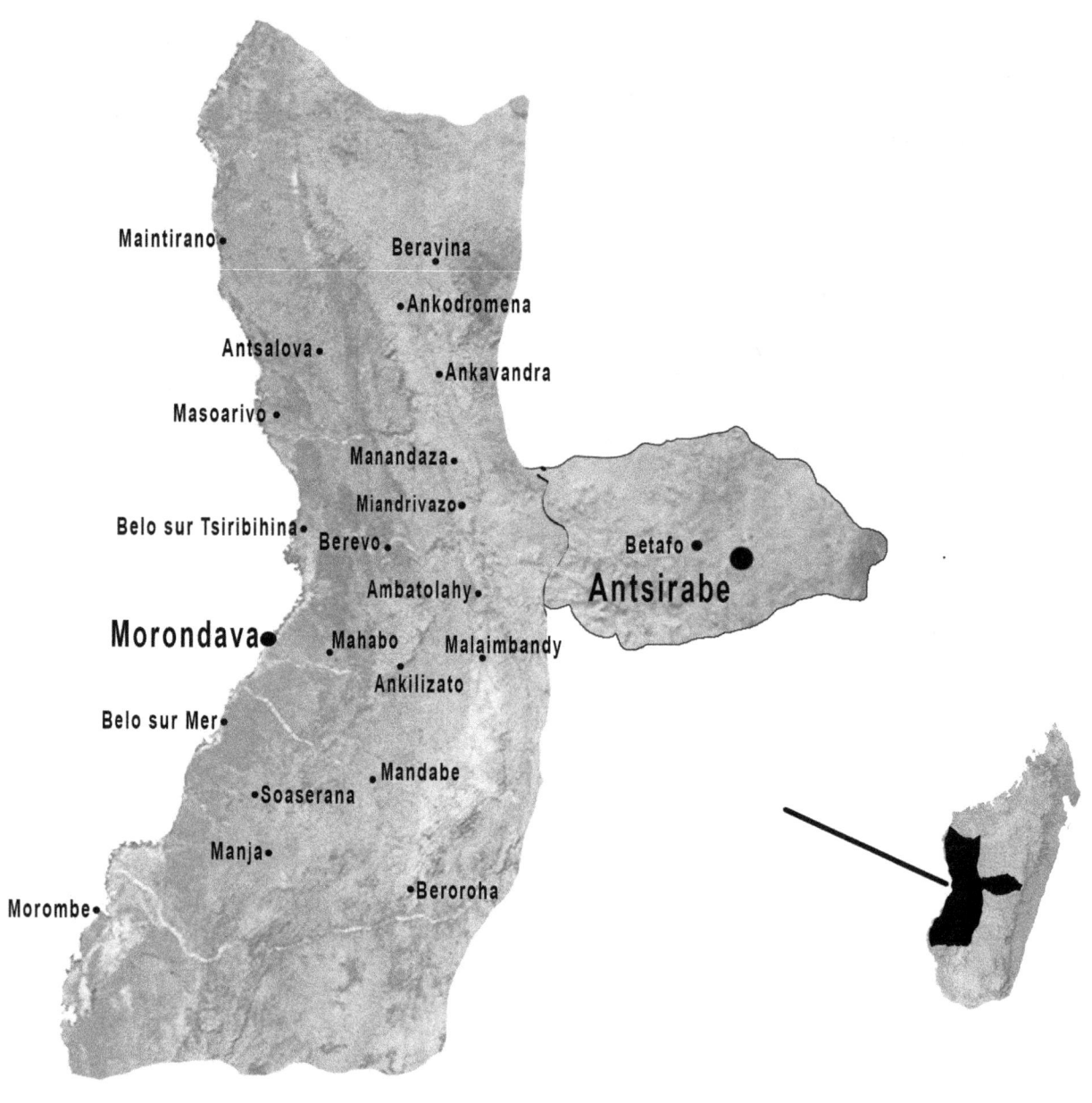

Chapter 3 —
Fr. William Breault, M.S., A Visionary on Mission

Young man, William Breault, in front of his birth home

While Father Coté's mission was short and plagued with frequent bouts of fever, Father William Breault (1894-1974) on the other hand, enjoyed excellent health. He served for seven years in Antsirabe and, later, for five years as founder and superior in Morondava. Before leaving on my own missionary journey to Madagascar in 1958 I, Donald, visited Father Breault at a nursing home in Central Falls, Rhode Island. Not only did he give me his blessing but admitted that leaving Morondava had been the greatest mistake of his life.

I can well understand his misgivings, as God had truly given William Breault the qualities needed to found the Mission as well as great love for the people he served. Not only did he still remember the language after being away for twenty-two years, but was excited as he spoke of villages, rivers, and areas I would someday discover for myself.

From 1919 until 1927 Jesuit missionaries had made frequent and prolonged visits to villages and towns on the West Coast, and specifically to Morondava. Hence, we have reason to consider these Jesuits (after the laymen and laywomen, of course) as the actual founders of the Catholic Church in the region of Morondava. Those Jesuit missionaries had all insisted that, if they had to give up a Mission, it would be better to leave the established churches in Fianarantsoa and Ambositra and focus on Morondava. But their Superiors had other views. As a result, the grace and privilege of establishing a permanent residence in the region of Morondava would be given to the American La Salette Missionaries.

Breault was the first to take up permanent residence in Morondava in 1928. Though there was nothing official, everyone concerned – the local Bishops, the Propagation of the Faith in Rome, and even our very own General Administration – gave a favorable nod to a separate Mission on the West Coast of Madagascar. From the very beginning of his missionary endeavors, Breault dreamt of a Mission in the West. What joy for him in 1922 when Bishop Dantin sent him and Father Clément Michel to explore the territory. The account can be found in *Our Lady's Mission-*

(from left) Frs. Breault and Spielman among a group of young seminarian candidates

ary of 1923. For more than two months, Breault and Michel travelled through the territory, on horseback, in river-barges, in ocean out-rigger canoes, in filanjana chair and on foot.

Carrying on St. Paul's Missionary Spirit

With his catechist by his side, Fr. Spielman mounts his horse for visits to the bush communities

Again, reminiscent of St. Paul, many hardships awaited these young missionaries – neither hunger, nor thirst, nor mosquitoes, nor sleepless nights. No, nothing could dampen their enthusiasm as they witnessed the generosity of the isolated Christian communities and their desire and hunger to have priests in the area. It was heartbreaking for both Michel and Breault to leave all these communities alone with no priests and return to the High Plateau. After such an experience we can understand Breault's great concern to found the mission on the West Coast. How he prayed and worked to convince the authorities of the urgency to take over this mission territory.

At the same time as Breault was undertaking his annual visits from Antsirabe to Morondava by way of the Tsiribihina River, Jesuit missionaries were also frequently visiting the West Coast, working their way west from Ambositra. As we have noted above, they also recognized the great need for the presence of missionary priests in the West. Bishop Dantin was in a quandary. His first concern was, of course, for the evangelization of the area of Antsirabe. He needed all the fathers he could get.

The 1911 visit to Miandrivazo had impressed him favorably, but he was not too keen on La Salette missionaries expanding their ministry to the West. One of his fears was that, if the La Salettes moved to the West Coast, it would result in a shortage of priests and that the Jesuits would readily move in to work in the area of Antsirabe.

Evangelization of West Coast of Madagascar

Realizing the potential of the West Coast mission, Bishop Dantin finally decided that Breault could go and remain in Morondava, but only under one condition; namely, that another American priest would replace him in Antsirabe. Thus, it came about that in 1928, Rome finally confided the evangelization of the West Coast to the American La Salettes. New missionaries would be sent for this extensive region of Madagascar, and one of them, Paul Girouard, would replace Breault in Antsirabe.

The area of this new mission territory was vast. It included four major coastal cities: Maintirano, Belo sur Tsiribihina, Morondava and Morombe; each approximately 200 miles directly west of four corresponding major Catholic cities on the High Plateau: Antananarivo – the capital of the country – and Antsirabe, Ambositra, and Fianarantsoa. Those miles encompassed drastic changes in mentality, culture, language and religious practices.

As mentioned earlier, Father Spielman had been sent to Antsirabe from Hartford after Father Coté's death in 1923. He too wanted to "go west." Bishop Dantin would not allow it. Young and zealous, having already learnt the language, Bishop Dantin greatly appreciated Spielman's ministry in Antsirabe. Fluent in both the Malagasy and French languages, Spielman greatly impressed everyone with his generous service and respect for people and their customs. Bishop Dantin was most reluctant to allow him to join his American compatriots in Morondava. But after a few years he finally yielded, hoping that Spielman would eventually become Superior of the Morondava Mission, replacing Breault.

Although a separate mission territory, Morondava was still under the ecclesiastical jurisdiction of Antsirabe. There had never been a very warm or cordial relationship between Father Breault and Bishop Dantin. The latter did not always understand or appreciate Breault's sense of humor. When Bishop Dantin was a little disappointed with the annual statistics concerning missionary work in Morondava, Breault told him that if he were not happy with the numbers given, then the Bishop could just add a zero to all the numbers. After all, zeros count for nothing!

This was not an answer to please Bishop Dantin. Breault was a hardworking missionary, not a bureaucrat, and therefore not overly concerned about providing, at any specific time, the annual reports and statistics the Bishop required.

Defending the Rights of His People

Breault loved the people and was tenacious in defending them from injustice. He was not afraid of the French Civil Administration, going to court many times to defend the rights of the local people. He was also a "bon viveur", and Breault would enjoy aperitifs with the French Colonials. During those first years there was very little anti-malaria medication. The everyday remedy was a glass of Cognac or Rum and that suited Breault just fine. None of those early missionaries were ever alcoholics as moderate use was considered medicinal.

So it was that, shortly after his arrival in Morondava in 1933, Spielman was named Superior of the mission, much to Bishop Dantin's delight. It was also a fact that Spielman was a suitable candidate to serve as future Apostolic Prefect. In their own ways, both Spielman and Breault were giants and served the mission very well. Both contributed generously to the founding of the Morondava mission.

Their early years of missionary work in Antsirabe alongside our French Fathers proved to be very beneficial. They were able to grasp a deeper understanding of missionary pastoral care. They learned methods of organizing a missionary district which were so different from the way American parishes were structured.

Fr. Paul Girouard, M.S. arrives at the Madagascar mission

The arrival of Fr. Paul Girouard

When, in 1928, Father Paul Girouard (1898-1964) arrived in Madagascar, it finally became possible to relinquish Breault from obligations in Antsirabe in order to establish the Morondava Mission. Again, we would like to insist on the importance for our founding missionaries of their years working in Antsirabe. It was training that would prove to be very beneficial in Morondava. If they were successful in establishing and founding a new mission it was due in great part to their experiences in Antsirabe.

Bishop Dantin had forcefully made it clear that the Morondava Mission would have to be established without affecting the number of missionaries working in Antsirabe. Breault could leave Antsirabe only when he could be replaced by another American. Paul Girouard's arrival in 1928 was the catalyst that allowed this to happen. Only in 1934 would Girouard himself be freed to join his American confreres in Morondava.

His years in Antsirabe were most providential. The experience he gained ministering in a well-established Christian community would be very precious. His experience in training catechists on the High Plateau proved to be especially valuable. During his time in the district of Mahabo, he would be called to found there the first "Normal School" (School for the training of catechists) in the Morondava mission. Later, as Bishop, he would build a new school that served for many years for the training of our catechists.

On June 25, 1937, a few La Salettes gathered in Morondava: (seated from left) Frs. Futy and Garon; (standing from left) Dorval, Clossey, Girouard, Pra, and Le Blanc

The Arrival of Frs. Clossey and Mansfield

Girouard was happy working in Antsirabe. The French Fathers always enjoyed his company and missionary spirit. When Fathers Harold Clossey (1906-1963) and Thomas Mansfield arrived in 1932 they were also given the opportunity to study the Malagasy language in Antsirabe, and learn pastoral approaches adapted for Madagascar. Anxious as these three were to join their fellow Americans in Morondava they had but great admiration and gratitude to French Missionaries who had taught them well.

Chapter 4 —
Morondava, A Mission-Building Experience

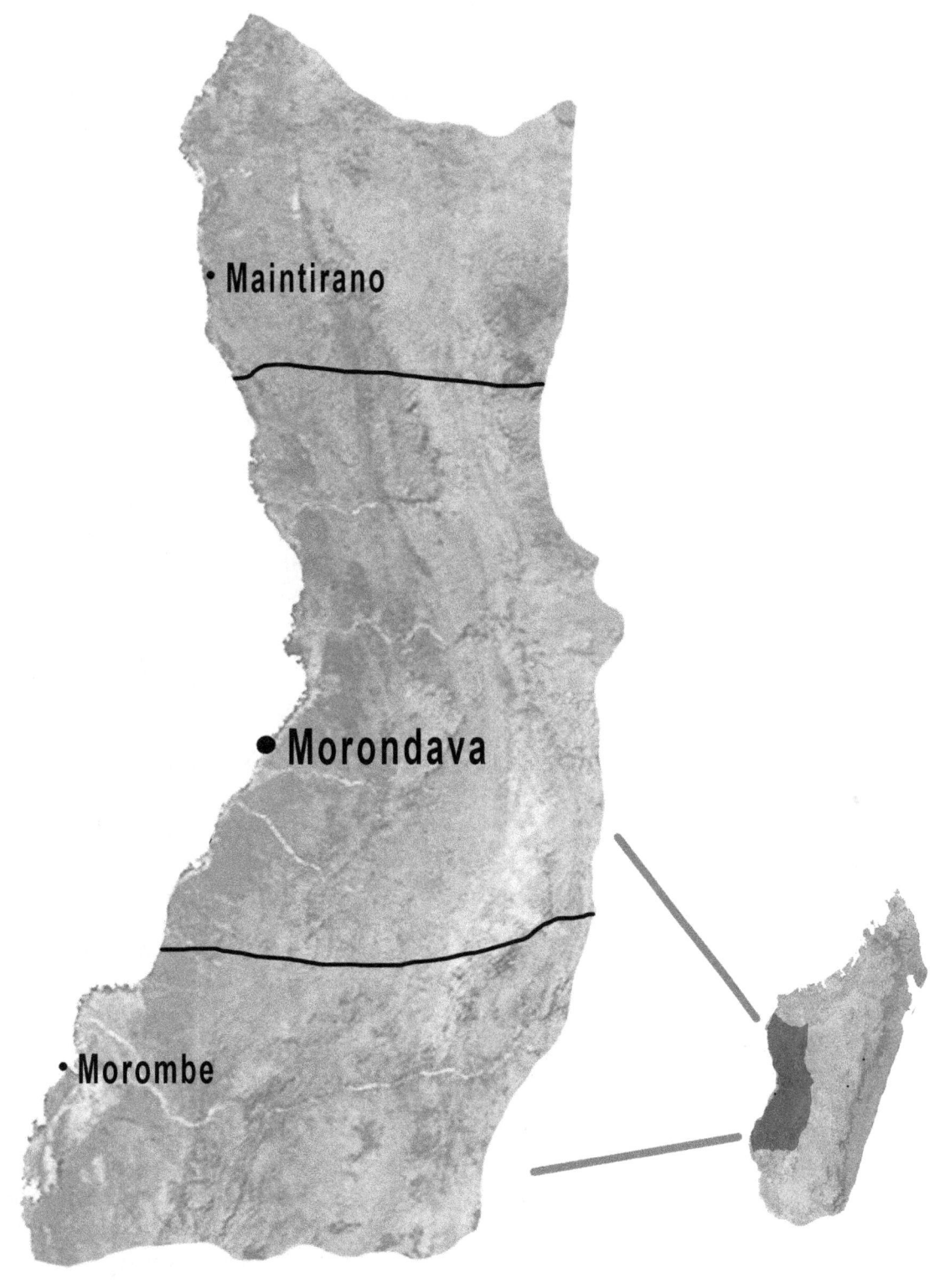

After so many years of preparation, of extensive correspondence between Antsirabe, Rome, and Hartford, the green light was given in 1926 for the new mission of Morondava. Yet, it would require another two years before the actual foundation occurred. Although there would be La Salettes in both Morondava and Antsirabe, this was not just a La Salette affair.

Although the new mission would have juridical connections with Antsirabe for a few years, it would not be a geographical extension of Antsirabe, but a separate mission. It involved bringing together territories touching the Vicariates of Fianarantsoa, Antananarivo, and Majunga. All of these were only too happy that the Americans would now care for territories they had never been able to cover adequately. Finally, the Menabe Region would have resident priests. Bishop Dantin was also extremely pleased but wanted to make sure that new foundation would in no way diminish numbers of priests ministering in Antsirabe.

Building our First Residence in Morondava

First house for La Salettes on Morondava beach

Father William Breault was therefore the very first to take up residence in Morondava on May 21, 1928. A few days later Father Cecil McDonald arrived, accompanied by Brother Stephen Levickas. They rented an old military shack by the ocean with plans to build a first residence as soon as possible. Breault already well-versed in the Malagasy language visited nearby neighboring villages while Father McDonald – always affectionately known as Mac – took time to study the language.

Mac did not waste any time, but began making plans for future buildings. Brother Steve, with a truck at is disposition, set about gathering materials. This was the "mustard seed," the first three men living in very Spartan conditions in a country unknown to them, under French authorities who could be suspicious of Americans. The little furniture they had consisted of crates which served as table and chairs. Their great consolation was, of course, the joy and faith of the Christians who were so happy to finally see Catholic priests taking up residence in Morondava.

First La Salette residence built by Mac and Steve in Morondava

A French Jesuit missionary who had visited Morondava in 1922 had been so impressed by the faith, generosity, and willingness of the people that he had prayed that this mission would remain under the care of the Jesuits. As Divine Providence would have it, the American La Salettes were called to found this new mission.

Morondava Growing by Leaps and Bounds

The total population of Morondava at that time was little over 7,000 people with only 600 baptized Catholics. In 2020 Morondava counted 100,000 people with about 20,000 of them Catholics. The French administration and colonials, who were nominally Catholics, would be present for the celebration of major Religious Feasts but few would attend services on a regular basis.

Some administrators were Masons; others were prejudiced against religion – and against the Catholic religion in particular – and therefore would not do anything that would favor the Catholic Church. France was known as a Catholic country but during those years there were many attacks on the Catholic Church. As mentioned above, when these attacks dealt with the welfare of the Malagasy people, Breault would not hesitate to intervene.

Breault did not wait for the arrival of the fourth member of this new missionary contingent to arrive; he left in July for three months, visiting many towns and villages throughout this vast new mission area. Father Arthur Le Blanc arrived in August.

With Mac and Brother Steve engaged in urgent building planning and execution, and Breault away, Le Blanc immediately delved into ministry. He did not have the good fortune to take time off to study and learn the language systematically as most missionaries were able to do. He plunged into learning through total immersion. He nevertheless always regretted that he had never been given the opportunity to study the language. By so doing, he freed Mac and Steve to concentrate on urgent construction.

the First Celebration of the Feast of La Salette

The original mud church was modified and enlarged; mud walls were replaced by wooden boards. In a month's time, the new church was ready for the first Celebration on the Feast of La Salette, the 19th of September. The first public procession was organized that same year from Morondava across the salt flats to Namahora – a distance of about 4 kilometers (2.5 miles).

The Catholic population of Morondava gathered for the La Salette Feast Day

From the very beginning the missionaries made sure to place their ministry under the care of Our Lady of La Salette. Thus, the original founding fathers were facing the challenge of setting up a new church structure in the city, of establishing Christian communities in the larger Sakalava Kingdom of Menabe, and of constructing needed buildings for residence and worship.

Divine Providence had well prepared the men needed for such a venture. Breault, with his zeal, energy, determination, generosity, and pastoral experience was the leader. Mac was a gifted civil engineer destined for construction. Working in tandem with Steve, they gathered materials, made plans and supervised workers. Le Blanc, known as Whitey, was quiet, calm, unassuming, friendly, humble, generous, and always cheerful. In this way, they formed two teams; one to focus on pastoral care and ministry, and the other for construction of needed edifices – churches, residences and eventually schools.

As a result, the first solid residence with four rooms was ready in February of 1929 while a second was ready in July of the same year. Fortunately, that first house, which is still standing today, was barely finished when a cyclone – we would call it a hurricane in the western hemisphere – destroyed the military shack on the beach where the La Salettes community had been living.

Setting Up Hartford's Madagascar Mission Office

As often happens, disaster opens the door for creative opportunity. In this case the destructive force of the cyclone provided an occasion for the administrative center in Hartford, Connecticut, which was responsible for the new mission, to set up the first mission office. Father Paul Regan, M.S. (1897-1943) was the director. It became the responsibility of his office to finance the new mission in Morondava. Many of the relationships established with U.S. dioceses in those early years are still strong today.

The local Sakalava people had offered a large-forested area of land to the missionaries. From the local colonial administration, the missionaries subsequently obtained a land permit (known as a "concession") allowing them to harvest from the forest the wood needed for construction. In that forest there grew a very precious camphor wood that resisted termites. The first church, dedicated to Our Lady of La Salette, was built in 1930 of that camphor wood. It still stands proud and solid today.

In an effort to generate local income, the fathers began a very profitable business selling boards and beams to the local people. But when Bishop Dantin heard of it, he stepped in and told them that they could not undertake commercial activities, and this project had to be abandoned.

Fresh milk was a sought-after commodity and, on a property bought in Namahora, they were raising milking cows. Fresh milk was a delicacy. They could not, however, supply the demands of all who sought fresh milk. This became a cause of controversy and discontent among the colonials. As a consequence, that activity was also discontinued.

Original Morondava church, residence and other buildings in Morondava

Chapter 5 —
Mission Activity Flourishes

This vast mission territory was organized so that as Breault would visit the distant outlying communities, Le Blanc would do ministry in Morondava and the surrounding villages, and Mac and Steve would do the building.

Where There's a Will, There's a Way

The La Salettes gathered in Morondava in 1949: (front row, from left) Frs. Joseph Ihhof (Superior General), E. Garon, R. Lanfranconi; (middle row, from left):F. Dorval, B. De Boisseson, L. Haridon, Bro. John, A. Le Blanc; (back row, from left): Czosnek, P. Girouard, Costiou, C. McDonald

Later Le Blanc loved to relate the experience of his first Christmas in Morondava. Because of the pressures placed on him, Le Blanc had neither the time nor opportunity to do a methodical study of the Malagasy language; he learned it by speaking with the people. Sacramental ministry was, at that time, still all in Latin. To minister on that first Christmas, only four months after his arrival, he had faculties to hear confession, but only in French and not in the Malagasy language that was still mostly unknown to him.

As people wanted to receive the Eucharist for Christmas and confession seemed a necessary prerequisite, people really wanted to receive sacramental absolution. Those who could speak French could come to confession. But where did that leave the uneducated people? They found a way. They would tell their sins to the catechist who would write them on a piece of paper in French. Then the repentant sinners would approach Le Blanc with the paper on which their sins were written in French and thus Father would give them absolution.

Even today we could ask whether such confessions were licit; but we know God in his great mercy forgives all sins. Most surely, in such a case the catechist would be held to the secret of confession!

For the first year, Breault did most of the trips to the vast bush area, visiting Christian communities from Maintirano to Morombe – an area of some 90,000 square miles – while Le Blanc held the fort in the city of Morondava and a surrounding area of about 6,000 square miles. Mac and Steve were only too busy with needed, urgent construction projects. There was a strong bond among the four missionaries, and there was little time to foresee or even dream of how that mission would grow and prosper.

Fr. McDonald built this house in 1931 at Belo sur Tsiribihina

Medical Ailments were Part of Daily Living

They all suffered with bouts of malaria and fatigue while Le Blanc had serious and unbearable pain from very bad teeth. The only solution was to pull them out! He always laughed later when telling of how he would put a tight noose around the tooth, attach a strong string to a door, and then slam it shut! The painful tooth – and the pain – were history!

He had his first dentures made in Morondava by a local dentist. Years later when Le Blanc got a chance to return to America for a vacation, he visited an American dentist who insisted that Father's Malagasy-made dentures should be sent to a dental museum!

The Wonderful Ties that Bind

The missionaries had few comforts but many consolations, and a great love and admiration for one another. They bonded in their love of Christ as very few men have. Years later, on February 9, 1972, Le Blanc visited with Mac who, worn out from ministry and building projects, was resting at the Sisters Clinic in Antananarivo. Le Blanc spent all afternoon and part of the evening with Mac reminiscing about those first exciting years in Morondava. The next morning, February 10th, Le Blanc learned that Mac had passed away in his sleep during the night.

Serving their People, Near and Afar

(from left) Frs. McDonald and Breault with Brother Steve

It would always be difficult for him to share with us his appreciation of and love for Mac. The Christians of Morondava were so happy to have a resident priest that there is nothing they would not do for their priests. Even the French Colonials and the Administrators soon showed their appreciation for the American Missionaries.

There were no paved roads, no bridges spanning the rivers, and the costal salt-flats were often covered with thick mud from fluctuating tides. This gave new significance to what it meant to travel a mile or a kilometer. Breault's tri-monthly trek, mostly on foot, oxcart or filanjana, from Morafenobe in the North to Beroroha in the South – a distance which, in a straight line covers over 250 miles, and closer to 500 when traveled on land – was an exhausting one, yet necessary for keeping in touch with, building up, ministering to, and sustaining the life and faith of Christian communities.

The area covered by Le Blanc to visit families and churches in Morondava and surrounding villages was smaller, but somewhat more densely populated. From the very first years there were many Baptisms, First Communions, Confirmations and Marriages. Most of the ministry was centered on ministering to the existing Christian communities of Catholics who had migrated to Morondava from the High Plateau regions of Antsirabe, Ambositra and Fianarantsoa.

As much as they would have wanted to reach out to the local non-Catholic Sakalava population, their first concern was to look after baptized Catholics who, too often, had strayed from the Catholic faith to adopt the pagan customs of the area. It would take many years before the Catholic Church could have any real impact on the local people. There was much work to be done and these four men were giants.

Chapter 6 –
Belo Sur Tsiribihina,
A New Mission Endeavor to the North

**An Austronesian outrigger canoe used by the first ancestors of the
Malagasy people who once sailed from the Malay Archipelago
(between mainland Indochina and Australia)**

The first three years they worked out of Morondava, radiating to the extreme corners of the mission. Breault never tired of his visits to the far away areas, traveling on foot, filanjana, canoe, or any vehicle possible.

With the arrival, in 1931, of Father John Henry Newman (1902-1973), brother of Bishop Thomas Newman who would later establish the La Salette mission in Burma, there was already talk of opening a second residence in Belo about 100 kilometers (62 miles) north of Morondava.

While Morondava was the French administrative center, it was Belo which was really the capital of the Malagasy Sakalava Kingdom, better known as Menabe. It was the residence and tombs of the Sakalava Kings, and the Fathers thought it would be very appropriate to assure a presence there.

In fact, in 1845, a French Jesuit visited Belo and had an audience with the King and his court. The King listened attentively and was captivated by the portable harmonium or foot-pedaled pump organ that Father played for him. Yet he would not hear of converting or allowing the missionaries to establish a church. It was this same Jesuit priest who, in speaking of the Sakalava people, asserted: "The Sakalava sleep at night and rest during the day."

Without a doubt, the excessive heat during the day had an influence on daytime activity! Belo was, however, a strategic place at the delta of the mighty Tsiribihina River, and establishing a residence there would be a solid move. Mac did not trust Morondava, which was at sea level, and thus was easily threatened by the strong tides of the Indian Ocean. Mac was convinced that eventually Morondava would disappear, submerged by the ocean. The danger remains real to this day, especially with the general rising of ocean level. Every time the city of Morondava is flooded by high tides we wonder if Father Mac's prophesy will someday be fulfilled.

A New Residence for La Salettes in Morondava

(left to right) La Salette Frs. John Newman and Harold Clossey near an oxcart, an ordinary method of transportation

Nevertheless, in 1940, under the vow of obedience, Mac built the new large spacious residence. But later, in 1945, so convinced was he that Morondava was destined to disappear into the ocean, he refused to have anything to do with building a large school on adjacent Mission land.

Belo remains a very important cultural center while Morondava remains the largest city and center of the diocese. John Newman had already been in the mission since 1929, the first arrival after the founding fathers. In Morondava alongside Le Blanc, he was able to learn the language, as well as pastoral guidelines for the Mission. Father John Henry Newman had received some medical training that served him well; thus, he could care for sick people who came to him.

Finally, in 1931, Father Spielman received permission to come down from Antsirabe. This added to the number of American missionaries in the Morondava mission. In March, together with Newman who is considered the founder of the Belo Mission, they crossed the Tsiribihina River and arrived in Belo.

We must not forget these were the first priests ever to take up residence there. Though the fathers had purchased a spacious property, there was no residence for them. As they walked about town with their white cassocks and bearded chins, they were the talk of the town. Having seldom seen a white man in a flowing white cassock, the frightened children ran away and kept their distance from them.

A Princely Welcome

Fortunately, Prince Kamamy, successor of the king who reigned there back in 1845 and had refused the Jesuits hospitality, welcomed the newly arrived missionaries and offered them one of his many houses as a temporary lodging. That very year in July, work started on what would be Mac's first major residence outside of Morondava. It was incredible, almost miraculous how Mac could organize a work site, keeping sixty, seventy workers busy all day. His construction projects were so masterful and workers so skillfully apprenticed that each project served as a trade school, and Mac formed some of the best carpenters and masons of the area. A worker had only to say he had worked for Father Mac and he would be hired by anyone on the spot!

Opening a Second La Salette Mission Post

In March of 1931, hardly three years after the original foundation, those stalwart American La Salette Missionaries had now opened this second mission post, from which the northern part of the mission would be served by Spielman and Newman working out of Belo. Breault and Le Blanc ministered in the south from Morondava. Mac and Brother Steve continued building wherever needed. Before going to Belo, Mac had already finished two residences and the new church in Morondava.

On January 23, 1932, less than a year after their arrival in Belo, the Fathers moved into the large spacious residence that still stands proud in the center of the Mission compound in Belo. It has stood solid, surviving even extremely violent cyclones that razed every building in Belo except the Mission House.

Frequent visits to the Bush Communities

Newman took care of the town of Belo, whereas Spielman went out on frequent visits to the distant areas of Miandrivazo, Morafenobe, Ankavandra and Maintirano. His experience in Antsirabe was most beneficial as he set out on these long journeys. As one reads the journals of these first missionaries, one has to be impressed by their zeal to visit the bush communities. Not only are there page after page of their constant trips but also how often they were sick with fever caused by malaria and blackwater fever.

With Spielman in the north, Breault could now concentrate on Morombe, Manja, Mahabo and Malaimbandy where Christians were always very happy to have fathers visit. There was much joy, enthusiasm, and hope for the future of the Church. The Americans had arrived and everyone admired their sense of American know-how and enterprise.

Fr. Aloysius Spielman, M.S., sends his picture with a note of thanks to his many Mission supporters

For the celebration of the Feast of the Sacred Heart at Belo in June 1933 over a thousand people came from the entire mission to attend the celebration, something unheard of for Belo. It is interesting to note the annalist's remarks concerning this important meeting.

> June 25. This was the biggest day in the history of the Belo residence. The procession of the Blessed Sacrament was a huge success with exactly 1,107 persons taking part in it. The people come mostly from the following places. Morondava, 124; Antanambao 41; Bemanonga, 14; Mahabo, 27; Miandrivazo 29; Antsalova 27; Tsiandro 23; Beroboka, 30; Ambato, 25; Maintirano, 9; Bevilo, 46; Ankavandra 28; Mandroatsa, 7; Mandabe, 2; Masoarivo Avaratra, 26; Trangahy, 21; Berendrika, 28; Bekily, 8; Marovoay, 19; Berevo, 28; Antshoa, 31; Serinam, 130; Tsaraotanana, 51; Soaserana, 27; Andranomiely, 18; Ambonara, 26; Masoarivo (36), Serinam 38; Ankirondro, 22.

We can not only trust but must admire those figures of 1933. I don't know if, today, we could gather so many people from distant areas to attend a celebration. They were now five priests ministering in two mission districts and there was great hope for the future.

The Founding years – 1933 until May 1936

Yes, the Jubilee for the Universal Church, announced by Pius XI for 1933-1934, was another remarkable year for the Morondava mission as with the arrival of three more men from America — Fathers John Brady (1907-1970), Harold Clossey, and Thomas Mansfield. With assurance that Girouard would also soon join the team, it seemed that all was set to raise the ecclesial status of the mission from a Separate Mission to that of an Apostolic Prefecture. As Breault left for a well-deserved vacation in the U.S., Spielman was handed the administration of the Morondava mission.

There were now eight young American priests under his leadership ready to convert the entire Sakalava Kingdom of Menabe. There was an excellent spirit of comradery among them. One only has to read Mansfield's letters to see how happy they were. No doubt there is an extraordinary grace given when young men respond generously to God's call to evangelize a very poor and difficult area. They had to contend with excessive heat in the summer, non-existent roads, malaria infected mosquitoes, few and distant churches, fragile and paganized Christian communities, scant vegetables, few comforts; clean water and electricity were not even in the picture! Yet they were so happy to serve, and so happy, even at a distance, to live in a spirit of comradery, and dedication to the mission activity confided to them.

We can only marvel at how often they would visit with one other and how they looked forward to meetings and retreats together. How they would make every effort to be together for a special feast. These were the best of the founding years – 1933 until May of 1936.

A Greek Orthodox Layman, a friend of La Salette

It would be difficult to speak adequately of our American La Salettes in Belo without a word about Mr. Emmanuel Frangkialokis, a Greek Orthodox layman and owner of Belo's Grand Hotel. He befriended the Fathers on every occasion and in every need. The Fathers could not have worked and built without his friendship and support.

He would advance large sums of money for construction and was ever ready with services and materials. The Fathers of Belo always insisted that his name should never be forgotten in the Annals of the Mission. It would have been difficult for the Fathers to establish themselves without his help and friendship.

In light of authentic custom and local history, it is interesting to read notes in reference to the *Fitampoha*. It was the most important ceremonial gathering of the Sakalava people. They came to wash the bones and relics of their Royal ancestors. It was a solemn and sacred liturgy.

Today, however, the festival has lost its relevance. It is done all too frequently as local folklore with a commercial interest that has little to do with respect for Royal relics. I quote from "Annals."

> Prince Kamamy paid the Père [Father] a visit today to assure le Père that the approaching feast of the

The original church in Belo sur Tsiribihina

Sakalava was all above board. No sacrifices, etc. etc. He invited Newman over to the opening of the house in which the relics of the Kings are preserved. P. Newman went in and, with Mr. Martin of the Crédit Foncière of Morondava and the Prince, they were the first ones to view these chosen remembrances of once great men. The feast promised to be a great display of Sakalava customs and it seems impossible that everything will be carried out without some witchcraft or other. (We will see.)

On October 18 he continues:

> The Sakalava feasts are starting this A.M. with fireworks, shooting of guns, etc. They are to last a week celebrating: "Les grandes fêtes du bain royal des reliques des Rois du Menabe" (The Grand celebrations for royal baths of the relics of Menabe Kings) as the sign at Kamamy's house indicates. The latter is chief and director of the festivities in which three or four thousand Sakalaves are expected to participate.
>
> The sand bars on the Tsiribihina near the bar are all decked out with flags, etc. As it is at this spot that the king's bones, rifles, spears, etc. are to be washed and given the royal bath after fifteen years enclosure in stuffy coffins.

There would be much to say about how differently this celebration is performed today. It is nevertheless interesting to note how the Prince invited Newman to be the first to view the relics. This is an indication of great respect and trust, because a foreigner would normally not be invited to such a viewing.

Today many of the relics have disappeared. The celebrations that are performed today are meant to be a source of financial income for the people of Belo. Life seemed to have been much simpler in the 1930s.

Chapter 7 —
Manja, a Further Mission Initiative to the South

In 1933 the mission residence of Manja was inaugurated, thus creating three major mission posts: North, Center, and South from where the territory could be covered. The first Catholic school was opened in Belo. Morondava was preparing to receive a community of Sisters to open up a school for young girls. We learn from the letters and articles they wrote how these men were ready to face the enormous challenge of establishing the Catholic Church on the West Coast of Madagascar.

Fathers' house in Manja

Meeting the Challenge of Their Ministry

What a challenge; yet with their youth and American know-how, they were determined to go forward. This they did. It seems they were always out in the bush, travelling by filanjana, or canoe or eventually by car during the dry season. No hardship seemed unbearable. They were always on the move. Although each had his primary mission post with its responsibilities and commitments, it seemed they worked as one team helping one another out. One can read in the "Annals" how they were so often out visiting Christian communities, crisscrossing the territory, that it is not easy to determine just where they were stationed.

With the creation of a new southern district, personnel changes were inevitable. Teams were now quite stable: Newman, Spielman, and Brady were based in the north, Breault and Clossey covered the central area of Morondava, Le Blanc and Mansfield held down the south.

As the work flourished, one discovers Mac and Steve moving freely from one post to the other, supervising and building churches, rectories, and schools. One can frequently read in the "Annals" how Father Le Blanc is sick with the fever and must rest, or that Father Clossey was debilitated with a strong fever. The only one who seemed to have been spared was Father Mansfield. But when he finally did succumb to a fever it proved to be fatal. Much more will be said about Manja later.

Football (Soccer) field in Morondava

Chapter 8 –
Brother Stephen Levickas, An Unforgettable Missionary Brother

The Story of a Life Well-Lived

Brother Steve, a true master builder

An important part of the story of the Morondava mission would be incomplete without special mention being made of Brother Stephen Levickas, known to everyone as simply as Brother Steve.

He was born in Vilcaviskis, Lithuania, on August 26, 1889, and his baptismal name was Joseph. Sometime around the year 1912, he migrated to the United States. On May 13, 2014 he entered the postulancy program in view of becoming a Professed La Salette Brother. During novitiate training, he discovered that being a Religious with vows was too awesome a task for him. He left – only to come back, requesting to be an La Salette Oblate Brother in 1919.

The vocation to be a La Salette Oblate Brother is unique. He would continue to live in the community, but as a lay person with a special contract. He wanted to cooperate in La Salette ministry and share in the life of the community, but without taking religious vows.

Steve's specialty was carpentry. In 1928 he volunteered to accompany Fr. Cecil McDonald to Morondava. Brother Steve was a most unusual character – one you would never forget. As the sidekick of Fr. Mac, he was a skilled builder/carpenter who, without knowing the local language, taught his workers by example, and taught them well.

The Gift of Building Churches

The church he and Mac built in Morondava is still in use as the parish church for the city. Benches built in the 1930s still serve the faithful as they kneel and sit for Mass and other services. For a few years this church served as the Cathedral until the new one was built in Namahora. Brother Steve was known to be very comfortable sleeping in the forest, so one should not be surprised to find lemurs,

Interior of church in Morondava, built by Brother Steve and Fr. McDonald

snakes, and chameleons in is room! His legend lives on in Morondava.

Together with Father Newman, Brother Steve returned to the States in 1936. He lived and worked for many years at the seminaries in Altamont, New York, Hartford, Connecticut and Milford, Iowa. Many young Fathers – and I, Jack, are one of them – and Brothers who came years later to Morondava from America had lived with him in one of those seminaries. Even there, people remembered some of his eccentricities.

Never one to seek comfort, when he was helping to build the new Seminary in Altamont, Steve chose to live out in the barn, with his dog, Wooly – and only the Lord knows how many other of God's creatures! He would entertain the students with stories, and sometimes even act them out so wildly that the students questioned if they could be true.

Brother Steve and his dogs

Chapter 9 –
A New Phase of Mission Activity: Catholic Schools

Children in a La Salette School

New phases of mission activity were being explored, and the first Catholic school was inaugurated in Belo. February 24, 1935 was a red-letter day in the history of the Belo mission; it was marked by the blessing of the first Catholic school established in the Menabe Kingdom.

The very first Jesuit missionaries to visit Belo in 1845 had spoken of opening a school as a means of introducing the Catholic faith to the Sakalava people. His request was denied. It took only 90 years before that plan fully unfolded and, on this day, the first school could be established. Written documentation from that time gives this account:

Fr. Brady had celebrated the first Mass of the day at 5:30 am. The inaugural ceremonies began at 7:30 am with Fr. Newman presiding. A very nice procession was formed which went along the main road from the church to the school. The Church and School buildings, as well as the route the procession would follow, were well decorated with flags and banners.

After the blessing the people returned to the Church where Fr. Brady gave the sermon for the occasion. This was followed by a High Mass sung by Fr. Newman. After Mass the entire congregation assembled at the School where a group picture was taken by Mr. Istasse, with Mr. Roch's camera which the latter had kindly lent us for the occasion. The people remained in the school building and on the school grounds throughout the day.

Dinner was served on the School grounds and a Family Feast was enjoyed by all. February 28, 1935 was the First Official Day of School. About seventy pupils were on the list. All seem pleased with their instructor, Raphael Ratsimba. Bishop Dantin sent his blessing to pupils, school and people.

Catholic Education in a Challenging Environment

Most adults and youth were illiterate – their culture had indeed a well-developed oral tradition and keen memories – and few parents saw the need of sending their children to school. God uses seemingly unbelievable ways to draw people to Faith. One way is through schools. The founding Fathers, overwhelmed by visits to Catholic communities scattered over the vast territory of the mission, did not feel capable of maintaining schools. Now, however, that one priest could remain as a stable presence in the city or town, while his partner covered the bush, they knew the time had come to focus more on schools.

Schools would combine to improve many elements of life, including education and formation of social skills, along with providing an opportunity to teach the religious principles of the Catholic Faith.

Religious Sisters and Brothers in the Morondava Mission

Traditionally, Catholic schools were one of the principle services of Religious Sisters and Teaching Brothers. Although we will be getting a bit ahead of history, it seems that this would be a good place to speak of the importance of Religious Sisters and Brothers in the Morondava mission.

Indeed, no history of American La Salettes in Morondava would be complete without underlining the importance of religious communities of Sisters and Brothers who came to work with us, in particular various feminine congregations.

Canadian and Malgash M.I.C. sisters celebrate the Twenty-Fifth Anniversary of the foundation of their sisters in Morondava

From the very beginning, Breault had invited the Sisters of Providence of Corenc, France to administer a school in Morondava. Having built a convent and school, the first Sisters finally arrived in 1935, not too long after the inauguration of the school in Belo. These Sisters of Providence were the first pioneer Sisters to venture to Morondava. They are credited with opening a Girls' School, an Orphanage, and a Trade School. Thus, began the presence of other Religious – especially women religious, but also Brothers and Priests – who would work side by side with La Salette Missionary Priests and Brothers, in a partnership that goes on to this day. Due to a lack of native vocations and to communication problems, the Sisters of Providence left in 1952. God has his plans. In 2007, this congregation of sisters would return to work, not in the city of Morondava, but in the district of Ankilizato.

We all knew, most of us from personal experience, how religious brothers and sisters contributed to the growth of the Catholic Church in the United States through their work in schools and hospitals. It became the same in Madagascar where, in some way, their presence and mission is more extensive than that of a priest. As women, it is easier for them to approach and establish contact with children and women who represent more than two thirds of the population. So, when the Sisters of Providence reluctantly decided to leave, Bishop Garon sent Father Girouard to Canada in search of a missionary community of sisters who could come to work in Morondava.

I, Donald, was a novice in Brewster, Massachusetts at the time (1951) and I clearly remember how Girouard, accompanied by Father J. Alphonse Dutil (1896-1991), our novice master, left on a trip to Canada in search of a community of sisters.

The Arrival of the Missionary Sisters of the Immaculate Conception

They asked for our prayers so that their mission would be successful. And successful it was! The Missionary Sisters of the Immaculate Conception (M.I.C.) agreed to come to Morondava in 1952, to direct the Catholic school for girls in Morondava, to be known as the College of the Immaculate Conception. Beginning with only a few students, these Missionary Sisters of the Immaculate Conception, commonly known as the M.I.C. sisters, today care for the education of over 2,000 students in a fully accredited school system, ranging from Kindergarten to the conclusion of High School.

Ministering Together, building the Kingdom

From 1952 to 1965 we were the only two congregations of Religious in Menabe region – the La Salette Missionaries (M.S.) and the Missionary Sisters of the Immaculate Conception (M.I.C.) – and both were working in the same parish of Morondava. Special bonds were created and every La Salette knows how much we owe to these Canadian sisters.

Not only did they teach and direct the school; they also worked with us pastorally, going out into the nearby bush churches on weekends to help prepare both children and adults for First Communion and Confirmation. In addition, they assured that our laundry was done perfectly; they frequently shared with us their culinary skills. We especially appreciated the deserts of cakes, cookies, and pies which they sent our way!

Their full-time ministry was education but they were always happy to join us on our visits to the bush, where they helped prepare children and adults for Sacraments. The M.I.C. sisters would later open the first Catholic School in Mahabo and in Bemanonga.

The Franciscan Missionaries of Mary Join the Team

In 1965 Franciscan Missionaries of Mary (F.M.M.) came to Morondava. Their congregation was well-known because of their medical skills and management of clinics and hospitals. A new Government Hospital was built in Namahora, and the government health services in Tananarive considered the Franciscan Missionaries of Mary the best to administer it. The government even built the convent for them on the hospital complex.

The presence of five religious sisters was a tremendous boost for the mission. The government hospital was run effectively. The sisters, who worked in the hospital's administration as Director, Finance Manager and Nurses undertook visits to the nearby bush churches and villages on weekends to give personal attention to the sick, to teach catechism, and prepare children and adults for the sacraments.

In 1972 they accepted to re-open the school in Belo, which Father Normand Mailloux (1930-2010) was forced

Sr. Claire, one of the Franciscan Missionary Sisters of Mary (F.M.M.) ministering in Morondava

to close due to lack of financial support. Today it is thriving.

In 1979, they also agreed to serve in Berevo. Their ministry in Berevo has been one of witness. They quickly became known from trips to the market for food. They opened up their home for classes, teaching women and children to sew, improve family hygiene, to cook and to plant family gardens. Their work continues today. They administer a School in Berevo (350 students) and supervise four schools in the bush (Betomba, Ankalalobe, Mahavelo, and Tanandava).

The Arrival of the Brothers of the Sacred Heart and the Sisters of Jeanne Delanoue

The Brothers of the Sacred Heart (F.S.C.) meet with some La Salettes for fellowship in Tsinjoarivo

In 1967 the Brothers of the Sacred Heart (F.S.C.) came to administer and teach at the newly built St. Paul's College for boys in Namahora. Similar to the College of the Immaculate Conception in Morondava, the education they give continues to be excellent. Both schools are now mixed schools with boys and girls, mainly due to the long walk students had to make across the salt flats to get to their corresponding schools. The name "college" refers to a fully accredited school. In 1972, the Sisters of Jeanne Delanoue (J.D.) came to Malaimbandy. It was the fulfillment of Father Joe Silva's hard work and determination.

Brother Celse Scotton, an Italian La Salette, had come to Morondava after many years in Antsirabe. He too was an excellent builder, having just finished building the convert and school in Mahabo. With the school in Malaimbandy now ready for occupancy, the sisters arrived. Another blessing for Malaimbandy. They were all native Malagasy sisters from the High Plateau, but that did not protect them from the blazing heat of Malaimbandy. They assured a national school curriculum, and opened a small Medical

Dispensary. They visited distant bush churches for extended periods, taught catechism, family hygiene, and sewing. It was a marvel sight to see them walking for hours, crossing rivers and streams, walking up steep hills with a portable sewing machine balanced on their head!

In 1979, they accepted to re-open the school in Miandrivazo, also closed years earlier because of a lack of finances. Today the college of St. Peter in Miandrivazo is flourishing.

Later, I will speak of the Center for Handicapped Children, called the "Beautiful Gate." In 1982, these same sisters of Jeanne Delanoue, after studying to acquire special medical and psychological skills, were the ones who would open the Center in Morondava.

The Carmelites of Mary Immaculate Join the Ministry

The Missionary Sisters of the Immaculate Conception (M.I.C.) opened a new college in Morondava

These were the first four religious congregations to work with La Salette Missionaries in the Morondava Diocese. Over the years a strong community spirit was built up as we came together for prayer, for moments of recreation, of grieving, of religious renewal. Words will never be sufficient to express our gratitude for all the sisters and brothers who worked with us.

In 1987 a new community of Religious men, the Carmelites of Mary Immaculate (C.M.I.) from India, joined our diocesan ranks and are still ministering in Mahabo and Ankilizato. There work was not only pastoral, but formative. They quickly established schools wherever they served. And they arranged to have other religious sisters come to work in the diocese.

With the Jubilee year of 2000 it was as if flood gates opened so that today we have twenty-five communities of women religious in the diocese and ten communities of men religious. Their presence is giving an intense and renewed effort in all our social activities, especially education and health, in view of evangelization of the West Coast of Madagascar.

Let us get back to our founding missionaries. In early 1935, there were only La Salette Missionaries working in the Morondava mission.

Chapter 10 – The Mission Spirit Grows Strong

Newly ordained Fr. Aloysius Spielman, M.S., volunteers for Madagascar

The city of Morondava remained the central community post for the mission, with Fr. Aloysius Spielman fulfilling the role of Superior in residence after the departure of Breault for a well-deserved vacation.

From the residence in Belo the missionaries served the entire northern section of the mission. There were constant visits and exchanges between the two communities. Not only were the Fathers faithful to their daily community prayers but never missed the monthly retreat on the 19th and their annual retreat.

Though he had no formal medical training, Newman was rather gifted and graciously cared for the sick who came to him. When we, the younger generation of missionaries, arrived over twenty years later people still spoke of his skill in providing healing medicines. Brady on the other hand was known for his preaching. Even the French administrators had nothing but admiration for his sermons, especially when preached on July 14th, the French National Holiday. These were good years and there seemed to be a most promising future for these young American Missionaries so dedicated and so willing to accept the hardships of life in the bush.

In June, as was mentioned above, for the Feast of the Sacred Heart, all the Fathers assembled in Belo to celebrate with Christians who came from the entire mission territory. In September a similar gathering would be held in Morondava for the Feast of Our Lady of La Salette. Getting together around the time of major feast days, holidays and holydays was an indication of their total unity in pastoral activities. Both Mac and Le Blanc spoke with great animation and gratitude of those wonderful founding years.

With the arrival of new recruits, they were sure they could evangelize the entire Menabe for Jesus Christ. Three new missionaries arrived in 1933, and it was decided that Le Blanc and Mac would move to Manja-Morombe. They were the first resident priests in that area, and Le Blanc would remain there until 1950 (17 years) thrilled to preach and offer the Sacraments, and build churches and schools. He was the first Catholic priest ever to visit the many busy villages.

As the number of Christians increased, new churches and chapels were built. With the arrival of sisters in Morondava there was more and more talk that central mission of Morondava would become an Apostolic Prefecture and that Spielman would be the first Prefect. Bishop Dantin was only too anxious to be liberated from the overall responsibility of the Morondava mission. We can understand his concern as he had more than enough to do to assure the Pastoral Care of Antsirabe.

Interior of the Manabe church in Madagascar

Chapter 11 – Exodus of (Most) American La Salettes from Morondava

Madagascar Missionaries: (from left, bottom row) Frs. Edouard Rostaing, Etienne Garon, Edouard Follezou, Raphael Lanfranconi; (top row) William Breault, Alphonse Coté

It has never been too clear just what happened, who and what actually transpired between the Colonial Authority and the La Salettes, and, as a consequence, why Father Spielman could not assume the responsibility of Apostolic Prefect for Morondava. He had served well in Madagascar for thirteen years, was fluent in French, and very respectful of French authorities. Both the French Ambassador to the Vatican and the French Minister of the Colonies gave assurance that there would be no objection to Spielman being made Apostolic Prefect; that is, placing a priest at the head of a 'pre-diocesan' missionary jurisdiction or territory where the Catholic Church is not yet sufficiently developed to become a diocese. Though in the light of Faith we have to accept that God works through events wrought by human hands, it is, nonetheless, very difficult to understand why this unfortunate break came about.

Leaving the Morondava Mission

Already in June of 1936 decisions had been made in Hartford, and Americans were told they would have to leave the Morondava Mission. It was a most challenging time for these zealous missionaries especially because funds for Madagascar had been cut off. The Mission Office in Hartford was now preparing to accept a new mission in Burma. It was not only unfair; it was unjust that all help from the United States was withheld, while missionaries had to continue their work. Mansfield wrote on June 20, 1936 in his letters how they had no money even to buy food.

> As far as funds are concerned, we surely are suffering; money is as scarce as ice cream. Our own Fathers in America are not sending us a cent, just the stipends for our Masses, and that is all. We cannot accomplish our ministry with such meagre funds – it is impossible. It is sad to see our work going on the rocks because of no resources whatsoever. We are really bankrupt. I think that if our creditors demanded their money, we should perhaps all land in jail. We are certainly passing through a terrible crisis, and I don't mean maybe. All building, and even our trips unto the bush, had to be discontinued, for without funds we cannot buy gas or even pay natives to

carry us long distances.

Already in October of 1935 Mansfield wrote:

> Yesterday I received a telegram from Fr. Le Blanc at Morombe. He says that he is dying of starvation. Fish is the only stable food there, and he can't eat it: even the smell of it makes him very sick. He asked me to send him some money. I wrote back that I am in the possession of 15 francs (one dollar) and that I could not part with that, as it separates me from starvation. We receive practically no cash from the [United] States: the Superiors are holding it up so as to have a little on hand in case we leave here and go to another Mission. In the meantime, we are supposed to live on our good looks. If we do not get an American bishop here in Sakalava we may go to another country as it seems that the French want this colony all for themselves. The government fears foreign influence.

Le Blanc attributed this sad situation to Father Francis Kirby, then Provincial of Hartford, but we can't believe that our Fathers in the United States were aware of the privations our missionaries were enduring. Not only were the missionaries sad that they would have to leave, but they had no financial help during that last year. I believe Mansfield was speaking in the name of all of them when he wrote:

> I shall shed tears when the order comes for us to pack up and leave. To say good-bye forever to these dear good people surely will be hard. One grows attached after a few years; I now can see easily how missionaries usually return to the Missions.

Such were the powers of the time, and then a letter came from the Superior General in Rome stating that the Sakalava mission would be turned over to the French Province. It was a sad day; yet we must see God's Providence at work and we shall see how God intervened so that American La Salettes would remain in Madagascar.

The Provincial Administration in Hartford had decided that the men in Morondava could volunteer for the new Mission in Burma but that, as an American Mission, Morondava would be closed. The provincial had so decided, but God had other plans! The Burma mission was indeed founded in 1937, and to this day remains a great tribute to the missionaries who worked there.

Fr. Francis Kirby, M.S. (1896-1958), first La Salette Provincial Superior in the United States

Chapter 12 –
Fr. Thomas Mansfield, M.S., Remaining in a Garden Watered by Tears

Fr. Thomas Mansfield, M.S., at his departure to Madagascar

Meanwhile in Morondava, Americans were still very present. Some had already received orders to return to the United States. How God intervened is a most interesting story that is worth remembering. Breault, who had gone home for a vacation with every intention of returning to Morondava, decided to remain in the United States. Newman and Steve had left in May of 1936 and Mac was getting ready to leave for an extended vacation, with some time in Ireland.

One of the most popular, generous missionaries, one whose constant smile and laughter had impressed the people, was Father Thomas Mansfield, M.S. Christians, non-Christians, Europeans, loved him as a brother and father.

Everyone knew how he had a sweet tooth and how he loved honey. People would give homey to Le Blanc and say, "This is not for you but for Father Mansfield." He served for a short time in Belo, and then in Morondava before being transferred to Manja-Morombe to work with Le Blanc.

Manja was the residence where the two priests lived together. Mansfield, however, wishing to serve with greater generosity, would spend extensive periods of time in Morombe. In late 1936 Mansfield had journeyed to Morombe. He decided not to return immediately to Manja, but to remain in Morombe during the rainy season (from December through March each year) to work on church and school.

January is not only the rainy season but the time of year when it can become extremely hot and humid. Mansfield had gone to a bush village for a visit and it was there that, on Thursday January 7, 1937, he came down with a sickness known as "Black Water fever" and which all too frequently was fatal.

Father sent word to the doctor in Morombe to send a vehicle that could bring him back to the mission compound in Morombe. As soon as the doctor saw him on Friday it was apparent that there was little hope. All day Friday Father sweated from an intense fever while being in a semi-coma. He spoke English and Latin so no one really understood what he was saying.

Prayers for a Special Priest

The entire population of Morombe, alerted by this serious illness, was in communion with his suffering as all tried to help him. The mission compound was filled with Christians in silent prayer. He was accompanied by a good Christian who helped him pray while holding up the cross to him. On Saturday Father asked that the Christians be allowed to enter his room so he could give them his blessing, and children were with him when he finally breathed his last Saturday afternoon.

Church in 1935 where Fr. Mansfield ministered with Fr. Le Blanc

In Fr. Emile Ladouceur's book, La Salette: *Ten Decades with Our Lady (1846-1946)*, he writes:

> The La Salette Missionaries from the American Province have left a fine record in the history of the Church in Madagascar, which has been aptly described as "a garden watered by tears, the tears shed by Our Weeping Mother of La Salette."
>
> There is a touching tribute penned by a native Malagasy, in farewell to the Fathers upon their relinquishing the Sakalava Mission to the French Province. We quote it in full:

"You may leave, valiant Missionaries, for your work, grand and beautiful and holy, remains. God has blessed it. He has set thereon the seal of sacrifice and has affixed thereto the stamp of suffering. One of you at least shall not be recalled. You will leave him here in Malagasy soil to perpetuate your remembrance. The memory of Father Mansfield will be the eternal, saintly echo of your sojourn in our midst."

> The efforts of the La Salette Fathers of Madagascar, beginning in Antsirabe and continuing to Morondava, have been so successful that Cardinal Laurenti did not hesitate to say that *"this mission is among the finest and the most flourishing of all the Catholic Missions."* Much of the credit for these splendid results goes to our generous French and American benefactors. The "Paradise of the Missions" earned that title through the sweat and tears of all who shared in the work.

The untimely death of Fr. Mansfield, a great dedicated missionary, would bring many graces to the mission, not least of which was that, because of it, the Americans would remain in the mission. Le Blanc was so touched and impressed by the sympathy shown by the natives that he decided not to return to the United States but to remain in the mission. When Girouard heard this, he also requested that he be allowed to remain. Mac had already sailed and was in England at the time. When he heard of the decision of Le Blanc and Girouard to remain, he immediately returned to the mission in Morondava without continuing on to America. So it was that, although the Provincial Superior had decided that all

Americans would leave, God had other plans for his Church of Morondava. Mansfield's death was the catalyst that made this happen.

Mansfield was buried in Morombe in the town cemetery. His was a simple grave, just like the ones of the people he had lived with and served. For years the Christians visited his tomb, bringing flowers in memory of one who had given his life for the mission. In 1964, Fathers John Repchick (1928-1998) and Joe Silva, who would arrive in the second wave of La Salette Missionaries, went to Morombe to collect his remains. They brought them to Morondava where he now awaits the Resurrection. He lies in peace next to Fathers Le Blanc and Girouard.

Simple tomb of Fr. Mansfield at Morombe

Write Home to Your Mother!

One will be greatly impressed by Mansfield's letters to his mother where he shares his inner feelings and emotions and his great love for his mother and family. In the distant mission as he journeyed through the bush visiting isolated villages, he would write to his mother. It was a way to remain close to her. How he longed for the day when he would be able to see her. In his last letter to her dated January 1st he wrote:

> You have prayed to the "Star of the Sea" to guide me back to you; well I really think that the "Star" is now shining, and it will not be so very long before our happy reunion.

Little did he know that the Star would lead him to his Eternal reward to meet his other dear Mother, Our Lady of La Salette. After Mansfield's death the people of the Morondava mission were both very sad but also consoled. Even though it was said that the Americans were leaving, they had left a most precious gift – one of their own would remain there.

By God's plan, the American La Salette Missionaries would continue ministering in Morombe until 1950. In 1950, the pastoral care of Morombe was confided to the Missionaries of the Holy Family – a Missionary Congregation founded by a Missionary of La Salette, Father Jean Berthier, M.S. The territory of the mission of Manja-Morombe was erected as a diocese in 1960 and is still served by the Missionaries of the Holy Family.

Plaque on Fr. Mansfield's tomb in Morondava

**Here lies our spiritual father
Thomas Mansfield, M.S.
Gone to God on January 9th, 1937
Being in his 30th year of life
"Pray for Him"**

Part Three — Apostolic Prefecture (1938-1955)

Early in 1937, the French Provincial, Father Joseph Futy, M.S. came for a canonical visit in view of the transfer of the Morondava Mission to the French Province. Spielman and Brady would leave in the course of 1937, and Clossey would be the last to leave in 1938.

Le Blanc and Girouard chose to remain as members of the French Province. They were soon joined by Mac. Those events brought to a close the first phase in the history of the Mission which is a great tribute to our American Missionaries. They were pioneers in the best sense of the word, on the road constantly to reach as many people as possible.

Today where they sowed the seed of Faith there are many churches, schools, young dynamic Christian communities ministered to by local priests. The churches, rectories, and schools they built are still there. Even though there are now few Christians who remember them, the baptismal registers are full of their signatures, authenticating the thousands of baptisms that they performed.

Bishop Dantin was greatly upset by the departure of so many young American La Salette Missionaries because he deeply appreciated their missionary zeal. With only the three original pioneers remaining, he also recognized that now missionaries from Antsirabe would have to fill the gap and staff the vast Morondava Mission. This meant fewer priests for Antsirabe.

Bishop Joseph Futy, M.S., first Prefect Apostolic of Morondava

So, we close this first part of an American La Salette Missionaries presence in Morondava. The official and published reason for the departure was France's refusal to allow Spielman to become Apostolic Prefect. This could very well be the reason. Yet all preceding meetings and discussions with authorities indicated that there would be no problem for the Americans to assume the responsibility for a mission in French territory. God alone knows, as he is the Master of History.

Once transferred back to the French, the mission of Morondava would soon become an Apostolic Prefecture, with the former La Salette French Provincial Joseph Futy becoming the First Apostolic Prefect. There would now be a complete Ecclesiastical separation from Antsirabe, even though both Antsirabe and Morondava would depend on the French Province for funds and personnel.

La Salettes were Leaving But Not Completely

So, after ten years of faithful service, American La Salette Missionaries were leaving without really leaving. Not only would the two tombs – Coté in Antsirabe and Mansfield in Morombe – remain as a lasting memorial, but three men – Le Blanc, Girouard and McDonald – would be the stable presence that for the next twenty years would keep the American spirit alive.

The next part of this amazing history will allow us to highlight the lives of three giants – three impressive missionaries, three men filled with a deep faith and great love for Madagascar and its people. Despite pressure from their American Provincial, despite the apprehension of having to serve under a French administration, their only concern was that they could in no way abandon the people. Their deep motivation was the love for souls and the establishment of God's Kingdom.

We can only hope that future generations of missionaries in Morondava will never forget the names of "Le Blanc, McDonald, and Girouard." They all died in Madagascar and are buried in their beloved, adopted country. The History of the Evangelization of Menabe cannot be written without their names being honored.

We in no way wish to underestimate the contribution provided by Breault, Spielman, Mansfield, Newman, Brady, and Clossey, along with Steve; but Le Blanc, Girouard, and McDonald, three stalwart American La Salette Missionaries, had the singular grace of giving their life to the very end for the mission. Their names are engraved in stone in the mission cemetery in Namahora, but even more so they are engraved in the hearts of those whom they loved and served. The three pioneer forefathers accumulated a total of 142 years of dedicated service for the evangelization of Morondava.

La Salettes with Many and Differing Gifts

These three pioneers of Catholic evangelization in Menabe were very different in character and personality. They had a great variety of talents yet they had but one heart, one spirit; it was to serve the people of the mission territory of Morondava. It was providential that, although in different years, all three died in the month of February to indicate how close they remained in life and in death. When we young Americans began arriving some twenty years later in 1958, they were still very active.

Malagasy men show their catch, a mighty crocodile

Not only did we admire their great missionary spirit but were blessed to inherit that spirit which had sustained their missionary endeavors. How fortunate and blessed we were to have these three pioneers to lead the way and help us understand the Malagasy mentality.

How we enjoyed listening to their stories, their adventures, and their love for the people. Mac could spend hours telling us how he welcomed Her Majesty's Army when, during World War II, English Forces took over the stronghold of Mahabo. We would get an even greater laugh when he recounted how, on one of his frequent visits to the bush with a catechist, they were forced to sleep by the river, and were visited at night by a hungry crocodile who, fortunately, preferred their roasted chickens to human flesh.

Our only regret is that we did not listen with greater attention and record their stories. Even we who have served here many years feel very small and humble when we look at these giants who led the way. Long years of dedicated, silent work in the distant bush country on the West Coast of Madagascar will remain alive in the annals of our history. Le Blanc was the last survivor, dying in 1990 after sixty-two years of active ministry. Jack and I feel blessed to be among the last living witness of the faith and love that inspired these three men.

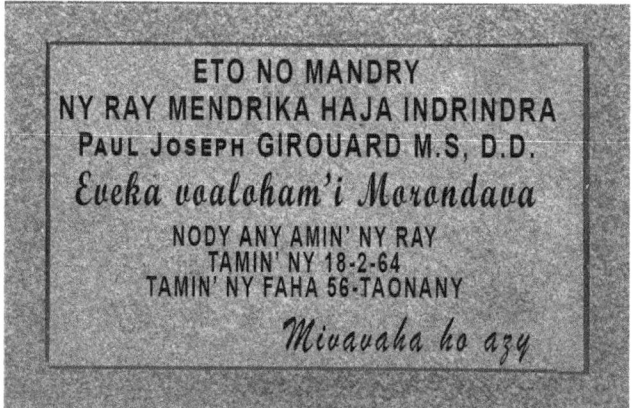

Here lies our beloved Father
Paul Joseph Girouard M.S. D.D
First Biship of Morondava
Who has gone to the Father
on the 18th of February 1964
At the age of 65
Pray for Him.

Chapter 13 —
Fr. Arthur Le Blanc, M.S., Who Lived the Longest and Won Every Heart

Fr. Arthur Leblanc, M.S., in 1928 before leaving for Madagascar

Father Arthur Le Blanc served the longest so we will begin with him. Originally from Saint Cecilia parish in Leominster, Massachusetts, he was one of the eldest children of a large French-Canadian family.

Like so many of us, the Sisters at the parochial schools had discerned a vocation and encouraged him to become a priest. Father Donat Fluet, a La Salette who also hailed from Leominster, encouraged him to join the La Salettes in Hartford, Connecticut.

The Call to Priestly Ministry got Stronger

This possibility seemed like a distant dream, because the family was poor, and Arthur had to work to help the family. However, with prayer and insistence, a year later his father finally allowed him to enter the College Seminary in Hartford.

In his first years, reading the life of Theophane Venard, M.E.P. (the French Foreign Mission Society) who was martyred in Vietnam and declared a saint, young Arthur already wanted to be a missionary. He always had a great devotion and spoke frequently of Theophane Venard. Whenever he had the occasion to speak of his own missionary vocation, he would always mention Theophane Venard. Le Blanc took his first vows in 1920 determined that he too would become a missionary in a foreign country.

After his first vows on July 2, 1920 – by the grace of God, all three took their vows on the same day – he was sent to Tournai, Belgium for his studies in Philosophy and Theology. Le Blanc was a bright, outstanding student, very popular and highly appreciated by everyone both at the University and in Community. It was his custom on Feast Days to prepare a poem and sing a little song for everyone's enjoyment.

Community was Central for Him

The French Fathers who studied with him had high praise for his community spirit and fidelity as a religious. Even in his old age, how he loved to be with the community. A community celebration would never be complete without a poem from Le Blanc and a song. This was perhaps a way of imitating his mentor, St. Theophane Venard, who had said: "Be happy, really happy. The life of a true Christian should be a perpetual joy, a prelude to the festival of eternity."

Le Blanc would never miss community meetings, prayers, or retreats. During his years in Tournai, while studying the Dominican school, known as the Saulchoir, he had great teachers, such as Father Sertilanges, who had a lasting influence on Le Blanc's spiritual life.

He was soon Off to the Missions

Yet always foremost in this mind was that desire to go to the foreign missions. After his Priestly Ordination he volunteered and was accepted for the Morondava Mission. Despite the fact that he had been absent from the United States for seven years, Father Crozet, the Superior General at that time, gave him – and Fr. Girouard who, after his studies in Rome, was also accepted for Morondava – only one month in the U.S. before leaving for Madagascar. Fortunately, the Superior in the U.S. was a little more understanding, and they were able to have three months at home. So it was, with great joy that young Father Le Blanc, realizing his boyhood dream, finally embarked for the long trip to Madagascar.

Upon arrival Le Blanc went directly to Morondava where he joined Breault, Mac and Steve. With no time to study the Malagasy language, he had no choice but to do his best with French. Liturgies at that time were in Latin, so he had no difficulty administering the Sacraments.

Mac and Steve were busy with construction. So that left newly-arrived Le Blanc to take over the pastoral care of Morondava and the surrounding villages. Breault was always in the far-off bush. Le Blanc remained in Morondava from where he continued to made visits to Mahabo (22 miles), Malaimbandy (120 miles), and the bush centers of Morondava. Le Blanc was very happy to work with Breault and they make a good team as they set about organizing the Parish of Our Lady of La Salette. Very kind and very charitable, Le Blanc always had nothing but good words and admiration for Breault.

St. Théophane Vénard, M.E.P. (1829-1861)

Opening of a Second and Third Mission Post

As mentioned earlier, with the arrival of new missionaries, a second mission post was founded in 1931 at Belo sur Tsiribihina, which undertook ministering to the vast territory to the north. With the arrival of more new missionaries from America in 1933, it finally became possible to open up the third mission center to cover the territories to the south. Its central post would be in Manja. Le Blanc and Mac were sent to open up this mission, becoming the first resident priests ever to live in Manja. They loaded two trucks with furniture and supplies needed to open the new post. We can understand the great joy and enthusiasm of the Christians who finally would have their priests living with them.

The new mission post in Manja would minister to three widespread mission districts: Manja itself, Morombe, and Beroroha, covering an area of roughly 12,000 square miles (by comparison, the entire State of Massachusetts is only 10,500 square miles). Le Blanc would end up staying there for a total of seventeen years. It was his first and greatest love.

La Salette Fathers' house in Manja with two other La Salettes visiting

During those years he had various assistants living with him, especially Mac who had come with him in the beginning; later, beginning in 1935, with Mansfield. Yet many times he was alone to serve that vast area.

A True Legend In-The-Making

Le Blanc became a legend. He traveled thousands upon thousands of miles, sometimes by *filanjana* but mostly by oxcart. For some reason he never saw the need to learn to drive; perhaps he found automobiles not only too expensive, but also too fragile and very prone to break-downs on the extremely rough paths that serve as roads in the bush country. He felt much more secure and far safer in an oxcart that would bounce along the dirt roads, or slush safely through mud and water on roads or passages inaccessible to automobiles.

God had given him a most remarkable gift; he was one of the very few who could sleep comfortably in an oxcart! Most missionaries considered the oxcart to be a torture chamber that would shake them up as if they were in a blender. But for Le Blanc, the sway of the oxcart was similar to being lulled into sleep like a child. He sat comfortably in a special chair and would pass away the long hours enjoying his pipe and the companionship of a catechist or a helper who accompanied him, drove the oxen, cooked meals, and served at Mass.

Spreading the Gospel Message to All Mary's People

When he could buy batteries for his portable Zenith radio, he would fiddle with it trying to tune into the *Voice of America* – his one opening to the outside world. Whether riding in an oxcart or being carried in the rhythmic swing of a filanjana chair, he found no difficulty reciting his Breviary and saying his Rosary. In the heat of the day, the oxcart could easily average four miles an hour, while in the cool of the night the oxen will trot about five and six miles an hour.

Le Blanc would come alive in his oxcart. How many little poems did he compose or how many homilies did he prepare during those seemingly interminable hours on the road? Years later, when he was in his 90s, his eyes would water with tears of joy when he climbed into his oxcart and headed out again into the bush. We always said that we would bury him with his oxcart – minus the oxen, of course.

Certainly, the best years of his life were spent in Manja, years during which he crisscrossed that vast area visiting church after church, leaving his home base for up to three months at a time, living on the road from his oxcart.

Fr. Le Blanc in a filanjana chair

The filanjana chair, suspended on polls and carried on the shoulders of four men, was the traditional way for dignitaries to travel. But having to pay eight carriers (two teams of four who would rotate with one another after carrying a certain distance), plus assuring their meals and lodging, was also very expensive. Two oxen, hitched to a cart, with a driver, who could serve as cook, companion, and when necessary as interpreter, was by far Le Blanc's preferred way to travel.

Why a need for an interpreter? There is one common language in Madagascar. However, there are eighteen different tribes of people, each with a hierarchy of sub-tribes; each tribe had its own dialect. Hence, at times the need for interpreters.

It is difficult for us to imagine the joy and consolation felt by a pioneer missionary as he explored virgin territory where the Gospel was unknown.

He was the first priest ever to visit many villages in this rough country which encompassed miles of sandy beaches along the ocean, wide expanses of prairie grass, and mountains that reached the 3,000-foot mark; and all this where no roads existed!

In some villages he might find a small chapel, usually constructed with the same materials used to build houses – mud walls and a straw roof – built by the few Catholic families scattered throughout the area. In other villages there were no Catholics, only non-Catholics who had never heard of Christ, and had never encountered a priest.

Soon, however, everyone came to know him, or at least know of him. Father related how at times he would decide to stop in a village just to pay a courtesy visit, to inquire if any Catholics lived around there. At other times he would receive an invitation to come, confirm a date for his arrival, and then go visit them. Contrary to the French Colonial Administrators who came from time to time with a list of demands on their time and possessions, Le Blanc had nothing to impose on the people, but rather a beautiful gift to bring – the Good News of the Gospel of Jesus Christ.

Welcomed with Customary Song and Dance

Whenever people knew Le Blanc was coming, whether by oxcart or *filanjana chair*, they would be waiting for the Father on the outskirts of the village and, with traditional Malagasy song and dance, would accompany him into the village. After a welcome speech by the village elders, he would be offered the most honorable house of the village. Once settled in, father would invite them to the Eucharist. Assisting at the "sacrifice" of the Mass, so different from their native sacrifices in which traditionally oxen were slaughtered, people would ask many questions – simple questions that could lead to deeper curiosity, and a desire to know more. Inevitably they would invite him to return.

Fr. Le Blanc enjoyed travelling in an oxcart

These became the first steps of evangelization – human steps which hopefully helped the people see the human side of Christ. What a grace it was for Le Blanc to have been the first priest ever to visit these villages!

They saw him Reading his Breviary and they Asked him Questions

In many villages there might be one person or a small handful of people who could read or write. Ancestral customs held large sway in the daily lives of the Malagasy people. Many parents could not read or write, and saw no reason why their children should do so. Many young boys and girls, however, were intrigued when they saw Father reading his breviary or the books from Mass. Inquisitiveness got the best of them and some would ask if they could learn.

Some village leaders refused to let their children study, ever fearful of what learning would do to ancestral beliefs. Others accepted and, when possible, father would find a capable teacher and open what was called a "garderie," similar to an Elementary School in the bush where children could attend classes for two or three years, be taught the fundamentals, learn how to read and write, to recognize numerals and solve basic mathematical problems.

Le Blanc's vision was always one of faith. The small "guarderies" were more than just a way to learn ABCs. They were paired with a vision toward evangelization. In fact, sometimes they progressed to what he called "juvenile parishes." We quote from an article he wrote after working in the Manja Mission sector in early 1950s.

> The best news from my sector at present is that my "juvenile parishes" are going strong. These juvenile parishes are composed exclusively of children. In many villages, while the adults refuse to respond to my advances as regards themselves, they are willing to allow their children to follow religious instructions and become Christians, but on condition that I found an elementary school in the village.
>
> This led to the foundation of several "juvenile parishes." The average number of children in such a parish is fifty. One native lay teacher takes full charge, giving the children religious instruction and the elements in the elements of reading, writing and arithmetic. So far, I am highly gratified by results and have good reason for hoping that little by little the adults will follow their

children in the Faith.

Already they like to assist at the catechism examination of the children and are proud when their children succeed well enough to be admitted to Baptism and First Communion. They showed good will from the beginning by putting up the school building at their own expense. I pay the teacher $100.00 a year. If I could afford it, I could get many more such parishes organized. I have already received formal declarations to that effect from several other villages. Before the year is over, I hope to be able to satisfy five of these commands. The other will have to wait as my numerous catechists and teachers already employed are a heavy charge on my limited means.

Faith and Education, Closely Linked

Most often the teacher would be a Catholic layman or women who would come with his/her family (also possibly in the company of family chickens, pigs, oxen, and goats) to live in the village. He/she would also serve as catechist, gathering people from the village and surrounding areas to pray and listen to the Gospel on Sundays.

Fr. Le Blanc in 1940 with a group of Christians

Father labored for ten full years before leaving for his first holiday in America. It was in August 1938. What joy to encounter those La Salettes who had been recalled to the United States a few years before. He was very happy that he would return to Manja after a year with his family, friends and community. The enthusiasm and team Spirit that had animated the American Mission were no longer there, but Le Blanc had come to serve the poor and he was extremely happy to be back with his flock.

Upon his return to Manja, Mac was there to build the large, spacious Church dedicated to Our Lady of La Salette that stands proud even to this day. He occasionally was given other priests to assist him in ministry in Manja or Morombe, but for the most part he was alone in Manja. He was able to open a Catholic School there which remains active to this day, while he opened many "garderies" in outlying villages.

Small in stature, and frail looking, Father had many bouts of malaria fever and other serious health problems. So much so that one French colonial doctor who treated him told his Superior that Le Blanc would not survive in the Missions, and his premature death would be his (the Superior's) responsibility. Once again, we see that doctors do not always have the correct diagnostic because Le Blanc lived to the graceful age of ninety-two, enjoying fairly good health. He would often get a good chuckle remembering how the doctor had predicted his early demise.

Hospitality was his Specialty

Le Blanc had an excellent memory and it is most unfortunate that he was not one to write his memories. He was a most hospitable priest and, whether living in far-off Manja or later on in Mahabo along the main highway, anyone who stopped in to visit would be invited to a good coffee, or, if available, a cold beer.

Le Blanc stayed in Manja for seventeen long years and how he was looking forward staying there. The war years of 1940-1945 were the most difficult. Not only were communications practically non-existent, but basic supplies were not even available. Without cotton their cassocks were made of raffia fiber. Nevertheless, with Mac as his companion, work went on, and New Church of Manja was dedicated in 1941.

A Second Visit back to the U.S.

Le Blanc went to America for his second visit in 1949. Although most of the young members of the La Salette Communities he visited did not know him, they were impressed with his simplicity and humility. Traveling man that he was, he enjoyed the "upgrade" from oxcart to plane, train and bus.

He visited most of the La Salette houses, giving retreats to young students, speaking and promoting wherever he could his mission that was in great need. There was a mission spirit among those young American seminarians, and in every seminary, there was an active mission-club. A surprising number of them were called "The Father Coté Mission Circle."

It was on his return trip in 1950 that, while in Paris, he received a telegram from Bishop Garon who was then the Apostolic Prefect in Morondava, informing him that he would not return to Manja but had been replaced by Father Joseph Burcklen, M.S. (1913-1998). Fortunately, he was already on his way back to Madagascar because that change in residence broke his heart. Even in his old age he would have harsh words for Bishop Garon because of his lack of sensitivity, not having consulted him before making the decision. A good religious, Father Le Blanc obeyed and took up residence in Mahabo where, once again, new vistas were opened for him in his ministry.

Celebrating Fifty Years as a Priest

It would be in Mahabo that, in 1978, Father Le Blanc would celebrate his fifty years of priesthood. Many French Fathers who had known him in Tournai, Belgium came to Mahabo to celebrate. The celebration was well organized and, humble as he was, Father was very thrilled with the recognition shown him.

Perhaps his greatest joy was that a very large delegation of Christians came from Manja. They publicly expressed their gratitude, assuring him that his ministry in Manja, Morombe and Beroroha would never be forgotten.

We also know that in 1959 those mission districts were transferred to the Pastoral care of the Missionaries of the Holy Family as a part of the new diocese of Morombe. The mustard seed planted by Le Blanc in Manja, Morombe and Beroroha became the solid, deep-seated roots of the tree known as the Diocese of Morombe.

Today, four diocesan priests and a deacon carry on the work Le Blanc had begun in Manja. Were he alive today, how he would be thrilled to see the School,

Fr. Le Blanc celebrated fifty years as a priest giving communion to one person he baptized

the medical center, the numerous bush schools and fervent Communities of faith flourishing throughout the district of Manja. The schools and medical center are under the care of the Holy Family sisters.

Fr. Le Blanc was Joined by Fr. Joe Silva

Though shaken and very much disappointed at being uprooted from Manja, docile Father Le Blanc moved to Mahabo where again he made all his visits with oxcart, happy as always to be in the bush. How

Four La Salette Bishops: Jean Guy Rakotondravahatra, Bernard Ratsimamotoana and Jean Marie Rakotoarisoa, with Fr. Le Blanc and Bp. Jean Samuel Raobelina

pleased he was in 1956 when Father Joseph Silva, a new young American La Salette Missionary, arrived to help him with the ministry.

Father Le Blanc enjoyed Joe's humor and especially Joe's great desire to serve the bush schools. These two, one young and one old, made an excellent team, bringing new life to the Mahabo parish. Except for some time spent in Morondava and in Berevo, Father Le Blanc remained most comfortable in Mahabo with people he knew so well and whom he had served with so much love and care.

Part of the Malagasy culture, which is based on ancestral worship, has great respect for old age. Le Blanc now embodied that quality and, in so doing, became a legend, greatly respected and honored. With the death of his two companions – Bishop Girouard in 1964 and Father McDonald in 1972 – he was the sole survivor of the original three. People knew he had founded the Mission in 1928, so it was also quite natural that he would get all the recognition and gratitude for work of our American Fathers.

Enjoying good health – despite what the doctors had predicted years earlier – but with poor eyesight, he was very happy to have Fathers Joe Silva and Roland Bernier with him in 1958.

It was like Old Times…

In 1961, however, Bishop Girouard's health was failing and he called Le Blanc to Morondava to take on the ministries of Superior, Vicar General, and Pastor of the Cathedral. Needless to say, he accepted reluctantly – after all, he had always been a bush missionary only too happy to be out on the dirt roads. In Morondava he insisted on having his oxcart and was happiest when, as part of the ministry there, he went out again to Befasy, Bevantaza, Manometinay, Belo sur Mer, and all villages he had known in 1928-1933.

With Bishop Girouard's health failing, Le Blanc was the man of confidence and trust that kept us all together. A peaceful, quiet, prudent man he was a very able leader. Many wondered why, in 1956, he had not been named Bishop instead of Father Girouard. Much to his regret, Le Blanc was on vacation in the United States when in February 1964 Bishop Girouard died. So often Bishop Girouard would say, "Father Le Blanc left on vacation too early".

Upon his return and after the nomination of Bishop Bernard Ratsimamotoana, M.S. to succeed Bishop Girouard, Le Blanc was named to the district of Berevo in the geographical center of the diocese. Many wondered at the wisdom of such a decision considering Father's age and the isolation of Berevo. Father was never one to falter or hesitate but went with the zeal of a young missionary.

Why not Two Oxcarts for Fr. Le Blanc?

The district of Berevo is divided by the mighty Tsiribihina River; the name itself means "Impassable," and indicates well the challenge Le Blanc faced. How would he get his beloved oxcart from one side to the other? Undaunted, his creativity showed the way. He got a second oxcart! Now he had one for the south and one for the north. As always, he was never happier than when he was on the road visiting the bush churches. While in Berevo he opened five schools in non-Christian villages, knowing that the school would be a powerful tool for evangelization.

Father Le Blanc never complained and would have remained in Berevo. But everyone realized it was not prudent to keep him in a district that had no means of communication, no adequate medical facilities, no roads during the rainy season, and only the highly unpredictable Tsiribihina River as a way in or out.

Consequently, in 1968, he returned to Mahabo, which would remain his home. It is where he had served both as pastor and curate, only too happy to be curate once again. But then, because of the shortage of missionaries, he was called once again to take over the leadership of the parish.

At that time, the Mahabo residence needed maintenance and major repairs. It consisted of a small kitchen, a dining room on the open veranda, and four rooms which served as sleeping quarters for the priests, and parish offices. It was decided that major renovations were necessary for the entire building with a larger veranda and a second story. The Fathers moved into the former sisters' convent (the school had been closed and the sisters had left the Mahabo mission).

Father Jean de la Croix Rakotoarimanana, M.S. (1937-2014) was pastor while I, Jack Nuelle, supervised the new construction. Le Blanc was only too happy. Now, once again as curate, he could continue his visits to the bush. It was a special joy at Christmas and Easter when many of the smaller Christian Communities could to gather to celebrate in the larger Bush Church of Analamistsivalana.

Finally Fr. Le Blanc retires

Le Blanc was, we mentioned, a quiet peaceful man. He enjoyed the silence of his room where he was a rabid reader. At that time, the Morondava Mission received hundreds – I would even say thousands – of paperbacks from the United States, so there was no lack of reading materials. Father enjoyed novels and historical books as well as religious ones. Throughout the years he had only candles or kerosene lamps to read by. The poor lighting finally affected his eyes and he was unable to see well enough to read.

He had memorized a few Gospel passages used in the Liturgy, and the entire Canon of the Mass, so could say Mass from memory. With his oxcart driver to accompany him, he continued his trips to the bush communities. Fortunately, he had his Zenith Radio to follow the *Voice of America* and *BBC World News*. It was convenient for all of us. He would keep us up-to-date on the news and was only too happy to share with us what was going on in the world.

One Last Vacation

In 1985 he accepted to go on his last vacation and was able to spend a few days at the Shrine of La Salette in France. There, on July 2, 1985, he thanked Our Lady for his sixty-five years of Religious Life. Once in the United States, he made his home-base at the National Shrine of Our Lady of La Salette in

Attleboro, Massachusetts. While there he underwent surgery for a hernia and then suffered from a urinary infection. Of course, among the doctors he would visit, one was an ophthalmologist.

The ophthalmologist in Attleboro informed him that they could not guarantee any real improvement in his vision, so Le Blanc refused to have the proposed operation on his eyes. But later, while visiting his brother in Florida, he was introduced to a very proficient ophthalmologist who promised better vision.

The operation was a success and Father Le Blanc came back to Madagascar with vision that allowed him to read and use the Malagasy Roman Missal for Mass. This happy situation lasted for a little over two years. Then, once again, his vision began to decline tremendously. Even with diminished vision, Father was happy in Mahabo, content to listen to his radio and continue his visits to the bush villages.

By that time, I, Jack, was the pastor in Mahabo, all the while putting the finishing touches on the new residence. It was my sad obligation to stop Father Le Blanc from going out into the brush in his oxcart. Le Blanc's faithful oxcart driver was almost as old as he was, and the two of them were good company for each other, but both had diminished eyesight. A few times during the rainy season, when it was difficult to judge the depth of the holes in the road which were filled with water, the oxcart tipped over with Father inside. Twice he almost drowned when the oxcart capsized on him. So, Le Blanc was informed, "No more oxcart trips in the rainy season."

That was a terrible blow because it ended a way of life. He continued to visit the bush churches, but, as he was driven in a Jeep into the villages, the same "Father-Le-Blanc-charm" was no longer there.

The Carmelites of Mary Immaculate Arrived...

In 1987 the new house in Mahabo was completed, and a new Missionary Congregation – the Carmelites of Mary Immaculate (C.M.I.) arrived from India. They were destined to take over the district of Mahabo, and I, Jack, would return to Malaimbandy.

It was also understood that Father Le Blanc would move to Morondava. Never one to leave a job unfinished, he asked to stay a bit longer in Mahabo to help the new Fathers, to introduce them not only to the district but to the pastoral methods of Madagascar.

Though three men – Paul, David, and Kuriakose – arrived to take over the ministry in the district, it was not long before they decided to split the Mahabo mission district into three sectors. Father Kuriakose left Mahabo to reside in Ankilizato to the east. Although only some 30 miles away, the road ascended over 2,000 ft to the summit of the Bemaraha mountain range, and then required dexterity to descend the only way down – through a pass named "the Mouth of Disaster" – into a fertile valley. For his part, Father David went to reside in Ankilivalo, a nearby town to the northwest. It was also located in a fertile rice-growing sector. This left Father Paul alone in Mahabo.

This division of ministry placed these three young energetic priests in different sectors. Father Le Blanc had apprehensions, first of all about them living in isolation, and secondly because, such a division left Father Paul alone in the most populated area of Mahabo. Would he have time to care for the needs of the city and visit the churches in the bush surrounding Mahabo? With Le Blanc's help and advice, he would do that and more, establishing churches in villages that had previously refused the Faith.

As very often is the case in religious communities, Father Le Blanc's transfer to Morondava took two years. Fr. Paul was more than happy to have Fr. Le Blanc continue visiting the nearby Christian communities. But in 1990, when Father Paul went to India for his first vacation, Le Blanc would have to be alone in Mahabo. That was an untenable situation, and finally he left to join our community in Morondava.

Growing Old Gracefully

He was well over ninety and, due to very poor eyesight, his activities were limited. Yet he always honored the community by his active presence in all community meetings and prayers. Continuously faithful to the habit he started some seventy years before as a young religious, on Feast Days he came with a song or a poem.

He could take care of all his needs despite his poor eyesight. We can say that he enjoyed excellent health for his age. He had a very regular schedule and every Sunday he would go by car, now with a chauffeur to drive him, to a nearby bush church to celebrate Mass.

As the district of Morondava cared for an important Bush School in Marofototra (six miles east of Morondava), it was possible for Father to visit there every week. I, Donald, was pastor of the Morondava district at the time and brought him there on Wednesday, February 14th so he could say Mass for the students.

When I went to pick him up at 11:30 am, I found him sitting under a large Kily (tamarin) Tree, happy to be surrounded by the school children and their teacher, speaking and laughing with them. That happy scene was the catalyst that helped us decide that he would now go out twice a week, Sunday and Wednesday, to say Mass. And of course, that pleased him to no end.

The Time was Drawing Near...

On Thursday afternoon, however, we were alerted that Father was agitated and in pain. The local doctor diagnosed a severe heart attack, and slowly Father slipped into semi-coma. Someone was at his side all the time and though he had a few lucid moments – he even smoked his pipe on Friday – it was evident that the end was near.

On February 18, 1990, Father Le Blanc died as he had lived; no noise, no problem. He was sick for forty-eight hours and on Saturday evening, as the sun was setting over the Mozambique Channel just outside his room, Father Le Blanc breathed his last.

The Funeral for a Truly Holy Man

The turnout for the funeral was incredible. Father Le Blanc was a living legend, the last of the founders to die, and there were some who remembered 1928 when the young missionary disembarked on the beach of Morondava.

His remains are in Namahora (at Villa La Salette) next to his friends Bishop Girouard and Father Mansfield; Father McDonald is buried in Belo sur Tsiribihina. For all of us young Americans who arrived in the fifties and sixties, Father Le Blanc was not only a big brother but a father to all of us. For years he was confessor to all of us so we owe him a great debt of gratitude.

We think a book could be written about Father Le Blanc and his many little poems and stories but we hope that these few notes will keep his memory alive. We are sure that from Heaven he has a special interest and attention for Manja and Mahabo.

In his later years, Father Le Blanc was often asked how he managed to live so long. He would take a tall glass, places two fingers on the outside at the bottom and, pointing to the measure, say with a laugh: "I would enjoy a little nip of rum in a full glass of water before each noon and evening meal." Whenever possible, this ritual was part of a daily aperitif shared with community, emphasizing the social dimension of life that was most important for him.

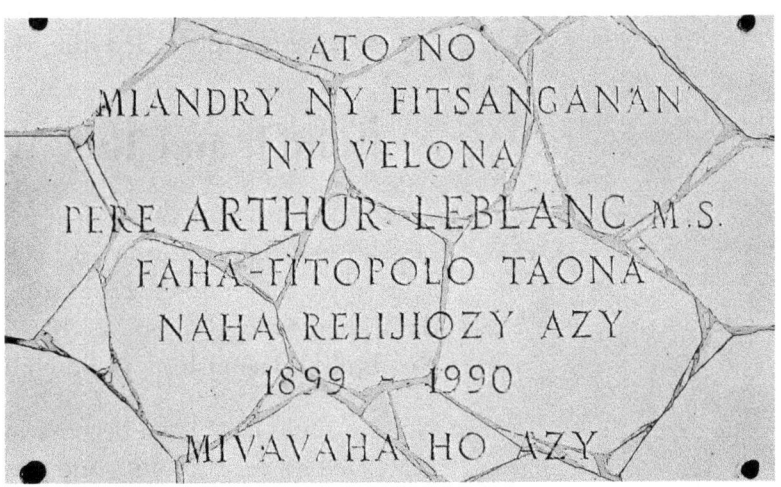

Plaque on Fr. Le Blanc's tomb in Morondava

Here Awaits the coming to fullness
Fr. Arthur Le Blanc M. S.
Having lived as a religious for 70 years
1899 - 1990
Pray for Him

Chapter 14 –
Fr. Cecil McDonald, M.S., the Master Builder

Fr. Cecil McDonald, M.S.

Our second giant is Father Cecil McDonald, M.S. (1897-1972), our proud Irishman who, though he immigrated to the United States, never became an American Citizen. He was always so thrilled to exhibit his Irish Passport. We simply called him Mac.

Build it and They Will Come ...

There was never any doubt that Mac's vocation was to be a missionary vocation to Morondava. When missionaries move into a new area, as was the case for Morondava, there is need to build – build Christian communities, build relationships, build churches and schools.

No one could have been better equipped to build than Mac. He had the diplomas and the know-how. But more especially he was equipped with a special gift to win the confidence of Malagasy workers who would follow his detailed instructions, work diligently, and get the job done. God, in His Divine Providence, having from all eternity seen the establishment of His Church in Morondava, had prepared Mac for the job. We can but praise and thank God's wisdom for having prepared Mac for the Morondava foundation.

Irish to the Core and Talented beyond Belief

Provincial archives have, without a doubt, information as to his birthplace, family and schooling. Mac would boast of his Irish blood and origin, but never gave details of his family and upbringing. He was 100-proof Irish and he would never allow you to forget it but I never heard him speak of his family. He was born Irish and very proud to die Irish and that was it!

His great dream had always been to have the La Salette Fathers establish a Parish, a Retreat Center, or a Seminary in Ireland. A Parish had, in fact, been established in Dagenham, England on the outskirts of London in 1928 just as Father McDonald was leaving for Madagascar.

That parish ministered almost exclusively to Irish immigrants who came to work in the new Ford factory. Father McDonald himself had contacted various Bishops and it seems there were good possibilities and openings in Ireland. But the La Salette administration in America would not budge. He didn't always have kind words for those who had not seized the opportunity to have a La Salette ministry in Ireland.

Fr. Mac and Bro. Steve, the Dynamic Duo

To speak of Mac and the construction work for which he was responsible, we must always remember to include Brother Steve who accompanied him from the United States. These two were a dynamic duo.

After Breault arrived from the High Plateau, Mac and Steve were the next to arrive in Morondava in May of 1928. Living in an old military shack by the ocean, it was evident that their first concern was to build a residence on a piece of land which already belonged to the Mission. Mac was given little time to learn the language.

Suitable accommodations were necessary for living quarters, and more importantly, the old mud Church required urgent repair to be made a worthy habitat as a permanent place for divine worship. In his own very easy, calm way, Mac was surely only too happy to open up his first worksite. He, like Le Blanc, was an avid pipe smoker. You would always see him with his pipe dangling from a corner of his mouth. Fortunately, Morondava grew some of the best tobaccos in Madagascar and there was always a plentiful local supply.

People Plan and God Provides

Providentially, there was an abundant supply of stone, sand, cement, and especially wood. In 1928, Morondava was surrounded by a large virgin forest, so it was not difficult to find good provisions of wood. But a very crucial part of construction is the people who would direct the work. Mac and Steve made a magnificent team who worked well together!

Those wonderfully inquisitive lemurs

I, Donald, never knew nor met Steve who was an immigrant from Lithuania. Always close to nature, he was very comfortable in the forest. When I arrived twenty-five years after his return to the United States, people still spoke of how he kept lemurs, turtles, snakes, and chameleons in his room. He never took a room in the residence but lived in his own little house on the property with his animal friends. I guess that one could say that he had a very Franciscan spirituality!

There is also a very humorous fioretti (little stories) of how, when Steve was serving as subdeacon during a Solemn High Mass, one or two of his inquisitive lemur friends jumped through the windows and into the Sanctuary. They not only disrupted the Liturgy but found a way to topple over flowers that decorated the altar. Needless to say, the young girls, and indeed the entire congregation, enjoyed the charming demonstration of lemur agility and mischievousness. Despite his peculiar lifestyle, Steve was a God's gift to Mac. He was a most precious helper.

It was Steve who would gather the needed building materials; Steve would drive the truck to the forest for all the wood needed for construction. He was only too happy to be in the forest, comfortable sleeping under an open sky rather than in his room. So, Mac had his work cut out for him and he continued to build until the very last years of his life.

On his way to Madagascar, he had the occasion to travel through parts of Africa where he examined their buildings and learned how to design buildings for a tropical climate. As a result, his Residences and Churches were built in view of excessive heat, always orientated to capture the maximum amount of airflow.

Building for the Future

Mac's first house in Morondava in 1929 and the center of the Mission Compound

I imagine his first real venture must, nonetheless, have been quite a challenge. As mentioned above, when they arrived, their first abode was an old military shack on the beach. A permanent dwelling was necessary.

The first residence would have four large rooms 4 x 4 meters (12 feet x 12 feet), with a large 4 meter (12 feet) closed-in veranda forming a protective belt around the building. There was plenty of space to walk or run all around the four rooms. The first house was finished in February 1929, and the second in July. Both houses are still standing today and very useful for the Mission work.

Today the first house serves as Parish Offices, Rectory, and the Catholic Bookstore. The second serves partly as storage space and partly as rooms for our La Salette Scholastic Brothers who come down to the West Coast to minister during vacations as part of their formation program.

It soon became evident that the old mud Church, even though it had already been enlarged, and embellished with wood, was much too small for the congregation. Breault, Superior in Morondava at that time, told Father Mac to build a "temporary chapel" in wood that would serve until a more permanent stone Church could be built. Breault then left on a three month visit to the bush.

A Temporary Chapel
Holding Eight Hundred People

Mac, however, figured it would cost very little more to add another 10 meters (30 feet) to the proposed construction. In the end, the finished "temporary chapel" was a Church was 40 x 14 meters (120 x 43 feet), seating 800 people with a large sanctuary and sacristy. That "temporary chapel" was so solidly built that, ninety years later, it is still serving as a parish church, having served also as the first Diocesan Cathedral from 1955 until 1991.

With large spacious windows, it is orientated to welcome the ocean breeze and to allow for some kind of comfort. Mac's creative thinking – dare we call it disobedience? – produced a monument in Morondava that has defied hurricanes, floods, and the ever-present termites. People love their church and many

French colonials, who were baptized and made their First Communion there, have returned to visit Morondava after many years back in France, coming to visit the simplicity and beauty of this wooden Chapel that Mac and Steve built. In 2020 for its 100th birthday it could qualify as a national monument.

Fr. Mac – Generous and Welcoming

Although building projects took up much of his time and energy it did not prevent Mac from having time for Pastoral Ministry. His easy, humble approach would draw people who were touched by the warmth of his smile. He had a heart softer than butter and I don't think he ever turned a beggar away without giving him something. He was generous not only with a smile and kind word but usually found something for the poor. The French and Indian merchants would lend him money, knowing quite well that it was meant to go for the poor.

And so it was that, after building the Church and two residences in Morondava, Mac went to Belo to build there what he considered to be the Main Residence and Center of the Mission Compound. Mac had a vision, and he fought with local politicians to have Belo, rather than Morondava, chosen as the Center of the Mission Region.

Why? Because the city of Morondava is barely two feet above sea level! Indeed, at high tide it becomes an island. During the equinox it was often flooded. Combine together the full moon, the monthly high tides and the equinox, and you have a yearly recipe for disaster! Mac prophesied that it would one day simply disappear into the Indian Ocean.

However, that was one battle he lost and Morondava remained the center of the Region. Had all the government money spent to keep Morondava afloat been directed instead to development in Belo sur Tsiribihina, the entire Region would have profited greatly. We still wonder if, with global warming of the oceans, someday Mac's prophesy will be realized, and the city of Morondava, invaded by the Ocean, will just vanish.

A Lasting Tribute to Faith, Ingenuity and Hard Work

It is astonishing – not to say miraculous – to recognize what can be done when faith leads the way. Three priests and one missionary brother arrived in Morondava in 1928 with their minds filled with dreams, their hearts saturated with love, and their spirits totally enlivened with faith. They used every gift, talent, and quality God had given them to establish a new mission. With the Mozambique channel to their backs, they fanned out through the Mission Territory confided to them to establish Catholic Church Communities to the north, east and south, while building a solid foundation in Morondava.

To Belo and Manja to Build the Kingdom

With new recruits arriving in 1931, they audaciously opened a district to the north in Belo. In 1933 a third district was opened to the south in Manja. One common thread that helped all these projects to have a solid foundation was the work done by Mac and Steve. The Churches and Rectories they build are still in operation today.

In 1933, from Belo Mac went to Manja with Le Blanc to open the new mission post. Every new beginning imposes construction projects, and no one was better equipped to do that than Mac. However, four years later, when he left for his first holiday, it was not sure that he would be returning to Manja because the order had already been sent out from America that the Fathers were to leave – dare we say abandon – the Mission. Never one to be idle, Mac managed, in his own special humble way, to squirm around it. He was on vacation, and made a pilgrimage to Israel. He spent much time in Ireland, his homeland, still convinced that La Salette could have a future in Ireland. He was in England, helping out at the parish in Dagenham, when he realized that Le Blanc and Girouard were still in Morondava, and going to stay there! He knew that his place was with them in the Mission. So, without setting foot in the United States, he boarded a ship back to Madagascar.

Mac built a new church in Manja

Bishop Joseph Futy, M.S. (1889-1956) the Apostolic Prefect in Morondava, was overjoyed with his arrival. Everyone knew how precious and necessary Mac was for the Mission. The mission could not find a more professional architect and contractor. His work was appreciated so much that he was even called to supervise and advise on Civil Construction Projects in Morondava.

Upon his return he immediately started building a spacious large residence that would serve as Bishop's residence until 1975 when it was turned over to the La Salette Congregation in exchange for their property in Namahora. Facing the ocean, that residence has stood strong and firm against some of the most powerful cyclones. Once during an excessively dangerous cyclone, the rafters lifted a few inches and we feared the worse; but Mac's beams held and there was little damage. The residence has the best location in town and from the spacious veranda we view some of the most colorful comforting sunsets you could want to admire.

After this monumental achievement in Morondava, Mac was sent, during World War II to Manja where he built the Church. Then he was off to Mahabo for a similar project. Few people are aware of the fact that during the war the English Navy invaded Madagascar and even made a landing in Morondava.

French colonial administration of Madagascar had generally sided with Maréchal Pétain, and therefore was not very favorable to De Gaulle's resistance efforts. Fearing that Madagascar would cooperate with Hitler, the Allies sent the British Navy to insure Madagascar's loyalty to the resistance. Books have been written on the British presence which was successful because the Colonial Administration finally accepted to fight with De Gaulle. Our French Fathers were generally favorable to Maréchal Pétain. There was, nevertheless, some resistance to the British invasion with fatal casualties in Diego Suarez, situated on the northern tip of Madagascar.

Mac built his "temporary" church in Morondava in 1930

When the British landed in Morondava, their intelligence services had been warned to beware of Fathers Lanfranconi and McDonald. Mac was not ordinarily one to get nervous or excited, but you just had to mention the British arrival in Mahabo and you were in for an hour of a very animated and emotional report of English ignorance and pride. As a true Irishmen, Mac had no special affection for the English so he took great pleasure challenging their arrogance when they arrived in Mahabo.

He was only too pleased to refuse them their afternoon tea, blaming them for the blockage that had cut off all supplies. Oh, Mac had tea in the house, but there was no way he would share it with these English gentlemen. Knowing the English would soon arrive, the Fathers had removed all tires from their vehicles which they set up on blocks to the disappointment of the British officers who needed transportation.

It is unfortunate we never convinced Mac to put down on paper his handling of the British invasion. He nevertheless lodged the officers in the Rectory for that evening. The British then realized that their intelligence services were ill-informed in calling Father Mac an enemy. Mac could get very excited and vocal when speaking of those anxious days when opinions were greatly divided in Madagascar between Maréchal Pétain and General De Gaulle. Father Futy in his journal has a complete and detailed account of the so-called invasion of the British Navy.

Back Home in Belo

Having finished the new church in Mahabo and a satisfactory residence, along with the Normal School for Catechists, Mac returned to Belo, his first and lasting love. Though he would still supervise construction sites in various locales, his home base now became Belo. It was his wish, which was respected when Mac died, to be buried there. He, as did Le Blanc, became legends. Everyone in Belo – Christians, non-Christians, and Moslems – could not help but love this humble, poor man who served so generously.

When the decision was made to build a new church in Belo on the site of the old one, Mac had other plans and a greater vision. The main street in Belo, which crossed the center of town heading north, actually cut through the grounds of the Catholic Mission. Mac managed to have the main street declassified and redirected so that it would lead directly to the main door of the new church. I don't know how he managed that, but I can see his little smile and hear his humble words as he convinced the Head Civil Administrator of Belo of the need to declassify the main street so that it ended at the church, along with creating two alternate roads branching around the mission compound. These would then rejoin and lead towards the north. People today still admire the strategic location of the Catholic Church in Belo, knowing nothing about just how Mac managed to pull that off.

In 1957 Bishop Girouard blessed cornerstone of new church in Belo sur Tsiribihina

Earlier it was mentioned that Brother Steve liked to have animals around him. Animals, whether wild or tame, have always been associated with human life, and in Madagascar they are ever-present – from a chicken as part of a meal, to the lemurs that embellish the forests, to the ferocious fossa who think the Lemurs are their special delicacy, to dogs and cats that circulate in villages and towns as cherished pets. All the fathers depended on oxen to transport them from village' to village where they instructed people in the Faith. Everyone knew that travel by oxcart was Le Blanc's specialty. Mac also had his favorite animal. His name was Jakob and he was a rare species, a radiated turtle. We never knew which of the two was the elder!

Mac built a new residence in Mahabo

Mac's Last Years

When a younger group of new missionaries began arriving in 1958 – and I, Donald, was one of them – we had the impression that Mac was already frail and worn out from years of hard work. He remained in Belo as assistant, known for his great charity and humility. We young missionaries enjoyed his Irish brogue, his natural and even humor, and his willingness to advise us on pastoral care. At one time or another, he had been pastor and director of the missionary districts in Mahabo and Belo. He had directed work sites in most of the mission compounds, but he never had major ecclesial responsibilities on the diocesan level, nor community leadership. He was a faithful, simple obedient soldier.

Tired from long years of hard work, Mac continued serving to the best of his capacities as assistant in Belo. When he went to Tananarive for a medical check-up in 1972, no one realized how serious it was.

At the Sisters' Clinic in Antananarivo he peacefully passed away in his sleep. Laurent Botokeky — (baptized by Fr. Clossey in 1936) — a Government Minister of Education and Culture during the First Republic of Madagascar (1960-1972) — was also a prominent and respected "Native Son" of Belo. As Government Minister, he was a very influential friend in Antananarivo, and had a great admiration for Mac. He took care of everything – especially the complicated paperwork – so that Mac's body could be transferred and buried in Belo.

This was in February, and it was the rainy season. Despite many delays due to heavy downpours, muddy roads, and crossing the intrepid Tsiribihina River which had flooded the area, Father Mac's body was laid to rest next to the Church he had built in Belo. It was later moved to a nearby burial site under a large Kily Tree in the mission compound. There is talk that the remains of Father Mac could find a final resting place either under the floor in the Belo Church or the community cemetery in Morondava with his brothers.

Tomb of Fr. McDonald next to his church in Belo

After so many years it is gratifying to see how people maintain the tomb with flowers, candles, and, in a great spirit of reverence, visit this missionary priest who gave his life for Belo. So, even though the community would like to transfer his mortal remains to the community cemetery in Morondava, people of Belo are not ready to give up this relic.

Chapter 15 – Fr. Paul Girouard, M.S., First American Bishop of Morondava

For the third, the last but not least of the American La Salette trio, we must now speak of Bishop Paul Girouard. He was the first American appointed to serve the Church in Madagascar as Apostolic Prefect (December 30, 1954) and the first Bishop of the newly-erected Diocese of Morondava (September 14, 1955).

We have here again one of the ironies of Church History. In 1937 there was no way an American could be Apostolic Prefect for the Catholic Church in Morondava – a situation which led, as we noted above, to the decisive event that saw almost all the Americans removed from that mission.

Fr. Paul Girouard, M.S.

The Completely Unforeseen Now Happens

Hardly eighteen years after that 1937 decision, and while still a French Colony, the Vatican named Paul Girouard as Bishop of the Diocese with no opposition from the French Government. Needless to say, Very Reverend Father Joseph Imhof, M.S. who was Superior General at that time, had been very hesitant to send in Father Girouard's name. He himself said that he was taking a risk in doing so. And it worked! He also said that, if the Congregation would have insisted a little more in 1937, Spielman could have been appointed the first Apostolic Prefect, and the Americans could have stayed.

It is true that, during those intervening eighteen years, there had been a World War and the Malagasy uprising of 1947 when France understood that there would be an end to their colonial empire. So, it came as no surprise when Paul Girouard was named Apostolic Prefect (1954) to replace Mgr. Etienne Garon, and then named Bishop the next year when Pius XII established the Hierarchy in Madagascar and Africa.

We agree with Father Josef Imhof, M.S. (1894-1986) that had a little pressure been used in 1937 the history of the mission would have been very different. With God there are no "ifs" and "buts," for God alone writes straight with crooked lines.

Differences of Opinion Arise

As always, we see God working in his Church. At this point we must consider another important decision that would have decisive effects on the history of the Mission. At that time, both Antsirabe and Morondava were under the tutelage of the French Province. Father Henri Gabier (1910-2001), Provincial of the French Province, made a three-month visit to Madagascar in 1955. Remember that the Mission of Morondava had been, since 1928, under mandate to the Congregation. Therefore, it was the Congregation that would present candidates for ecclesiastical leadership.

It was on the occasion of that visit in 1955 that Father Gabier proposed to Rome Father Griouard's name to become Bishop of Morondava. When Father Gabier finished his three-month visit, having consulted all the Missionaries, he was convinced more than ever that the French Province could no longer staff the two Missions – Antsirabe and Morondava. Knowing how limited the French Province was in personnel and knowing the ever-growing needs of Antsirabe, he considered it to be an injustice to focus on Antsirabe while neglecting the spiritual care of the Sakalavas.

There seemed to be no other solution but to return the Morondava Mission to the Propagation of the Faith who would then confide the Mission to a different Congregation. We can but admire Farther Gabier's intuition and courage for this decision.

This did not, however, please Father Imhof, Superior General, who, rather than turn the Mission over to the Propagation of the Faith, placed the Mission under the direct care of the General Administration. This included finding priestly personnel to staff various Mission Posts, as well as funding mission endeavors. For three years the Mission with an American La Salette Bishop was under the watchful eye of the General House in Rome. (Yours truly, Donald Pelletier, was the only missionary recruited directly by the General Administration to serve in Morondava.)

The French Fathers remained in Morondava knowing there would be no new recruits while awaiting a solution from Rome. It would be the General Chapter of 1958 that, having established the new American Province in St. Louis, the Province of Mary, Queen, gave it the responsibility of the Morondava Mission. That will be the object of another important era: St. Louis-Morondava: 1958-1988.

Fr. Paul in his missionary white cassock, cincture and La Salette crucifix

A History Worth Telling

Paul M. Girouard hailed from Hamilton, Rhode Island from a very devout Christian family which traced its origins to France in Rouanne and de Montlucon. To really do justice to Paul Girouard, our first American Bishop, an entire book would not suffice to relate his life history and missionary spirit. Upon his nomination, Father James P. O'Reilly, M.S. – a La Salette priest, author and historian – penned these words.

> One of the greatest events in the history of the Missionaries of Our Lady of La Salette took place at Hartford, Connecticut. On March 7, 1956, when the first La Salette priest from the United States was raised to the Episcopacy, in the person of Very Rev. Paul M. Girouard, M.S., who had recently been appointed the first Bishop of [the Diocese of] Morondava, Madagascar by Pope Pius XII.
>
> His consecration in the majestic precincts of St. Joseph's Cathedral [in Hartford], in the presence of a score of Archbishops and Bishops, of over two hundred La Salette Fathers and Brothers, of several hundred diocesan and regular priests and thousands of lay people, was a fitting tribute to the intrepid faith of the two founders of the Congregation in the United States.

He goes on to give us a few details of Paul's younger years.

> But the path to the missionary priesthood and eventually to the high honors of the episcopacy, was not strewn with roses. When Bishop-elect Girouard arrived at the Seminary on New Park Avenue, it was thirty-nine years since, as a young man, he had walked up the same steps to begin his long career of study, prayer and sacrifice. The fifth of eleven children, he had no money to pay for his education, and had to rule out the Diocesan priesthood as a result.
>
> He then tried two other missionary Orders, but both required a High School education before admittance. Even this condition was an obstacle, as he had been obliged to leave school early to help support his family. The Bishop-elect was about to give up his ambition for the priesthood and join a group of teaching brothers when a friend told him about the La Salette Seminary at Hartford. The reply came back: 'What are you waiting for? Classes have already started.'
>
> The Superior had judged rightly. Educated by a devout Catholic family, the new candidate from his earliest years in the Seminary gave proof of the supernatural strength of character, that deep faith and sound piety, that self-sacrificing zeal, which are the hallmarks of a priestly and missionary vocation.

The First Bishop of Morondava

Thus, Father O'Reilly gives us an indication of the virtues of this young man. He was an extraordinary man, a great missionary who became the first Bishop of Morondava. He would be very conscious of his responsibility and place in history. He had apprehensions regarding the future of the Diocese, not being able to visualize how the area would develop. It would be good for us to know better this outstanding missionary.

Though he was very proud of his family and remained very close to his brothers and sisters, he shared very little of his youth and early schooling. He was brought up in a very strict moral and conservative family atmosphere, very meticulous, a very neat and proud man who never accepted compromise.

He was born on December 27, 1898. Again, Provincial Archives must have details of his formation in our various centers. One sure date is that the three men, Le Blanc, McDonald, and Girouard, took first vows together July 2, 1920 in Bloomfield, Connecticut. Little did they realize that they would minister together in Madagascar and give the total gift of their lives for the Missions.

After his first profession in 1920 Paul Girouard was sent to Rome for his Philosophy and Theology which was most providential in view that one day he would be Bishop. He did have problems with scruples while in Rome, but thanks to the patience of a holy Spiritual Director, he overcame them, even though in his late year, suffering

Bishop Paul Girouard, M.S..
first bishop of the Diocese of Moronodava

Bishop Paul visits his bush communities

from a serious heart decease, the same scruples returned to haunt him.

After Ordination, to his great delight he was sent to the Madagascar Mission. He figured that his very name Paul was a prophetic call for him to serve in the missions. Yet, contrary to what his two classmates had done, he did not go directly to the new mission in Morondava, but to Antsirabe. He replaced Breault who had already served seven years in Antsirabe, knew the language and had make several visits to the West Coast.

Naturally, Breault was the one chosen to open the American La Salette Mission in Morondava. His departure from Antsirabe would indeed leave a void in personnel that Bishop Dantin could not afford to have. Though his fellow Americans, Fathers Breault, McDonald and Le Blanc, along with Brother Steve were already in Morondava, Bishop Dantin insisted that Paul replace Breault in Antsirabe rather than go directly to Morondava.

This was also most providential, as Paul had the opportunity and time to study the Malagasy language and also to profit from the pastoral experiences of our French Fathers. Of all the American Fathers who worked in Antsirabe, Girouard was the one most appreciated by the French Fathers. Of the three missionaries he had the best knowledge of the Malagasy language being the only one to have had the opportunity to study.

He served for five years in Betafo with Father Garon who would later precede him as Apostolic Prefect in Morondava; then he served one year in Faratsiho with Father Louis Feuvrier (1881-1964). Though very generous in visiting and ministering to the bush churches, Paul nevertheless suffered much from the lack of cleanliness and hygiene. He made sure to bring his own supplies, along with beddings that were neat and clean. He was a bush missionary and very happy to visit the bush villages but he made sure to be well organized, bringing with him all necessary supplies.

There were few roads, even in the Antsirabe Region, and missionaries would travel either by horseback or the filanjana carrying chair. Though he was looking forward to the day when he would join his American brothers on the West Coast, Paul was extremely happy to serve in Betafo as there was so much ministry to be done and so many people to care for.

The mortal remains of Father Coté were in the cemetery on the Betafo mission compound and Paul would frequently visit the tomb to be imbibed with and help carry on Father Coté's missionary spirit. He was greatly influenced by Coté's missionary zeal that he considered a model.

Lay Catechists – a Gift to the Church of Madagascar

His time in Antsirabe was most beneficial. It afforded him the means both for the study of the Malagasy language and for an in-depth initiation into missionary pastoral work in Madagascar. Well ahead of his time in ecclesial thinking, he was totally and completely convinced that evangelization would be accomplished with and through Lay Catechists.

The pastoral care of thousands of isolated and distant Faith communities was dependent on qualified catechists. He experienced this in Antsirabe and thus, when he was allowed to join his fellow American La Salettes in Morondava, he was named the first Director of the Training Center for Catechists.

After his Episcopal Ordination, he used all gifts received to build the modern Center in Mahabo for the training of Lay Catechists. The Center is always there and continues to assure the needed formation for our Lay Catechists.

Joining his Friends, Le Blanc and McDonald

After six years in Antsirabe, in June of 1934 Paul Girouard was allowed to join his American confreres and his friends, Le Blanc and McDonald. Paul worked mostly in Belo with visits to Maintirano, Morafenobe, and the surrounding areas. Paul was a great missionary and never so happy as to be in the bush visiting Christian communities. He left some rather interesting stories of diabolical possessions that I can believe were true experiences. Some of the more dramatic possessions were published in the National Magazine for the Clergy.

In 1944 Paul was named Pastor of the District of Mahabo. This gave him the pastoral care of not only the main Parish Church, but of some forty bush churches. From his work both in Antsirabe and Belo, he was more than ever convinced that Lay Catechists were necessary. Once in Mahabo, despite the heavy pastoral load of parish and bush ministry, he opened the first Training Program for Catechists.

Some Exceptional Lay Catechists

Some of his students would become great church leaders, most grateful for the faith and missionary spirit received from Paul Girouard. Victor Maheny would be the first catechist of Belo sur Mer, south of

After directing the training program in Antsirabe, Girouard opened a similar school in Morondava

Morondava, where he served for over thirty years and established a vibrant community that remains today a witness to his years of dedicated service. Victor's children and grandchildren carry on the tradition while one of his granddaughters is a sister of the Congregation of Jeanne Delanoue, one of his grandsons is a catechist, and another is in the seminary.

Another celebrated catechist was Pierre Celestin who worked for years in Manometinay. Thomas Mampitoesty, a native Sakalava of the area, was not only catechist but inspector for over fifty years in the District of Mahabo. There are many others but these three men could vouch for the solid catechetical training given them by Paul Girouard.

Paul was in Mahabo until 1950 when he was named to take over the mission district of Malaimbandy – a district that had been founded three years earlier. As is true whenever a new mission district was opened, everything had to be done. His accommodations were at a minimum, and he lived in the local "gite d'étape" or "traveler's refuge," consisting of four walls and a roof. The few acres of land that surrounded this rustic abode were to become the center of the Mission Compound of Malaimbandy.

The Challenges of His Mission Vocation

Though he suffered greatly in Malaimbandy, due to a general indifference of the population, he would continually visit the bush villages, even where there were no Christians. The area was populated mostly by people from the Bara Tribe which to this day continues to be very reluctant to accept Christianity and generally indifferent to human development and education. Despite schools and efforts of many missionaries, Malaimbandy continues to be a very difficult district. Paul worked there for five years until he was named Apostolic Prefect and, soon after, Bishop of Morondava.

His nomination arrived in January, during the rainy season when rivers are rushing torrents. Today between Malaimbandy and Morondava there are twelve bridges. In 1955 there were four! It took Paul over a week to travel the 120 miles by oxcart, often sleeping under the stars by the side of swollen rivers and streams while waiting for the water to subside to a manageable level so he could proceed across.

His New Responsibilities

Episcopal Consecration in Hartford, Connecticut of Paul Girouard

Though he was most reluctant to accept the new responsibility his welcome in Morondava was a triumph. He was received with great hope, joy, and enthusiasm by the population – and what is more surprising by the French Colonial Administration. Christians were thrilled that an American had been named to shepherd the Mission. Several months later, in November 1955, he was appointed as the first Bishop of the new Diocese of Morondava.

Though Paul could have been consecrated Bishop in Antananarivo, it was important for the strengthening of relationship with the Hartford Province to celebrate this honor given to one of its men. Another equally important factor was that Bishop Girouard would be looking for new recruits coming from the United States because the French Province had already published its decision to leave the mission of Morondava. So, it was a great day for American La Salettes when Bishop-elect Paul Girouard was consecrated Bishop in the Hartford Cathedral by Bishop Henry J. O'Brien (1896-1976).

His Consecration as Bishop

Much publicity was given to the event; much was written so no need to give any details here. That very same year in May 1956 Bishop Girouard ordained priests and deacons at the La Salette major seminary in Ipswich, Massachusetts. We must not forget that, at that time, Father Joseph Higgins, M.S. (1915-1976) was Provincial of the Hartford Province, the Province of Our Lady of Seven Dolors, and not only was he justly proud of the Ordination but most generous toward the Mission. In 1956 he allowed two young priests, Fathers Repchick and Silva to leave for Morondava and in 1957 four more, Fathers James Hogan, Henry (Sam) McKay (1920-1999), Roland Bernier (1929-2000) and Joseph Shea.

Though the people of Morondava would have wanted their Bishop to be ordained in Madagascar, we realize that the ordination in the United States was a good move. Within one year, six new Missionaries would arrive in Morondava. Everywhere Bishop Girouard went in the United States, he was admired for his pontifical stature, his winning smile, and his missionary stories. He came back to Madagascar with a solid four-wheel drive covered Jeep, and money for urgent projects such as the construction of the Training Center for Catechists and a large, impressive boy's school in Morondava.

Though the Missionaries of the Holy Family from Switzerland had taken over ministering in the southern districts of the Diocese only five years earlier, Bishop Girouard was anxious for them to have their own Diocese and their own Bishop. After innumerable correspondence, it was a relief and a joy, when five years later, in 1960, the newly created Diocese of Morombe was confided to Missionaries of the Holy Family.

Fr. Raphael Lanfranconi, M.S. Arrived

Though Paul was fluent in French and could correspond in correct French, he lacked confidence in his ability to write well and thus relied greatly on Father Raphael Lanfranconi, M.S. (1892-1972). Father Franco, as he was affectionately known, had arrived in Madagascar in 1921 and had studied Malagasy with Fathers Coté and Breault. Then in 1938, after seventeen years in Antsirabe, was sent to work in Miandrivazo.

A very talented man, with great determination and extreme sensitivity, he had been religious Superior of the mission for many years and could also have served as first bishop of Morondava. Bishop Girouard was very fond of Franco who took on at the same time the duties of Pastor of the Cathedral, Vicar General of the new Diocese, Religious Superior, and Treasurer of the Diocese. He wielded much of the authority (too much perhaps); this was the reason why he was a source of discontent among the Fathers and Religious.

After the visit of Father Wilfrid Boulanger, M.S. (1898-1985) in 1959 and that of Fr. Alphonse Dutil, M.S. (1896-1991) in 1960, Bishop Girouard realized that, for the greater good of the mission, he had to distribute those responsibilities to others. Placing the responsibility and authority in the hands of others was a source of great suffering for both of them. It was a most painful moment for Bishop Girouard; one that, without a doubt, foreshadowed the first symptoms of cardiac weakness.

Fr. Raphael Lanfranconi served first in Antsirabe, and then came to Morondava

His Weighty Responsibilities take their Toll

Those were, nevertheless, good years during which, under the guidance of Bishop Girouard, La Salettes from various ethnic backgrounds worked together, and new, spacious, solidly built churches were inaugurated in Belo sur Tsiribihina, Miandrivazo, Ankilizato, Belo sur Mer, and Malaimbandy. Work was finished on the large new school in Morondava, as well as on the new school and sisters' convent in Mahabo. Construction of a new boy's school in Namahora had also begun.

Because of failing health, Bishop Girouard could not attend the opening of the Second Vatican Council on October 11, 1962, nor any subsequent sessions. Those were, however, the years that marked the arrival of other young American La Salettes. This gave him much hope and he thoroughly enjoyed initiating them [including Donald] to all the details and excitement of missionary life.

He loved to take one of us on mission journeys with him, during which every tree, every turn in the road, every bend in the river, every village, and every Chapel would be associated with his experiences and stories.

While we, the younger group of missionaries, studied the Malagasy language in Morondava with qualified local teachers, those trips with Bishop Girouard were most beneficial in our missionary education. We, of course, were a new generation with new methods.

New Missionaries and Their New Methods

(from left) Fr. Le Blanc, Bishop Girouard and Fr. Donald Pelletier leaving the residence for a Solemn Mass

When I, Donald, finally had my own district and Bishop Girouard came for Confirmations, he would often voice his disapproval of our new methods. For example, the older missionaries would always travel with their cooking and kitchen utensils – and even their cook – knowing that the Christians would furnish chicken, eggs, and rice. They carried with them sturdy boxes, known as "popote" that contained sugar, salt, cooking oil, vinegar, etc. and all utensils needed to prepare and serve a meal. We, the younger crew, thought this was too complicated. We were content to accept cooked food from the Christians and actually we thought they prepared excellent, tasty meals!

When Bishop Girouard came to Befasy, Beleo, and Belo sur Mer, he did not always enjoy the cooked meals presented by the Christians. He, as well as Franco, told me on many occasions that I would not last very long as a missionary nor survive many years in the bush living without the "popote."

Actually, I have survived both of them and have spent many years in the bush doing very well with meals prepared by the Christians. In many villages I would eat with the family, thus establishing a closer relationship with them. Maybe not the healthiest method but we have survived as well as, and even better than many of the older missionaries.

A Truly Good Shepherd

As first bishop of the Diocese of Morondava, Bishop Girouard was a good Shepherd who loved his people and cherished visiting with them. He was a good preacher, always preparing his homilies well. In 1960, Madagascar gained its independence from France. There was great fear of the Communist Party which was very active in Madagascar, and had established solid support in the Morondava area. We were all encouraged to preach against Communism which again was not an urgent matter for us. In fact, I had good friends in the Communist Party that, I, Donald, in fact would allow to receive Communion despite interdiction by Father Franco.

His Ailments Increase

In 1960 Bishop Girouard went to Switzerland for the Episcopal Ordination of the first Bishop of Morombe and it was in Switzerland that he experienced his first serious heart attack. Upon his return he was never the same person and had to lighten his workload. He considered sending in his resignation to the Apostolic Nuncio but was advised to ask rather for an Auxiliary Bishop, which he did not see as a viable solution.

Considering his failing health, he continued to guide the Diocese, making needed decisions especially after Morondava had been handed over to the new Province of St. Louis, which would furnish both missionary personnel and financial aid. His classmates, Fathers Boulanger, Provincial of the St. Louis Province and Dutil, Superior General, supported him and encouraged him to continue his ministry. He delegated much authority to Father Le Blanc, his Vicar General, ministering at the Cathedral Parish.

In the late afternoon three to four times a week he would ask me [Donald] to drive him out to Marofototra to Pignolet's concession that bordered the Morondava River. There I would let him off and with his cane he would go and walk on his own for thirty to sixty minutes as I waited in or around the car. While he was enjoying his walk, I would catch up on my reading.

**Bp. Girouard,
the first bishop of Morondava**

How he enjoyed those walks, how he would be revitalized by the quiet and peace of the river! I can't say that I was thrilled to be the driver, but then I wanted to believe that I had enough faith to say I was doing it for Christ. It was a consolation for him to be driven out to Marofototra. I could never drive too slowly, so that he could take notice of every new house or new construction along the road.

The long caravan of cars and people in the funeral procession

Living with him on a daily basis, joining him for prayer, and at an evening game of cards I didn't realize just how sick he was. His doctor had us move his living quarters from the second floor to the ground floor so he would no longer need to climb stairs. But even that did not alarm me. He was strong enough to preside at the Pontifical High Mass in the Cathedral for Christmas 1963 and again for New Year 1964.

Not being able to preside at Mass on the Feast on February 2nd, nor on Ash Wednesday, were indications that he was weakening. As we entered the Lenten season, he would not hear of going to the Hospital or the Clinique in Tananarive. He wanted to die in Morondava.

On February 18th, as the medical plane was flying overhead to take him there, he breathed his last. With great faith and peace, he had received the Last Rites two days earlier with all the Fathers, Sisters, and some Christians in attendance.

His Funeral was a Local Day of Mourning

His funeral was one of the greatest in the history of Morondava. The Cathedral, which Mac and Steve had built in 1929, was too small to hold all the government officials, Muslims, Protestants, and non-Christians who joined the faithful Catholics of the Diocese in praying. In his honor, all stores, schools, and offices throughout the city were closed. It was declared a day of mourning.

The Trio Served Well and Left a Legacy

He was buried in Namahora under a Kily (Tamarin) tree as he had desired. In 1964, Bishop Girouard was the first of the trio to die; Mac would die in 1972, while Le Blanc would outlive them all until 1990. If American Missionaries were here to carry on the legacy, it was because these three men had decided to remain in Morondava even after Superiors in the United States had ordered them to return to the United States.

Fr. Jeremy Morais, M.S. visits the tomb of Bishop Girouard

They preferred to join the Province of France and remain in Morondava rather than to abandon the mission that had been so integral to their lives. We will have more occasions later to mention these men as we continue our memories but their presence and work was vital during the years of 1938 to 1958 when the mission depended on the French Province.

Chapter 16 – Faithfully Filling the Gap

Before moving on to the St. Louis years, we need to give great credit to two American La Salettes who came from Immaculate Heart of Mary (IHM) Province in Attleboro, Massachusetts to serve in Morondava during the years of Bishop Etienne Garon, M.S.

We recall that when, in 1936-1937, the La Salette American Missionaries were recalled to Hartford, both personnel and finances from the Mission Office were discontinued. All the Missionary efforts of that Province were now directed to the new mission in Burma. Morondava was stranded, existing with a skeleton crew – roughly three priests for 90,000 square miles.

Soon a few French La Salette Missionaries came to minister there: Father Franco was one of the first to come to fill the gap. After World War II others, some of the French priests liberated from military service, came to help. An appeal was made to other Provinces, and among the few who could be liberated were two Americans: Fathers Gerard Langlois (1913-1979) and John Berube.

(from left) La Salette Fathers Léon Mousset, William Breault and Etienne Garon with some young seminarians from Betafo

Fr. Gerard Langlois, M.S.

Fr. Gerard Langois, M.S.

Gerard Langlois was a native of New Bedford, Massachusetts. He had always dreamt of a Missionary vocation and, as a young La Salette, had been impressed by both Fathers Girouard and Le Blanc when they came to the Province of the Immaculate Heart of Mary (IHM, Attleboro, Massachusetts) while at home on vacation.

Among the first class to enter Enfield in 1928, he was among the first ordained from the IHM Province. Years earlier, there had been a question of IHM Province taking over the Morondava Mission. But Asia beckoned, and the IHM Province launched a Mission in the Philippines. Father Langlois did not feel the call to serve in Asia but when the occasion presented itself, he volunteered and was accepted for the Morondava Mission.

He arrived in Morondava in 1949 and was stationed in Belo with Mac. Despite his great zeal and generous spirit, Langlois did not have the physical capacity for the bush life of Madagascar. During the many years that he spent in Belo, he made very few visits to the outlying bush churches, and only once ventured to travel on the river to Berevo – a long and fatiguing sixty mile up-stream journey.

Madagascar was still a French colony, and many elderly French expatriates still lived and worked there.

Cathedral Maria Manjaka

With a good knowledge of both the Malagasy and French language, Langlois found in Belo a very fruitful ministry. His was a very discreet presence. He administered the Sacraments, celebrated Mass, preached Retreats, performed Weddings, and was especially generous in visiting the sick and elderly – both Malagasy and French. His presence and his ministry were both highly appreciated. He took his first vacation in 1958.

In 1961 he was named to Morondava. There he continued his ministry among the bedridden and sick in the hospital. He had a wonderful approach with French expatriates who had lapsed in the practice of their Faith, and many died with the Sacraments due to Langlois' visits.

Because of constant bouts with health issues, he was sent, in 1965, to the milder climate of Antsirabe where he served as Chaplain at a retirement home for elderly French expatriates whose active lives had been in Madagascar and wanted to die there. He was very happy to continue with a ministry he enjoyed. However, after a few years, and with deteriorating health, he returned to Attleboro.

The 2000 Jubilee Year Emblem

Despite his physical handicap he contributed much to the life of the Belo parish. Many elderly people still remember him; among them are elderly couples who remember having been prepared for Marriage by him, and are proud of the fact that they were married by him.

When we, the younger American La Salettes, began arriving in 1958, he advised us very fraternally that we were not to try to change the Malagasy… "they will get the best of you and wear you out." This was a word of wisdom that served us well.

Father John Berube, M.S.

Another young American La Salette who felt called to serve in Madagascar with Bishop Garon was Fr. John Berube. He hailed from Springfield, Massachusetts, and was also from the Province of the Immaculate Heart of Mary. He arrived in 1954 and served until 1960.

John was very intelligent, gifted in languages and adapted quickly to Madagascar. A good organizer and a gifted speaker, he always impressed people with his smile and friendly approach. After learning the language, he first served in the isolated northern missionary district of Ankavandra with Father Bernard De Boisseson, M.S. (1908-1980), a rugged Frenchman who had survived World War II and was known locally as "the donkey priest" because he always travelled with them. At home, he had them corralled next to the house. They are noisy creatures, and it was more than John had bargained for. So, after a year John was named as Director of the southern mission post of Mandabe. He served there for two years where he was a good pastor and a spirited animator with all the parish groups, while not neglecting his visits to all nearby bush churches.

Fr. John Berube, M.S.

In 1958, Father Joseph Shea, newly arrived in Morondava, was named to be his Curate. In 1959 John was named to open the new mission district of Berevo with Father Henry (Sam) McKay as his Curate. Since this was a new post, John was the man sent to organize and set up all the structures of a Parish. The following year he left, never to return to Morondava.

However, John Berube's work in Madagascar was not yet over. He returned, in 1961, to Antananarivo, the Capital of Madagascar. There, with the blessing of the Bishops of Madagascar, he opened a Regional Office of the U.S. Catholic Relief Services (CRS) in Madagascar. Again, John was the man needed for this type of ministry. His goal was to establish contracts between C.R.S., the Malagasy Government and the Episcopal Conference of Bishops in Madagascar. His facility with Malagasy language and culture helped pave the way for smooth relationships on all sides.

Today the CRS office is the largest non-governmental organization (NGO) in Madagascar involved in some of the most needed projects for both the civil and religious development in Madagascar. John therefore, despite his brief tenure in the Morondava mission, did leave a lasting memorial of his presence in many cities and Dioceses of Madagascar.

With his work finished in Antananarivo, he returned to the United States. Once back home, Berube worked in the Seminary in Jefferson City, Missouri. I, Jack, taught there with him for a year. With his first-hand experience in Morondava, his presence helped generate lively interest among the seminarians in the Father Coté Mission Circle.

Later he left the congregation and went to Canada. We were never able to know of his residence. Occasionally people here will ask of him. Many had been blessed by his presence and ministry.

Part Four – St. Louis Province, 1958-1988

Fr. Henry Lenz, M.S. (seated, front row center), Provincial of St. Louis Province, visits the International Missionary Group in Morondava

With the recall of five priests and one brother in 1936-1937, there was a gap of twenty years during which, except for Langlois and Berube, no Americans came to serve in Morondava. Then the second wave began which included:

1956:	John Repchick, Joseph Silva
1957:	Henry McKay, James Hogan
1958:	Joseph Shea, Roland Bernier, and Donald Pelletier
1960:	Lawrence Deschenes
1963:	James Jacobson
1964:	Arthur Lueckenotto
1966:	Mark Koenig, Normand Mailloux, and John (Jack) Nuelle
1971:	Mark Gallant, Peter Kohler

1982: Gerard Biron

1983: Ernest Corriveau

1987: Jeremy Morais

As mentioned earlier, the French Province had decided that it could no longer administer the areas of both Antsirabe and Morondava. Since the original mandate of the French Province was the care of the Vakinankaratra area of Betafo/Antsirabe, they decided to relinquish the Mission of Morondava.

A New Arrangement of Support for the Madagascar Mission

But rather than turn over the mission of Morondava to the Propagation of the Faith, the Superior General, Father Josef Imhof, opted in 1953 to take a different route; the Morondava Mission would depend administratively and financially on the General Council in Rome for the next five years, awaiting the General Chapter of 1958. What would the future hold?

God's ways are indeed mysterious. The General Chapter created a new American Province, centered in St. Louis, Missouri, covering the Midwest, South and West of the United States and parts of Western Canada. It was decided that the Morondava Mission would henceforth depend on this new Province for recruitment, finances, and animation.

The original Provincial residence in St. Louis housed the Mission Office for Madagascar

This was not pure chance. The nomination and consecration of Paul Girouard as Bishop was already an important factor that determined that the American Provinces would, once again, help the Morondava Mission. The future of the Morondava Mission, from the beginning, was part of the agenda of the 1958 General Chapter from the beginning. The presence of Father Le Blanc, attending as Special Delegate for Morondava, helped keep this before everyone's eyes. How would the Spirit lead the Chapter?

There was no way the Chapter could really consult any of the men in the mission itself about their preferred future. The resulting General Chapter decision was that Morondava and the new Province of St. Louis – to be known as the Province of Mary Queen – would journey together.

From the Mission's point of view, this was a very beneficial and providential decision. It brought not only new life and hope but also an unprecedented mission thrust to Morondava. For the home Province of St. Louis, this mission was a blessing and grace that would bring abundant life and a universal outreach for a young Province seeking its identity.

A New Province and its New Start

They were excellent years that brought both personnel and financial assistance to Morondava – greatly appreciated by La Salettes ministering on both sides of the world. This cooperation energized a missionary spirit in that western part of the United States that is still alive to this day.

Years later, in 2000, with the amalgamation of all four American Provinces to form a single Province in North America – Mary, Mother of the Americas – all this became history. But the Mary Queen Cathedral of Morondava will remain as a monument to record the excellent work that was accomplished during those years. The then-new St. Louis Province was not always able to send all the men needed, but the financial support offered was over and above the actual needs of the mission.

It must be noted that other Provinces of the Congregation – France, Italy, and Poland – were also very generous in sending personnel while St. Louis continued, through its Mission Office, to finance all the projects. No history would be complete without mentioning these other Provinces, but for the moment we are concerned mainly with our American Missionaries.

God in his great wisdom knew that someday the Americans would return to staff Morondava and carry on the tradition of those founding Fathers. For thirty years, St. Louis and Morondava journeyed together closely. Morondava is only where it is today because of the work accomplished through the St. Louis Province.

Chapter 17 – An Overview of the Political History of the Country

Agriculture is important

Before we move into these decisive years (1958-1988) it may be good to give an overview of the political history of the country that greatly influenced the social and economic growth that always has consequences for the spiritual life of the country. After sixty-five years of French Colonial rule, Madagascar regained its independence on June 26, 1960. It was a day of great joy and hope, when promises were made, pledging new prosperity and economic growth for everyone. You can well imagine the joy of the people when they regained their national sovereignty.

The First Malagasy Republic

The First Malagasy Republic offered a fairly good form of government, even though it appeared to be, in reality, a form of neo-colonialism. It was a smooth transition, without a bloody war. The people were pleased with the new government. As always happens when new power is gained, it did not tolerate opposition, while the ruling class profited from newly acquired power and wealth.

We, in Morondava, had two very influential government ministers and we realized how their wealth increased after only a few years. Apparently, everything seemed to go well while the French presence was still very visible in various administrative services.

Education showed a Need for Change

After twelve years of this neo-colonialism, the bubble burst. The first unrest came from students who demanded a change in school curriculum and programs which were not only taught exclusively in the French language, but were identical to programs in France – exams in Madagascar were prepared and copied from France.

It was rather ridiculous to be teaching in Madagascar that the longest day of the year is June 21st when actually in Madagascar it is the shortest! The manual stated that June 21st is the longest day of the year, so teachers had no choice but teach the error. It was also rather ridiculous trying to teach and convince Malagasy children that their ancestors were a blond haired, blue-eyed Gallic people from Central Europe! "Nos ancetres les Gaulois."

In 1972, throughout the island, all schools – public and private – went on strike. There were very peaceful and orderly demonstrations. Yet this was unheard of, and counter-cultural in a society where youth always obeyed and respected elders. The government, unprepared for such protests that were not politically motivated, did not know how to respond.

Resignation of the Government

As strikes continued and pressure mounted, the government panicked and over-reacted with violent military intervention; there were casualties and the government had to resign. Thus began a series of unfortunate upheavals which continue to this very day. Government leaders, unable to contain the uprisings, turned power over to the military. There was only one military General at the time. This was Gabriel Ramanantsoa. He was not a politician, yet he was named to take over the country.

Only three short years later, after incompetent leadership, he was forced to resign. In 1975 he named another military leader, Colonel Richard Ratsimandrava, head of the National Gendarmerie, to lead the government; he, in turn, was assassinated within a week.

The Second Malagasy Republic

A Military Directory of sixteen officers then assumed power. In June 1975, they gave power to another military leader, this time a naval officer named Didier Ratsiraka. He was subsequently elected president, and in turn inaugurated the Second Malagasy Republic, based on a newly proclaimed Socialist Constitution wherein the State would take over all important services and, supposedly, assure equality among all citizens.

The Third Malagasy Republic

It was a Communist ideology that would not only ruin the economy but bring a decline in social services, simultaneously fostering wide-based corruption in the government. Under the guise of controlled elections, it became de facto a dictatorship.

This launched a gradual decline that would actually last until 1991 when Ratsiraka was ousted. The Constitution was once again changed, which inaugurated the Third Malagasy Republic. In what was, somewhat, a free election with multiple candidates, Zafy Albert, a University Professor, was elected President. An honest simple man he would be impeached within five years.

Education and recreation are crucial; Sharon and John Markowicz (front center, kneeling) visits St. Peter's College in Miandrivazo

In a twist of irony, six years later the Socialist dictator, Ratsiraka, managed to be reelected for another six-year term. Soon, however, people had had enough of this corruption and in 2002 more street demonstrations occurred, and a new President was elected. Although the new President changed the Constitution, again, he did not wish to declare a New Republic. Unfortunately, pride got the best of this man; corruption, which he had vowed to stamp out, once again became rampant and again (in 2009) street demonstrations forced him to resign and flee to South Africa. Progress was impossible with so many complete changes in governments, ideologies, presidents, and administrative practices.

The Fourth Malagasy Republic

Next, a disastrous transitional government, which prolonged its six-month mandate to five years, inaugurated the Fourth Malagasy Republic which is finally getting off the ground as we write. Yes, after a little more than fifty years of independence we are on our Fourth Republic. All this was to indicate that, though we have had no civil war and no major violence, the political history has been catastrophic for the economy of the country especially after these five years of transition. Of course, the 26 years of socialism saw a constant decline in all social services, health, education, etc.

Madagascar – One of the World's Poorest countries

With corruption rearing its ugly head and so easily contaminating values, Madagascar remains one of the world's poorest countries. It is the reason why we have not managed to assure financial autonomy for our Churches. As subsidies from Europe and the United States diminish; most, if not all religious communities of men and women have one of their local communities working in rice fields, on farms, or in some other form of agricultural work.

This is also providential; religious are witnessing solidarity with the farmers of Madagascar. Even Dioceses need to have some form of work project that will produce needed revenues to operate Pastoral Services of the Diocese. Our Catholic Schools and Medical Centers, the best on the island, are very popular because similar governmental public facilities are not only corrupt but perform poorly.

Amidst the Turmoil, We Missionaries will survive

Underprivileged Malagasy children in the Morondava
Mission waiting for their new school to be completed

In trying to write the history of these years of La Salette presence in Madagascar it is important to have a general idea of the turmoil, confusion, frustration, and corruption we have had to live with and work with. This has had a very negative influence on a population, especially in rural and distant areas of the country, which are unable to cope with the new reality of globalization.

People frequently ask why Madagascar is so poor, since there are great possibilities, with so many natural resources. Certainly, one of the main reasons lies with our corrupt politicians. This has had a debilitating influence on the general mentality of the people who have lost hope in a better future and have lost all confidence in their political leaders.

Chapter 18 – All Missionaries Left Part of Themselves in Madagascar

La Salette Community Cemetery in Morondava

Another general consideration that needs to be clarified before we move forward in this history, is why some or so many of our missionaries opt to leave the Mission after years of generous service.

In the pioneering days of the Morondava Mission there was a natural – or shall we call it a supernatural – attitude that being a Missionary was a life-long commitment. As was mentioned earlier, five of our pioneer Missionaries are buried in Madagascar – Fathers Coté, Mansfield, McDonald, Le Blanc, and Bishop Girouard. Through their life and death, they sowed the seeds of faith, hope, love and life which blossomed "for the good of the Kingdom of God."

Others among the first pioneers were regretfully called back to America. Indeed, each and every American La Salette Missionary who served in Madagascar would proudly and truthfully say that "he left the better part of himself there" when for one reason or another, he was called to another mission.

The Climate can be a Health Hazard

For many of our La Salette Missionaries, a major reason for departure centered around health concerns. The climate is not easy. Many forms of fevers are endemic, and malaria parasitic infections can easily be considered "an occupational hazard" – and sometimes are deadly.

Health facilities, including access to doctors, are quasi non-existent. Not only are pharmacies rare, but, when accessible, medication is excessively over-priced. Procuring medication even for the most basic ills is virtually impossible. Unless you are somewhat suicidal, you may consider that it is more prudent to seek a place where health services are available.

Good health for Missionaries is a basic and an ongoing concern. From the earliest days, our American Missionaries knew that there was a good possibility they would die in their adopted mission land of Madagascar. Coté and Mansfield succumbed to fevers; early in his life, Le Blanc narrowly escaped death from Black Water Fever, and we don't know of any Missionary who avoided being literally stopped in his tracks by malaria.

Advances in Healthcare and Travel

As rapid air travel replaced extended ocean voyages, many things changed. Vacations at home in the States became more frequent. In the beginning, a vacation after ten years was the usual custom. Later it became seven years, then five, and now every three years is regular. These more frequent trips home provided access to better medical care.

Seriously debilitating illness and accidents could be treated better at home, allowing for a quick return to mission ministry. It has now become a La Salette policy to send our indigenous priests and brothers to France, La Réunion or Mauritius when there is a serious medical problem.

Neither the best of intentions nor meticulous hygiene can ward off all diseases. Coupled with inadequate medical facilities in Madagascar, the latest generation of Missionaries has often been required to spend their last days in the United States. It would be a grace to die in Madagascar but today most missionaries give their lives for Madagascar from the United States.

We need to say a word about the Covid-19 pandemic, 2019-2021. Of course, Madagascar was not spared; many died not knowing the cause. Many more suffered. A collective sense of preservation, amid very limited medical care, saved many lives. Praise the Lord, the La Salette Missionaries in Morondava remain safe. Both Donald and Jeremy were able finally to receive the vaccine.

Most second-generation American Missionaries, who served so generously from 1937 to the present, were not given the grace of being buried in Madagascar. Both Joe Shea and Arthur Lueckenotto wanted to finish their days in Morondava but God had other plans. Both died while in America.

A Significant Language Barrier

A second reason why Missionaries would leave is the language barrier. For most Americans, coming to minister in Madagascar requires learning two languages: French and Malagasy.

The International Community working in the Diocese of Morondava in the 1980s

All ministry, pastoral work, and evangelization is done in the Malagasy language which is a fearful challenge. Malagasy, belonging to the Austronesian or Malayo-Polynesian family of languages, has nothing to do with our Anglo-Saxon or Latin languages. Learning it requires a major mental conversion. Unless one can become relatively fluent in the Malagasy language, there is no reason to remain there; and this is why some of our men, after years of constant effort, opted to leave the mission.

During the French colonial era, a sufficient knowledge of French was required in order to minister in Madagascar. The incident cited earlier regarding Father Le Blanc's hearing Confessions shortly after his arrival illustrates that point perfectly. Despite age or education, it often happened that the best way to learn the Malagasy language was from an encounter with children. When speaking with them, one could often hear them giggle, indicating that they found something funny about the words or expressions we used. They were not disrespectful, but truly childlike. Mostly they were candid enough to explain what we said wrong. When I, Jack, was learning Malagasy, I would begin my day by walking across the street from the language school to a local Catholic elementary school. With permission, I would sit in on the catechism class with children five or six years old. I learned vocabulary that would be later useful in my ministry. Just imagine the scene. I am six-foot-three inches tall. I'm sitting on a stool built for a small child, surrounded by children who are less than half my size. After a few days, we all got used to starting the day together. I mostly listened, but when asked, tried to respond. There were plenty of giggles!

Obligations to Family or Community

A third and important factor would be family or community obligations that are also decisive elements in the process of an honest discernment. Some men have had to deal with family concerns while others were called to serve in a variety of capacities on Provincial or General Councils.

The model of more frequent vacations and taking advantage of better health services is a general pattern today for most international Missionary Communities. Having served in Madagascar for many years, there is an increasing portion of their members returning to their home countries. With the reality of globalization, some missionaries consider that it is more expedient, once the indigenous clergy have become sufficiently numerous, to leave the task of evangelization in the hands of their native brothers and sisters in faith.

For Missionaries returning home, this trend has happily helped create, in their home countries, many programs to help them re-insert themselves in their home culture after years in a foreign country.

Loneliness can be a Factor

Our present-day Morondava residence

A fourth ever-present factor in Missionary life that contributes to departures is loneliness. When embarking on their Missionary journey, young men knew that they would have to face loneliness in one way or another. We noted earlier how often the Fathers would leave on journeys to the bush that lasted from a week to three months.

They recognized – and counted on the fact – that Jesus had said that he would be with them always. But feelings of loneliness can creep up on a moment's notice. It has often been remarked how joyous the Missionaries felt when returning to a Central Mission Post after prolonged trips.

Although not always possible, a regular rhythm was slowly built into life in the Morondava Mission. Three times a year, usually in January, May and September, all the fathers and brothers were expected to come together for a week or two, for prayer and possibly a retreat, for comradery, for planning and counseling, for sharing stories, laughter, and of course, a game or two of cards in the evening.

But in the distant mission posts, where roads were often eroded, bridges easily wiped out, rivers impassable, and communication almost non-existent, loneliness could hit like a lightning bolt. Mostly Missionaries learned to endure it – and even thrive!

We later tried to establish a policy whereby no one would be alone in an isolated mission post. That was, however, not always possible. For some temperaments such living conditions could become unbearable. In that case, leaving the Missions was the only spiritual and healthy solution.

So it was that through the years our numbers diminished; but for some reason known to God alone, the American presence remains discreet, humble but very much aware that we carry on a tradition that is very precious and must not be lost. The five tombs of the original group of American Missionaries is a quiet but constant reminder.

Our La Salette Lay Associates Mission With Us

It is also interesting to note how some of our La Salette Lay Associates from St. Louis, Missouri and Enfield, New Hampshire have long taken an active interest in Madagascar. Today, with the speed of travel, they can visit the Mission area, not so much as tourists but particularly to be of service to the people.

Al and Maureen Daniels from the St. Louis La Salette Associate Group went numerous times to introduce the concept of "parish nursing" whereby the Parish fosters nursing care for the poor in their midst who might otherwise not have access to ongoing medical care.

A couple from the U.S. is providing workshops in Parish Nursing to parishes in Madagascar

John and Sharon Markowitz from the Enfield La Salette Associate group also went various times, introducing solar ovens which allow people to cook their meals without depending on wood, charcoal, or combustible fuels, thus preserving natural resources.

Both Associate couples also went to gain a first-hand knowledge of Mission Work, and use their experience effectively when giving weekend Mission Appeals to various parishes. God uses every opportunity to enlarge our Vision of Mission.

Our Gratitude to St. Louis Province for supporting Madagascar Missions

Before we continue on with our history, one last factor that must be clarified. This concerns the St. Louis Province's contribution to the Morondava Mission. If the Mission prospered and is today one of the most flourishing Dioceses on the Island of Madagascar, we must recognize the positive and important contribution of the St. Louis Province.

We who remain here – and I, Donald – could well be considered credible witnesses and want it to be known that we could never have survived nor done the work without the support of the St. Louis Province.

Father Boulanger, the first Provincial in 1958, was determined to bring the men together as a Province and also to create a Mission Office to support the financial needs of Morondava and to create a Missionary Spirit among all Province members.

Bishop Donald Pelletier, M.S., has supported and facilitated a new ecological program sponsored by John and Sharon Markowicz, using solar ovens instead of wood fuel

Subsequent Provincials showed the same determination. To express the reality that the deep mission spirit was shared by everyone in the province – not as an obligation to be endured, but as an acknowledgement of a personal and provincial commitment – all provincials visited the Morondava Mission. All Provincials visited the mission: all Mission Procurators spent time here, and there was a very intense, active, generous interest in the Mission. Regular shipments of supplies were sent from the Province Mission Office, which, among other things included vehicles, clothing, books, and containers of fruitcakes spiked with rum – needed as a preservative, of course!

Funds were not excessive, but we were never deprived. When funds were needed, they were always available. If the Mission Office itself was not able to help, provincial funds would fill the void. The Province sent very good members, but no one could have foreseen the drop in vocations. For thirty years, Morondava and St. Louis journeyed hand in hand. If today the Morondava Mission is where it is, we can be grateful to the member of the St. Louis Province.

Chapter 19 –
Second Wave of Trailblazers,
Frs. John Repchick and Joe Silva

Fr. Joe Higgins, M.S., sees off Frs. Repchick and Silva on a ship to Madagascar

After this long introduction to this second wave of missionaries, we think you are all ready to see faces, flesh, sweat, humor, laughter, tears and blood of the men who were ready to head out to the bush on foot, oxcart, jeep, motorbike, or out-rigger canoe – and even in a small airplane – to preach the Good News.

Again, I would like to insist that for some men an entire book would be needed to relate their Missionary work, accomplishments, and many adventures. We limit ourselves to our memories and the important events of the Mission.

The first men in this second wave began with young priests who were ordained in Ipswich, Massachusetts in May 1956 by Bishop Girouard himself. What a providential event! This first Ordination group would include not only those two priests, but also the Ordination of two transitional deacons destined for his Diocese in Morondava.

The two priests who had volunteered and left America to begin this second wave in 1956 were Fathers Joseph Silva, M.S. and John Repchick, M.S., and we must admit that they made for an odd couple that could not help but impress people. They were the trailblazers, the first Americans to arrive after Paul Girouard's Consecration as Bishop. Though people knew Father Repchick as "George", we will call him by his proper name, John.

Two Very Differently Gifted Missionaries

Joe was outgoing, extrovert, glib, short, and stout while John was tall, reserved, and strong with tender and compassionate eyes. John had been baptized and educated in the Eastern Rite Catholic Church. He brought with him that attentive and tender smile of his Oriental Tradition. On their way to Madagascar they spent five months in Rome to study French which provided the students – yes, I, Donald, was one of them – an opportunity to know and admire their Missionary Spirit. Bishop Girouard was not impressed with the knowledge of French they acquired during their stay in Rome – too much sight-seeing and skipping classes. These two adventuresome young Missionaries made for an impressive, friendly couple and many of us La Salette brothers in Rome would have been very happy to join them as they continued their Missionary journey to Madagascar.

A Journey from Here (Eventually) to There

Fr. Repchick stops to speak to two little Malagash girls

After their stay in Rome, their ocean trip to Madagascar, to the despair of the Fathers waiting in Morondava who were so anxious to welcome them, remains unique in the annals of Missionary travel.

It was the year of the Suez Canal crisis, so their Ship was obliged to take the long way around the Horn of Africa, with frequent stops along the Western Coast and, of course, pleasant visits in Durban and Cape Town in South Africa.

They, as obedient religious, had been told to disembark at Tamatave on the Eastern Coast of the Island. With the altered trajectory of the Shipping Company, their first port-of-call in Madagascar was not the East Coast city of Tamatave, as had been foreseen, but that of Majunga on the West Coast. This port was in reality the closets seaport to Morondava. Did they disembark there? By no means! It was "Tamatave or bust." So, they remained on the Ship, going on to Mombasa (Kenya) for an extra week of travels before reaching their destination at Tamatave. I do not have the exact figures but their trip from Marseilles to Tamatave was close to two months!

Their long-delayed reception in Morondava was all the more festive as it marked the return of young American La Salette Missionaries to the Mission. Both Joe and John had a rudimentary knowledge of French and both, despite this handicap, did remarkably well in learning the Malagasy language. Their teacher was Mister Felix, a School Teacher who had founded the Catholic Boy's School of Morondava. Always a little tipsy, and often red-eyed, he managed to teach them very well. Both became very fluent in the language which explains their success as Missionaries.

They Each had a Varied Background

As a child, Joe Silva had been tutored by his mother, an English Teacher. Consequently, he was extremely precise in his speech and use of words. While learning Malagasy, he was not only meticulous in pronunciation but also precise in grammar and his choice of Malagasy words. He loved to correct us and we appreciated his determination to speak the language precisely.

Joe, enthusiastic to move on, did not wait to finish the full course of studies or even to have faculties, but asked to go to Mahabo where he could join Father Le Blanc, who was anxious to build schools in the bush.

John, on the other hand, had his first assignment with an eccentric old French Missionary in Manja. Only John's easy going way and humor could have survived a full year with the whims of this character. John had the sympathy and love of the Christian community who suffered also from this eccentric French priest. It also indicated that John would be able to survive the hardships of missionary life.

When I, Donald, arrived in December of 1958, the rainy season had already set in but John made the exhaustive trip from Manja to Morondava because he wanted to welcome me to the Mission. He brought along guinea hens that he had shot along the road on his way to Morondava.

Except for a two-year stint in Berevo, Joe Silva worked mostly in Mahabo and Malaimbandy while John, after Manja, served in Mandabe, Ankavandra, Belo and a short period in Malaimbandy. Joe and John were trailblazers for the new arrivals and their community spirit contributed tremendously in helping the new arrivals integrate and adapt to the Mission.

Fr. John goes off to serve in the isolated district of Ankavandra

Chapter 20 –
A Closer Look at Fr. John Repchick, M.S.

(from right) John Repchick congratulates Fr. Sam McKay on his new beard

We often referred to John as "the gentle giant." He had a wonderful way with people. Although he awed them with his 6'3" build, his winning spirit and charming smile quickly put them at ease. I don't remember meeting anyone as sharp and clever at playing cards as John. I don't think he ever lost at a game. It might have been his ancestral Russian mind that allowed him to follow and know just where all the cards were. We spent many evenings enjoying one another's company playing cards – often by candlelight because there was no electricity. It was really remarkable how evenings in Morondava found us playing various card games while we enjoyed just being together.

After his year in Manja, John went to Mandabe, a distance of fifty miles. Once there, it did not take him long to be comfortable but more so, to win the hearts of the people. John always had plenty of candy in the pockets of his cassock, and a friendly greeting for everyone he met.

Stopping by the Roadside for Available Food

The dirt roads were quite good at that time so John would be a frequent visitor to Morondava where he would, of course, always beat us at cards. Bishop Girouard enjoyed John and was thrilled when John arrived, cassock stained with blood – an indication that he was bringing wild ducks and guinea hens for our next meal.

Driving along the bush roads one would cross flocks of guinea hens that were always an easy target. John enjoyed the bush and was very happy as a Missionary serving the people of Mandabe.

In 1964 he was transferred to Ankavandra, the most difficult and isolated district of the Diocese. Once again, with his pockets full of candy, he was a very popular and happy Pastor serving the Christian Community. The District of Ankavandra covers a vast area and John was only too happy to reach out to the distant Christian Communities. He was happy there especially when Father Bernier became his Assistant.

As we learned earlier, it was the Bishop who named the Superior of the mission. That changed in 1964.

Guinea hens roam the country

Though John was in distant Ankavandra, it did not prevent his confreres from electing him to the responsibility of Regional Superior in 1964. John was soft spoken, of gentle temperament yet had good leadership qualities and was not reluctant, when the situation required it, to take strong and even uncomfortable decisions.

Having finished his tenure as Superior in 1968, he returned to his first love – Mandabe. There he remained for the next eleven years ministering extremely well, building Christian Communities in various bush villages. Mandabe was not an easy district because the population of Sakalava and Bara Groups remained very indifferent to religion and education.

Fr. John often popped into the homes of his parishioners in the bush, asking "What's cooking?"

With his easy and winning way, John found pathways around barriers. Often in the evening he would walk through the village with an encouraging word to everyone. One of his habits was to approach families as they were preparing their evening meal, bend down to poke his head in through the small doorways and ask in English, "What's cooking?" Soon the people learned the response he taught them – it was perhaps the only English sentence most of them would ever know – and they would answer, also in English, "It's chicken and rice."

As the Mandabe community grew, John built a large spacious Church that could seat eight hundred people. The Church was dedicated in 1975 which was the 50th anniversary of the founding of the first Catholic Community in Mandabe. It was a most successful celebration with thousands of people coming from all over the Diocese. It was certainly one of the most comforting and consoling days for John.

A Very Close Call and a Mission of Mercy

In late 1977, John almost died. For an evening meal, he had been served some meat which had been cooked in a tasty sauce. Unknown to John the pork was slightly spoiled – something that could easily happen where there is no available refrigeration. It didn't smell bad, and the cook made a delicious sauce. The next day, John got seriously sick, vomiting almost everything he ate. People surmised it was food poisoning.

John lived on papayas for a month or so due to food poisoning

The only food he could digest was papaya. He lived on that for a month or so. The rainy season had begun. The rivers were still swollen, and the roads quite impassable. Phone service was non-existent. And there was no doctor in Mandabe. Finally, word arrived in at the Mission in Morondava.

Immediately Joe Shea, pastor in Morondava at that time, organized an expedition to bring John to Morondava where at least basic medical care was possible. He loaded his Toyota Land Cruiser with long, heavy ropes and cables, extra spare tires and other necessities. There were three rivers to cross with no bridges. The largest river, the Andrangory, was swollen to over 500 feet wide, and its fast-flowing water covered a sandy bottom.

Pulling and pushing, with the help of nearby villagers, they made the 150-mile round trip in four days. Once back in Morondava, the Sisters at the Hospital cared for him until he could get to a larger Hospital in Tananarive. It took over six months to get him more or less back to normal.

John moved to Malaimbandy in 1979. While there, he became one of the victims of our pastoral options of leaving men alone in the solitude of the bush. Without realizing it, he very slowly became addicted to the cool refreshing beer so readily available from a nearby storekeeper.

Once he realized this addiction, he accepted to seek help in the United States. His rehabilitation was most successful and John returned thrilled to be able to continue his ministry in Madagascar. Since alcoholism is often a wide-spread phenomenon in much of Madagascar, he brought what he had learned and used his expertise to help others.

An only child who immigrated to the United States from the Ukraine with his mother and grandmother, John felt a particularly delicate and sensitive responsibility towards his aging mother who, after the death of his grandmother, was very much alone in Olyphant, Pennsylvania. Doctors told John that the only remedy that would keep his mother alive and healthy would be his nearby presence.

Fr. John said Goodbye to Madagascar

So it was that, in 1984, broken hearted and with tears in his eyes, John said goodbye to Madagascar – he hoped it would be temporary – and returned to the United States. He was assigned to the parish of Prompt Succor in Sulphur, Louisiana. His plan was to work there where airplane access to his mother would be easily accessible. He would stay to work there until after God took his mother to heaven. Then, after her death, he would be only too happy to return to Madagascar.

John served in Sulphur, Louisiana where his outgoing personality easily won the hearts of people. His special ministry was visiting the students in Our Lady's School located on the Parish grounds. Sometimes, as he had done so often in Mandabe, he would have some candy in his pockets. The teachers did not like the children to have a lot of sweets, but John would surreptitiously sneak them a few pieces. He was always ready to regal-them with stories from Madagascar.

The children of Our Lady's School in Sulphur, Louisiana dedicated a plaque to Fr. John in their playground

Saying Goodbye to Fr. John

John called his mother several times each week, and visited her every few months. One day he fell sick and died shortly afterwards, on June 11, 1998. Jack Nuelle, who was Director of the La Salette Mission

Center in Hartford, Connecticut at that time, went personally to break the sad news to his mother. John had returned to America to be with his mother, to be there to comfort her in her final moments of life, but she was the one who had to bear the sorrow of his death.

Many La Salettes came to his Funeral, including Missionaries returned from Argentina who had known him as a young man before entering the seminary. The students of Our Lady's School honored him by erecting a small memorial to him on the edge of their playgrounds. It was their way of asking Father John to continue watching over them.

The Basketball Black Devils Versus the White Devils

During his many years in Madagascar, basketball quickly became a very popular sport. Even Morondava soon had some fairly good teams. The name of the local championship team was "Diables Noires" or "Black Devils." The team was very popular and they were justly proud of their record, even on a National level. So, when we –Jacobson, Lueckenotto, Jack, and Mailloux as players, with Mark Koenig and I, Donald, as supporters – were all together in Morondava, we formed a makeshift team that came to be known as the "White Devils."

Fr. Repchick's memory lives on in a school in Mandabe

The local team played some good games. The Black Devils generally got the better of us. They were younger and had better training, playing together almost every day, and so much better coordinated. And they had great incentive. There was not another team on the island that could boast of "beating the Americans!"

People wanted us to be called White Angels but we were happy to be known as the White Devils who always lost. The games attracted thousands of spectators and it was a good way to evangelize the young people.

In the year 1998, a new Catholic School was opened in Mandabe. Needless to say, it was named The Father Repchick Catholic School. Years later it was re-named Our Lady of Lourdes. Nevertheless, John's memory lives on in Mandabe and someday a monument will be set up so people will never forget this gentle, very kind missionary who every evening would go out visiting the families in the town of Mandabe asking, "What's cooking?"

The Tobacco Habit

The older Missionaries, our founders, were children of their time; they were all smokers. Girouard, Le Blanc, McDonald smoked the pipe, cigarettes and cigar on a daily basis. The modern Missionaries were in general also smokers, but then many quit because cigarettes were rather expensive, despite the fact that tobacco was locally grown.

The smoking habit became expensive, not so much because the Fathers smoked excessively, but because, when the natives saw Father with a cigarette, they would approach and ask for one. Whenever one of the fathers or brothers lit a cigarette, everyone standing around would automatically become a smoker and ask for a cigarette. As it was difficult, if not impossible, to refuse to dole out cigarettes to everyone. With the constant demands, many figured it was simpler – if no to say cheaper – to stop smoking.

Chapter 21 –
Fr. Joe Silva, M.S., God's Use of Creativity

Fr. Joe Silva, a dedicated Missionary

Father Joseph Silva was no less spectacular or gifted as a Missionary. It must be noted that John and Joe were both gifted singers which is a big plus in Madagascar where people easily express all their feelings through song. There is a traditional form of gospel-type singing called zafindaraony where the storyline is based on biblical stories, sung on a very slow balanced rhythm and tone, and with four-part harmony. The zafindaraony singing has been part of Malagasy culture ever since Christianity was first introduced in Madagascar.

Songs as a Means of Evangelization

These are not only very popular but a great means of evangelization. They cover the entire bible; and much of the Catechism finds expression through this form of singing. Joe picked this up very quickly and used it very effectively as a means of evangelization.

We all marveled on how well he mastered these songs and would perform them with greater spirit than the natives. He would juggle singing soprano parts as well as bass; and sometimes his facial expressions would give joyful meaning to the storyline.

They are especially popular during Christmas, Easter and Pentecost. Each local Church would spend months preparing a new rendition of a biblical event. One song could take as long as fifteen minutes to sing.

They were also a means of bringing family and Church together when a family member died. The Malagasy will wake their deceased all night long and you can well imagine the atmosphere created by ten hours of these bible stories in song. This tradition lives on today especially among the older generation. Joe certainly contributed much to their endurance.

Joe's Ministry Forming Bush Schools

Joe worked mostly in the districts of Mahabo and Malaimbandy where his memory lives on. In his first years, Joe was able to open many bush schools that he financed through the efforts of his Mission Club back in the United

Joe welcomes other La Salettes in Malaimbandy

States. A very ambitious project Joe wanted to realize was a large school in Mahabo that would be directed by a Community of Sisters. The building went up through the competent work of Brother Celse Scotton who supervised and creatively engineered the project. The school opened with small class attendance. But it grew and today Our Lady of La Salette School has over one thousand pupils.

Children's Need for Education

There was a clash of generations and it wasn't easy to convince the older generation of the need for solid buildings to complement the teaching done in government schools – teaching that was devoid of religious content. Joe was successful. In 1964 Sisters arrived in Mahabo and the School of Our Lady of La Salette was opened, setting traditional education into a Christian framework. Today the Grammar School has over a thousand children while the High School enrollment is over seven hundred. Little did Joe realize that the school he began in 1964 would become the largest and best school in Mahabo!

He Built Convents for the Sisters

Transportation into the bush was helped by a four-wheel drive Unimog

Everyone was so impressed with Joe's ability to envision building schools and sisters' convents that the Bishop sent him to Malaimbandy, together with Brother Celse, for a repeat performance. Malaimbandy was over 120 miles from Morondava with very bad roads. It was noted above that in February 1955, when Father Girouard was named Apostolic Prefect of the Morondava Mission, it had taken him a week to make the trip from Malaimbandy to Morondava. Ten years later, not much improvement had been made.

As a result, the transportation of building materials was a major problem – to say nothing of added cost. Joe always tried to find some new way to respond to the challenge of bad roads. His creativity always placed him a step ahead of everyone else in this department. He was the first to use a trailblazer motorbike with both front and back wheel traction, the first to use super-wide sized tires on his Jeep, the first to buy, the first to get a versatile four-wheel drive Unimog. When he was in Mahabo, even with his creativity, he remained docile to Le Blanc, his mentor, and he would use the oxcart when no other means of transportation could be found.

Race Relations were Challenging

Those were not easy years. They were times of political turmoil and social conflicts. Mahabo was at the center of some violent attacks on White Colonials. Yet they were also years of economic growth for the region: in many places cotton farms replaced tobacco plantations, the largest orange plantation (a projected 5,000 acres) directed by the Israelis, brought many new jobs to the area, the new dam on the Morondava River at Dabara, just east of Mahabo, opened up enormous irrigation projects, and contributed greatly to widespread agricultural growth of the region. And Joe was there in the midst of it all to represent the Catholic Mission.

In 1974, Joe returned to Mahabo where, together with Le Blanc, he expanded work in the bush. In 1977 he was transferred to Berevo where he was initiated into river travel. It usually took two days to work his way up-stream to Berevo on the Tisribihina River from Tsimafana on the southern bank of the river near Belo.

Evangelization by the Sisters

Joe was the first to convince Bishop Bernard Ratsimamotoana of how invaluable the presence of Sisters always was for distant outposts like Berevo. Quite often the Sisters assigned to Mission Districts were indigenous Malagasy. Their daily trips to the local market for fish or meat, vegetables and other supplies, afforded an opportunity to have conversations with women, men, youth and children on a vast variety of subjects, including the Lord Jesus, Mary his mother, hygiene, education, sewing, etc. This inevitably broke down fears on those subjects.

Soon the women would ask that the Sisters teach them how to sew, prepare more healthy meals, take more pride in their homes, eagerly enroll their children in School, and come to the Mission for Religious Instruction. Although Joe had the wisdom to urge the Bishop to look in this direction, he would no longer be in Berevo when Sisters finally arrived in 1978. Again, as in Mahabo, the Catholic School in Berevo remains a testimony that Joe had the true vision for evangelization.

In 1987 the Congregation from India – the Carmelites of Mary Immaculate (C.M.I.) – arrived to help in the Diocese. They took over the District of Mahabo from the La Salettes. Other Religious Congregations also came, and presently there are also five different Women's Religious Communities working in the district.

Over the years, the La Salette priests and brothers working in the Diocese of Morondava grew in number – coming not just from America, but also from Poland, Italy, France, and India. The French, and especially Franco, did not or could not understand Joe's humor, which at time was cause of conflict.

Clowning is a Good Thing

In 1982 Joe asked for a Sabbatical Year and after serious discernment decided to remain in the United States. We miss him. His speaking and singing talents were most precious for all our meetings. He was the clown in the best sense of the word.

During community meetings and celebrations, we could count on Joe for songs and humor to the great satisfaction and enjoyment of the community. He was also a very good secretary and we are very grateful for some of his notes as we write these memoirs.

He also set up a file system for Parish Registers where complete information on Baptized Catholics could be found on one card. Unfortunately, these precious files have been lost or were destroyed when Mahabo was flooded out in 1989.

Joe had a Broad View of Who is Family

Joe treated his workers and Catechists as family, He showed great consideration for their needs and concerns. I, Donald, spent four years in Mahabo with Joe, and learned to admire his patience and charity in treating with the Malagasy people who would come to the Mission.

When Mrs. Marchandise (the wife of a French expatriate) and her children were threatened by angry crowds during a time of social unrest, Joe did not hesitate to drive them in the middle of the night to safety in Morondava.

Their Lasting Legacy

With their departure from Ipswich, Massachusetts for the Morondava Mission in 1957, Joe and John were to blaze a path where many others would follow. They both served for more than twenty-five years, leaving a legacy that continues to inspire our Malagasy priests who follow in their footsteps.

Le Blanc was thrilled with the arrival of young Missionaries from America, and how he enjoyed our companionship! But the older French Fathers did not always understand or appreciate our new way of doing things. For health reasons, both John and Joe returned definitely to the U.S. in 1982.

Chapter 22 – The Second Wave Continues to Grow

(from left) Frs. James Hogan and Sam McKay embark together on their journey by ship to Madagascar

Joe Silva and John Repchick were already seasoned Missionaries in their respective Mission Stations when, the following year, four new recruits arrived. Two were older men, Fathers Henry (Sam) McKay (1920-1999) and James Hogan. Both men had originally volunteered for the mission in Burma. The process for obtaining visas for Burma, however, seemed interminable. Desiring at all cost to serve in the Missions, they offered to go to Madagascar – always hoping, nevertheless, that a Burmese visa would materialize.

At the same time two younger men, Fathers Roland Bernier and Joseph Shea, had volunteered to serve in Madagascar. They had been ordained transitional deacons by Bishop Girouard while he was still in the United States. Even before Ordination to the Priesthood, they requested to go to the Morondava Mission. They prepared by following special Missiology Courses at Fordham University in New York City.

As it turned out, no visas for Burma arrived, and all four – McKay, Hogan, Bernier and Shea – left together for Madagascar. Jim Hogan, however, had hardly finished his six-month Malagasy Language Course when his visa came through. The only snag in his swift departure for Burma came in the form of an appendectomy in Tananarive. The Burmese visa for Father Henry McKay never arrived, so Madagascar became his home.

Fr. Sam McKay, M.S., Open to a Variety of Ministries

Fr. McKay, whom all affectionately called Sam, was born in Boston, Massachusetts in November 1920. He was small, thin and his health was frail. He entered the La Salette College Seminary in Hartford, Connecticut in 1938 after completing High School. Even though illnesses caused delay, he was ordained in 1948, having volunteered for Burma before Ordination.

During the nine-year wait, he served in Parish Ministry in Lufkin, Texas, and as professor in both Hartford, Connecticut and Jefferson City, Missouri where he animated the Father Coté Mission Circles and generated lively interest in the missions. I, Jack, who would disembark in Madagascar nine years later, was one of those students.

The New Arrivals were Missioned Out Far and Wide

(from left) Frs. Roland Bernier, Sam McKay and Joe Shea relaxing in La Salette's Morondava residence

Following the same course of action as had been used for Joe Silva and John Repchick, these new arrivals stayed in the area of the Morondava Mission to study the local language. Also, like Joe and John, Bishop Girouard had not been impressed with the French that Joe Silva and "Rollo" Bernier had picked up during their three-month stint in Rome and insisted that future missionaries would not waste time in Rome. Fr. Sam was of good Irish descent, and was only too happy to join Mac in Belo. Bernier went to Miandrivazo with Father Pierre Lardière, M.S. (1908-2000), and Shea to Mandabe with Berube.

This was all new young blood and enthusiasm which meant new life and new outreach for the Diocese. Bishop Girouard was so excited to train these new men for Missionary service. He could spend hours sharing his experiences while giving good advice on Pastoral Care in the Morondava Diocese.

We will have much to say later about these three men who served the Mission for many years and who came from the Hartford Province. We must not forget that they volunteered for service in Morondava before the foundation of the St. Louis Province when the Morondava Mission still depended on the General Administration. They were American La Salettes, and only too happy to join the earlier pioneers.

In July of 1957 I, Donald, was privileged to attend the Departure Ceremony for those four Missionaries, and was greatly impressed with their generosity. I still remember well the homily given by Father Harold Clossey, who had been in that first founding wave of American Missionaries to Madagascar. He was so happy to see that young men would continue the work they had started in 1928. He admonished them to be very prudent, to beware of excessive work and to always sleep under a mosquito net, drinking only well-filtered water.

Chapter 23 –
The Arrival of Fr. Donald Pelletier, M.S.

Donald in white cassock in 1957 prepares to leave for Madagascar

I, Donald, was finishing my studies in Rome in 1957 when Father Imhof, our Superior General, accepted my willingness to serve in Morondava. Yet the transition did not go as smoothly as I would have hoped. Father Wolfgang Fortier (1900-1966), Provincial of the Province of the Immaculate Heart of Mary in Attleboro, Massachusetts, to which I belonged at that time, was against my going to Madagascar.

Father Josef Imhof, the Superior General, compromised, saying that the decision had already been taken at the General level, and I would go to that Mission. He agreed, however, that I could remain one more year in the Province before leaving. So it happened that, after one year at the Seminary in Attleboro, I also left for Morondava in October of 1958, arriving that December.

I was the first missionary to arrive in the name of the new Province of Mary Queen in St. Louis, which had been created in May of that year, and which had been given the care of Morondava. True, I came from the Province of the Immaculate Heart of Mary, yet I arrived in the name of the newly-formed Province.

Travelling by Ship to Madagascar

When I read the accounts by our old Missionaries of their ocean voyages, I can identify with their experiences through the Suez Canal and along the East African Coast. It was a most memorable and exciting trip. Later I realized how much future Missionaries would unfortunately miss the extraordinary experience of slowly traveling on long, relaxing ocean voyages. I know that in 1964, Jack and Mark Koenig were the last missionaries to come to the mission by ship.

From then on, travel by plane would cut the time from two or three months to a day or so. Today ocean travel is non-existent except for cruises.

Father Mansfield, who never returned home once he arrived by ship in Madagascar, did not enjoy ocean travel. For him, the quick plane trip would have been a delight. He could not understand why anyone would want to take such a long ocean trip unless it was for a very serious reason. Others had a different appreciation of ocean travel.

The Mission Team was Expanding

When I arrived in December there were already ten Americans waiting to welcome me: the three pioneers and seven of the recent arrivals. Soon they dispersed to their respective Mission Districts. Though there was a special Language School in Ambositra for Missionaries, Bishop Girouard decided that I would study the language in Morondava and that classes would begin in January, right after the New Year. Needless to say, that first month was not my best, as I now found myself a stranger among older men with little or no way of communicating with the native people.

Going to Language School Together

At the same time, "Rollo" Bernier was also experiencing some difficulty learning the Malagasy language. It was decided that he would return from Miandrivazo to Morondava and join me for studies. I was very happy to have a companion. Our class schedule was set up to allow us time to go for an afternoon swim in the Mozambique Channel, much to Franco's displeasure.

In any case we were very happy to have this time to learn the Malagasy language and slowly get accustomed to Malagasy culture. Our teacher was Jean Pierre Rakotobe who was in his first year of teaching at our Boy's School. Jean Pierre was a pleasant young man, originally from Morondava, and he managed to teach us rather well, giving us a love for the language.

Fr. Rollo Bernier at prayer in the chapel of the La Salette residence in Morondava

Bishop Girouard asked us to dedicate four hours a day to the study of the language. My personal schedule was divided between prayer, meals, giving at least eight hours to study, along with two hours of tutoring and, of course, the time for a swim in the ocean. Months went by too quickly, and slowly both Rollo and I were able to communicate and make friends especially with the young men at the School.

A New Diocese in Morombe

May 1959 was soon upon us, and it would harbinger many changes. Our mission in Morondava was to establish the Kingdom of God. We knew we were servants, and change was inevitable. The major catalyst for change came from the Missionaries of the Holy Family, who had come a few years earlier to help with ministry in the area of Morombe. They – or rather the Mission of the Church in the area of Morondava – were now ready to establish the new Diocese of Morombe, which would include the district of Manja.

The new jigsaw puzzle of assignments had Bernier returning to Miandrivazo to be with Lardière, Sam McKay and Berube were sent to open up a new District in Berevo, Repchick would remain in Mandabe, Joe Silva and Le Blanc returned to Mahabo, and Joe to Antsalova, Mac and Langlois went to Belo, and, for my first assignment, I would care for the thirty or so bush Churches attached to the Morondava Parish.

I visited three of the Churches with Father Bernard Ratsimamotoana – who later would become Bishop of Morondava – but was soon left alone for my solo flights. It was quite a shock when Franco handed me the keys to the Jeep, and then told me to go out in the bush for two weeks and visit ten Churches. I had two young men to show me the way, and all fears and anxieties were dispelled when I experienced the warmth and joy of the receptions given me in various villages.

The Perils of Travel and Ministry in the Bush

Oh yes, I had to deal with mosquitoes, rats, and dirt; I had to learn to shower with only a bucket of water; I had to exit early in the morning to find a remote area where I could squat and "go to the bathroom." All this brought back memories of camping days.

But the uniqueness I experienced was the great joy and peace that came from being with the people and trying out my hesitant Malagasy. I guess all Missionaries went through the same initiation. I was well equipped with a camp bed, a water filter, and a Mass kit. I felt I would soon convert the entire world.

Young Donald Pelletier in the Jeep, a God-send for bush ministry

From the very beginning I enjoyed the bush, and felt comfortable with the people. I experienced no major problems with food: rice and chicken were the main diet. For the next three years, I spent at least twenty days a month in the bush getting to know all the villages scattered throughout the Morondava district. It was about 7,700 square kilometers (or 3,000 square miles, a little larger than Delaware) which included 120 kilometers (or 45 miles) of coastline on which some twenty small fishing villages were located.

It's Language Immersion Time

This was total immersion for the language and, as I felt very comfortable with the people and only too happy to share their way of life, I did feel God was calling me to the Mission. There were many times when I had to walk long distances, times when I learned how to travel in an oxcart, but the most enjoyable trips were experienced on the ocean, travelling in the outrigger canoe, the wind in my face.

Bishop Donald visits the familiar beach in Morondava

I got to know this area very well because I worked there until 1972. Years later, after I became Bishop, I was able to revisit most of these places. I imagine that the other young Missionaries – Shea, Bernier and McKay – had the same experiences to which I was being initiated, as they too began their Pastoral Care of bush villages. It was not always easy fighting mosquitoes, rats, experiencing hunger, thirst, fatigue, and sleepless nights, but they were good years.

Chapter 24 –
Fr. Roland Bernier, M.S., A Deep-Hearted Desire to be a Missionary

Fr. Roland Bernier, M.S.

Father Roland Bernier hailed from Waterbury, Connecticut. We called him "Rollo." He was born on September 4, 1929. Already thinking of going to the Missions when he began studying Theology, the fact that Bishop Girouard had ordained him a Deacon sealed his fate. He arrived in Morondava with Joe Shea in January of 1958.

Like Joe, Rollo had profited from a Missiology Course at Fordham University in New York City after his Priestly Ordination. Hence, he was anxious for Missionary work. With Joe Shea, he had a course of Malagasy here in in the Diocese, the last course given by Mister Felix, a seasoned school teacher at our boy's school. Having passed the exam that allowed him to hear confessions, his first assignment was with Father Pierre Lardière in Miandrivazo.

Together at Language School

Lardière was one of the French Fathers who had come to serve in Morondava after the Americans had departed in 1937. He had many years of experience, was very patient and understanding and would surely be a very god teacher for Rollo. After six months in Miandrivazo, however, Lardière thought it would be good for Rollo to have a language refresher course. As I had arrived in December and would be taking Malagasy courses, it was decided that Rollo would be my companion.

I was extremely happy to have Rollo come, as I had fears of having to study alone. Together in Morondava, I learned to know and appreciate Rollo who was a very sociable brother and a "fun" personality. On the other hand, it did not take long for me to realize why Rollo was hampered in his attempt to learn Malagasy. The course was given in French, a language largely unknown to Rollo. We worked well together. However, I had spoken French since childhood, which gave me an incredible advantage. And, although Rollo had already taken the course before, I was understandably making better progress than he.

Every morning we spent two hours with our teacher, Jean Pierre. Then we had two hours of study; that was a good morning's work. Much to Franco's disapproval, every afternoon we would go to the beach for a swim before working on vocabulary. Studying side by side, I got to know how Rollo struggled with studies. It is often said that one learns a language better when helping others to do the same. Helping Rollo learn Malagasy helped me improve my language skills. After five months and having passed the exam for confessions, Rollo went back to Miandrivazo while I remained here at the Parish.

Back Again in the Challenges of Ministry

Miandrivazo was and remains a vast Mission District, some 13,000 square kilometers of extremely rich soil, with many rivers and lakes. When Rollo arrived there in 1959 there were still many French Colonials working on tobacco plantations. Miandrivazo at that time produced Virginia and Maryland tobacco for export to France. This helped him feel comfortable with visits to brush Churches because often he could room and board with the French Colonial. The District had over forty chapels and Rollo, like all of us, soon learned to enjoy and not just to endure the hardships of visiting bush Churches.

From Miandrivazo Rollo later went on to Ankavandra, where he joined up with John Repchick. He was much more comfortable being with another American. Not only is Ankavandra very isolated from other Mission Districts, but the sizeable distances between its Churches had to be covered on foot.

He and John made a very good team, and Rollo was happy in Ankavandra despite his frequent bouts of malaria. While he could speak English with John when together at home, ministry in the bush provided him a total immersion. After his second course in the language, he felt much better with the language. His capacity to understand the people improved greatly. Yet he was not always able to answer adequately, and this became at times a source of misunderstandings.

Later he spent some time in Mahabo with Le Blanc. Then he was named treasurer here in Morondava where once again we worked, prayed and enjoyed being in the same community. Rollo was a great community man, always entering fully into community activities.

Fr. Pierre Lardière, M.S. (1908-2000) from France

Health and Government Challenges Arise

In 1976 he was back in Mahabo as Curate, until Le Blanc insisted that he take over as Pastor. But then Rollo ended up with serious health issues – a urinary infection that required an operation in Tananarive. Back in Mahabo Rollo still struggled with the language.

This was a time of civic unrest and Rollo was having difficulty, feeling very uncomfortable dealing with changes that the government was forcing on Malagasy culture. One consolation was that Rollo was in the parish and I was at the Training Center for catechists – both lodged on the same mission compound – we bonded and spent much time together.

A Painful Decision - Leaving the Morondava Mission

To leave the Morondava Mission was a very painful decision for him to make. He wanted so much to be a Missionary and he really loved the people, but his health was deteriorating and his Superiors decided it would be better for him to return to the United States. Strange that once he was back in the United States, he would love to speak Malagasy and when we spent time together while I was on our home visits, I couldn't believe how well he could still speak the language.

Serving in Louisiana

A beautiful thing happened to Rollo while in Louisiana. Father Remi Ralibera, a Jesuit whom Rollo had known in Madagascar, was the editor of our national weekly Catholic newspaper "Lakroa" (meaning The Cross). He visited the United States as a guest of the American Government. Rollo guided him around, visiting our Parishes in Texas and Louisiana. Due to Rollo's guided tours, Remi Ralibera was able to write several excellent articles on life in Louisiana. Needless to say, Father Ralibera had nothing but praises for Rollo's service in discovering America. Although Father Ralibera's trip had been planned by the United States Government, they allowed him to go out on his own with Rollo.

Our Lady of La Salette watches over the stunning Betsiriry Valley

Once a Missionary, Always a Missionary

Rollo and I kept our relationship alive even at a distance through regular correspondence. He shared deeply with me his struggle with lung cancer (Rollo had been an avid smoker). He was extremely pleased when I was named Bishop and, at his death, left all his Patrimony for the Mission of Morondava. He had left the Mission, but his heart always remained here.

Chapter 25 –
Fr. Henry (Sam) McKay, M.S.
Little to Say but Well Said

Fr. Henry McKay, M.S.
Arrived in Madagascar in 1957

Among the newly arrived group, Henry (Sam) McKay was already thirty-eight years old, and a little older than the rest of us, having done almost ten years of Priestly ministry in the United States. No one knows where he acquired the name Sam, but somehow it just seemed to fit his personality.

We all naturally looked up to him. Sam was very understanding and compassionate. He had a dry wit and never used more words than necessary. His debut to Mission Ministry was in Belo with Mac while he studied Malagasy. His initiation into Mission life finished, he was named to open the very difficult post of Berevo with Berube.

When Sam was in Belo learning the Malagasy language, Mac had been busy building the new Parish Church. Sam would visit the bush Churches where, despite his limited knowledge of the language, he quickly won the affection and confidence of the people.

An Easy Manor and a Fine Sense of Humor

Working with Mac in Belo was an excellent initiation into the Mission that awaited him in Berevo. Two good Irishmen, both avid pipe smokers, they were extremely happy to work together. Mac had visions of how Sam could be the one to carry on his work in Belo. We all loved Sam, respected him and admired his easy manor and fine dry sense of humor. In discussions and meetings, Sam would always have a final comment, often to bring about sincere laughter.

When Berube returned to the U.S., Sam was left alone in Berevo. Even before coming to the Missions, Sam suffered from an alcohol problem that many hoped and prayed would be solved in the Missions. Alone in Berevo, Sam was brought face to face with the gravity of his problem and could have easily died had it not been for a special intervention.

With an Alcohol Dependency, He left for Home

It was a very somber day in 1961 when he left the mission to return home. We were very anxious about his voyage home. God accompanied him.

At home, help was available, but Sam's problems continued. Finally, after numerous failed trials, Sam was able to overcome his dependency. He went on to do an exceptionally fruitful ministry throughout the United States helping others to overcome alcoholic addiction, just as he had.

He always remained very interested in the Mission and we can never forget the pain and suffering of this great man who served in Berevo. He truly loved the people and often shared his regret for having often been an occasion of scandal for them. You could tell that, despite his addiction, he was otherwise very comfortable in the mission, very happy, enjoyed the climate, the people, and the challenges; but again, God had other plans for him.

The people in Berevo understood and never forgot the great love and compassion he showed for the poor. In the history of Berevo, Sam's name will be written with golden letters. Once Sam was driving his Jeep after he had indulged too much and as he drove through a very deep hole filled with water, the Jeep tipped over. He fell into the water hole and Sam would have drowned had it not been for his companion who pulled him out of the water.

Fr. Sam McKay became a seasoned veteran missionary

At that time Berevo was blessed with an extraordinary man who served as a Catechist. We are grateful for this holy man who did much to help Sam. In his later years Sam would have very grateful words for the kindness shown to him by Antoine Ratsimanosika.

To this day, Berevo still remains quite isolated. The roads have deteriorated, and now Berevo can be reached only by the river. When Sam was in Berevo we could, at times during the dry season of the year, reach the town by road, but today a long journey by river is the only way to get there.

Chapter 26 –
From Brother Steve to Brother Larry

In 1960, while Donald was still trying out my wings in the bush of Morondava, Brother Lawrence (Larry) Deschenes (1923-1990) arrived from Hartford. There was a time when we had many brothers in the Congregation and Larry, with his determination and talents, stepped into the shoes left by Brother Steve.

Larry was a blessing for the mission. Originally from Norwich, Connecticut, he was born on October 30, 1923, and became a La Salette Missionary Brother on September 19, 1944. He had worked well at the Ipswich Shrine with Father Joe Higgins, M.S., where he had already shown his talents for construction and maintenance.

Bro. Lawrence (Larry) Deschenes was a man of daring and vision

Larry was a Mover and a Shaker

When he arrived in 1960, the Mission Compound was far from orderly or attractive. The old Church was still there, shacks served as garages, and there was really little harmony in various structures. It did not take Larry long to tear down all garages, shacks, and the old Church. Once he had cleared the area, he built a large five-car garage, created a La Salette garden embellished with shrubs and flowers, with a Shrine to Our Lady of La Salette in the center.

He then set up a large spacious carpenter shop needed to make doors, windows, and furniture for new buildings and construction. Then, facing the Sisters' School, he added still more garages where mechanical work would be done. It took a lot of determination and courage to envision, organize and execute these plans, because there was out-right opposition from Franco. Even Bishop Girouard hesitated to give a green light for such a drastic change.

This was new planning, and required a new attitude. Larry was the only one who would dare go ahead with the project, even making plans and beginning construction before permission was formally given.

He Managed to Communicate with His Workers

Larry was never really fluent in Malagasy but managed well enough to communicate with his workers in French. He was naturally talented, and he loved a challenge that would test all his creativity and determination. No doubt his way of doing things did not please everyone, but he would accept to be corrected and could ask forgiveness when he had offended someone. He would not hold a grudge and could approach someone he had hurt to seek forgiveness.

He brought in new ideas and a new way of looking at things and was not afraid to implement American standards in his work projects – no half-way measures. He was the first to use paint, soap, and tiles in the bathrooms where he installed running water. Disinfectants and insecticides helped keep many little – and not so little – critters at bay.

He was a True Godsend

Basically, Larry was a Godsend to the Mission. He brought a new fresh honest way of looking at things. His direct personality was what was needed to convince the likes of Girouard, Le Blanc and Franco that the Residence needed a top-to-bottom cleaning and refurbishing. How justified he felt when they were happy with the changes.

He bought the first electric refrigerators and insisted we have cold beer available at all times, especially since this Residence was the center for hospitality in the Mission. He organized his own vacation time and was the first to have his own vehicle; needed for his work, yes, but also for his recreation and vacation.

We were probably a little too lenient, while being very happy with his work and therefore hesitant to confront him on his private lifestyle. The years were good and in a short time Larry accomplished much, indeed way beyond our expectations. When Bishop Girouard died in 1964 in less than twenty-four hours Larry had finished an impressive tomb where Bishop Girouard could rest in peace. Larry was a great help in organizing the Funeral Mass and Reception.

Always on the Lookout

He was really a jack-of-all-trades and could do well in the kitchen, in the garden, in the workshop, in planning and executing his construction projects. He had good ideas and knew how to implement them. He could convince anyone of a good buy, and he always got his way in a bargain. As the French Colonials were departing from Madagascar, precious equipment was left behind. Larry would never miss the opportunity to acquire some of it, if it could serve the Mission.

We owe to his talents all the original buildings on the Mission Compound in Namahora as well as the Churches in Belo sur Mer and Befasy. For many years, Namahora was but a vast tract of land waiting to serve the needs of the Mission. In a few years Larry built the Campus of Saint Paul's College, the Minor Seminary and a workshop for future construction needs.

It was Time to Go Back Home

The church at Belo sur Mer built by Bro. Larry in 1963

To make an omelet you have to break eggs and Larry was not always the most diplomatic. His determination could, and did offend people. There came a time in 1972 when the Superiors decided it would be better for Larry and for the Mission that he return to the United States. It was unfortunate, yet Larry held no grudge and remained on very friendly terms with the men in the Mission. In the United States he continued to send supplies to Morondava.

We are not to judge him but rather to thank God for all the work he accomplished for the Mission. He was really the one that dared to think-outside-the-box, and move from an outdated French Colonial Economy to a needed more comfortable lifestyle.

He Built Several New Churches

When the old wooden Church in Belo sur Mer was destroyed by a cyclone, Larry was the one to buy land along the bay and build a new, solid cement Church. With his team of workers, he spent six months in Belo building the Church, so very happy with the challenge of building in a difficult environment.

In 2018 the Church sustained significant damage from a tremendous cyclone, and was rebuilt on the same foundations. It still stands at the center of the new Mission District of Belo sur Mer.

A few years later, he built the new Church in Befasy. He spent an entire rainy season there, isolated because of floods and lack of roads and bridges. That December, as Jack and I were flying back from Mandabe to Morondava, Jack flew barely over the treetops in Befasy and "parachuted" down a few live ducks sewn into baskets. We wanted Larry to have the essentials for a good meal to celebrate the New Year. The ducks landed on a mound of sand in the middle of the worksite. They probably had a heart attack on their unexpected parachute jump, but we know that they were greatly appreciated for the New Year's dinner.

A year after Larry's arrival, after the visits of Fathers Dutil and Boulanger, Bishop Girouard finally decided to reorganize the leadership of the Mission. Le Blanc became the Religious Superior, Vicar General and Pastor of the Cathedral. As expected, this was the origin of much tension, unrest, discontent, anger, especially among the older members of our International Mission Community, most of whom were not Americans.

For us young priests, this was a difficult time because we could not understand why these changes prompted such violent reactions. From 1961 until 1964 Le Blanc was an understanding Father for all of us. He kept peace and did an excellent job as Vicar General and Religious Superior.

Many Necessary Changes Followed

It was only after Bishop Girouard's death, however, that the Mission was able to reorganize to reflect the two entities that it had become: a local Diocese, and an autonomous Religious Community which depended on the St. Louis Province. As such, there would now be an elected Regional Superior whose election did not depend on Diocesan approbation.

That was a vast change. John Repchick served as Religious Superior from 1964 until 1968. Then Normand Mailloux was elected to succeed him. It was during his tenure – 1968 until 1974 – that La Salette Property in Namahora was exchanged – becoming Diocesan Property, while the Diocesan Property in Morondava was handed over to the Congregation.

Art Lueckenotto was Regional Superior from 1974 until 1980, and then Jack accepted to serve for nine years until he was elected to serve in Rome on the General Council in 1988. Joe Shea was elected to replace him.

In 1988, the Region ceased to depend administratively on the St. Louis Province, becoming instead a Region of the Antsirabe Province. Financially, for three years the Region would still depend on St. Louis. After that the complete change would be ratified in a decision of the La Salette Council of the Congre-

The St. Louis Residence and Cross

gation which took place in Switzerland in 1991.

Joe Shea was, therefore, the last Regional Superior from 1888 until 1991 when the Region of Morondava was to be joined integrally to the Province of Madagascar in Antsirabe.

We Needed and Got Some Very Good Men

These men – John Repchick, Norm Mailloux, Art Lueckenotto, Jack Nuelle, and Joe Shea – are the five Americans who assured the leadership during the thirty years when Morondava depended administratively and financially on the St. Louis Province. Working all that time in conjunction with La Salette Missionaries from France, Italy, and Poland, there was an excellent community spirit, with all La Salettes committed to the establishment of the Church in Morondava.

Most of the improvements brought about by Brother Larry's initiative during those years of change still stand today. Larry would later serve in our Mission in the Philippines where he died in 1990.

Chapter 27 –
Fr. James Jacobson, M.S., First Mission Procurator

Fr. James Jacobson, M.S., a veteran soldier who become a veteran missionary

St. Louis was a fledgling Province in 1958 and it needed to set up its own new structures and spirit. Its members wanted to include in their essential structures the support of the Foreign Mission of Morondava confided to them by the 1958 General Chapter.

Setting Up a New Mission Office

In that first year of its existence, Father James Jacobson (1924-1978), born in Chicago, Illinois and known simply as "Jake," was given the task of organizing a Mission Office for the new Province. We had noted earlier that the Hartford Mission Office had ceased to support the Morondava Mission in late 1935. In the intervening years, young La Salettes from America had support for specialized projects from local "Mission Clubs" mostly coming through the efforts of family and friends.

In cooperation with local Diocesan Propagation of the Faith Offices, Jake Jacobson began giving Weekend Mission Appeals which served a double purpose; first, it helped educate people on the Mission Christ had given to the Church – that is to say, all baptized Catholics – and second, it invited them to contribute to the actual working of the Mission in Morondava.

A New Mission Effort – Getting Co-Missioners to Donate Monthly

Another initiative launched by Jake was to get people to contribute monthly to this new Mission effort. He began by writing to five hundred friends of the La Salette Community, personal friends and families of the Missionaries. He asked them to contribute $1.00 each month to the fund.

In response, he wrote a Mission Letter each month, commenting on the activities in the Morondava Missions to which they would become "partners" or "co-missioners". This initiative evolved years later into the Vision and Mission Newsletter, which in its hey-day was sent out every month to over 5,000 "co-missionaries". It continues today as an essential work of the La Salette Mission Center.

Jake soon found that interest in the missions can become contagious. After serving for 2 years as mission coordinator, he volunteered to go and to serve personally in the very mission of Morondava he was supporting.

It's Never Too Late

A wounded paratrooper of World War II, Jake was a belated vocation. He had a winning personality and an easy approach with younger people. Even though he spoke little Malagasy, he loved to get the youth out for physical training, having them do some rigorous calisthenics, jumping up and down, working up a healthy sweat, not just counting their simple push-ups.

From Morondava to Malaimbandy, Jake made every possible effort but, sadly, he just could not conquer the language. He was nevertheless anxious to serve and was sent to Ankavandra. Surprisingly, despite his faltering Malagasy he did very well and enjoyed serving the people there.

In a mission house where basic comforts were lacking, he installed a shower and toilet facilities that were fed from a deep well equipped with a small generator and an electric pump. Thirty years later the system was still working perfectly, with only one major upgrade – there is now a solar panel to furnish electricity rather than the generator.

Baptismal registers show that he visited the bush Churches on a regular basis and surely it must have been done on foot as there were no longer passable roads.

Fr Jacobson in a farewell ceremony in the Jefferson City chapel

"You're in the Army Now"

Jake had served in the Army during World War II. One thing he learned was the joy of occasional good times when tasty food and a little whisky were on the menu. The first time Donald ever went to a First-Class Restaurant in Tananarive was with Jake.

As mentioned above, he had a very easy friendly way with the youth who admired him. His battle scars, ever evident on his body, impressed them tremendously. Jake would dramatize his battle experiences. Many times, communicating in a very faulty Malagasy language but aided by very understandable gestures, he would have his audience totally captivated as he narrated how he had been an easy target of enemy fire as he was slowly coming down in his parachute.

This was not just idle show, but was part of his mission. He narrated to them how, with bullets flying all around him – and some through him – it was precisely when he had nowhere else to turn that his mind easily turned to God. It was there, in the midst of battle, that he vowed to become a Priest, should Our Blessed Lady bring him home alive. His presence among them, as a La Salette Missionary, was a result of his fidelity.

He Decided to Remain Home in the U.S.

In 1966, after six good years in the Morondava Mission, Jake realized he would never adequately learn the Malagasy language. Home on vacation, he decided to remain in the United States. He would have wanted to stay despite his difficulties with the language but it was decided that it would be better for him to remain home. He died in an automobile accident in 1978.

Chapter 28 –
Fr. Arthur Lueckenotto, M.S., A Man of Solid Dedication

Fr. Arthur Lueckenotto, M.S, after his priestly ordination

The next arrival, in 1964, was Father Arthur Lueckenotto (1935-2014), familiarly called "Lueck." He was born on December 22, 1935 into a farming family from the small farming town of Meta, Missouri, some twenty-five miles from Jefferson City, the state's capital. His robust health and strength were proof of hard physical work on the farm. He had volunteered for the Morondava Mission in 1961 while studying in Rome. Like many others, he spent a year in the U.S. after his Ordination in 1963.

Off to Language School

Fluent in French, acquired during his studies in Rome, he was the first American to be allowed to study the Malagasy language in Ambositra at the special school for newly-arrived Missionaries. The first five – Joe Silva, John Repchick, Rollo Bernier, Joe Shea and Donald Pelletier – had studied in Morondava, and had bonded closely. We now felt like veteran old-timers as we welcomed Lueck.

Coming from the St. Louis Province we felt and knew that Lueck would be a solid and good Missionary. Most of all we figured that the arrival of new Missionaries would be an annual event and that we would soon adequately staff all our Mission posts.

There was, however, an interval of two years before Norm Mailloux, Mark Koenig and I, Jack, arrived; then four more years before Pete Kohler and Mark Gallant arrived in 1971. Not a shabby group of newcomers for the 1960s! Jeremy would be the last to arrive in 1987. Gerry Biron and Ernie Corriveau would come in the early 1980s; their presence and support all too precious but also all too short.

He was Very Good with the Malagasy Language

Lueck was well equipped to profit fully from the Malagasy course in Ambositra and is probably our best speaker of the Malagasy language. A great and cheerful conversationalist he speaks the language as one who was born here. After his studies, Lueck worked in the District of Morondava for a year. Before speaking in length of Lueck, who was called back to the Father the 29th of October 2016, it may be well to speak of Betomba where Lueck worked with our two Brother Marks – Mark Koenig (1966), and Mark Gallant (1971).

Working on Our Dreams for Evangelization

Bro. Mark Koenig, M.S., loved to go hunting for wild boar

There seemed to be no barriers to our dreams of evangelization and development in the hopes that we would be receiving Missionaries from the United States. As the French expatriates were leaving, there were many very interesting large land concessions up for sale. Mac was more than enthusiastic as he knew this area and the great wealth of food and agricultural products that these colonial plantations represented. We also believed that, with a well-established agricultural farm which could serve as an Agricultural School, we would further local development and train strong leaders for rural areas.

Being a little naïve, some also thought the farm could be an important financial income for the Diocese. Little did we know. Madagascar is basically an agricultural country (85% of the people are farmers) and we wanted to identify with that population. So it was that in 1964 the large concession of Betomba (in the District of Berevo) was available and, having received a grant from Misereor (the official aid framework of the Catholic Church in Germany), we bought this concession in view of setting up a farm and an agricultural school. Little did we realize the personnel needed for such a venture.

Our Catechist School in Betomba

Having decided also to place our School for the Training of Catechists in Betomba, Lueck was sent there to set up the School, while a Polish Priest, Fr. Władysław Czosnek, M.S. (1912-1973) would be responsible for the training of Catechists. The plan was to train our Catechists not only for Pastoral Ministry but also to teach them how to earn an honest living through farming. Lueck, born and brought up in a farm in the heartland of Missouri, was the ideal man for the project. We can say that from all eternity God had prepared Lueck for Betomba. When Mark Koenig, who had been born and raised in the farmlands of Ohio, arrived in 1966, he was also a very gifted man to help Lueck in Betomba.

Dreams for Betomba seemed limitless, and we had two great farmers for the job. Tractors, river barges, thousands of acres or fertile soil; we were set to move

Meeting of catechists at our school in Betomba

and we did. There seemed nothing that would not grow in Betomba. Besides the large vegetable gardens, they planted cotton, beans, corn, squash, peanuts, wheat, rice; the barn yard housed pigs, milk cows, chickens, ducks, turkeys and geese.

A Deadly Crocodile

Mark Koenig, who loved to hunt, was bringing in wild boar and hunting crocodiles which endangered the lives of the local people. In fact, their cook, a stout handsome man went for a swim one day after lunch, was caught by the crocodile who hid the body in the mud. Crocodiles usually wait for the body to decompose somewhat before consuming it. People knew the whereabouts of the crocodile's burrow and, after killing it, were able to recover the mutilated body.

It's Very Hard Work to Keep a Farm Going

Betomba became the busiest Port on the Tsiribihina and thousands of people were very happy. The farm was producing tons of cotton, beans and peanuts. It was not easy work and even after Mark Gallant arrived in 1972, it meant hours of hard work under the hot sun. How they worked, how they produced excellent crops but then students were few and most were interested in theory rather than practice.

They went on, determined and really believing that Betomba could become an important agricultural center for the area where many farmers would come to get seed and better breeds of animals. At the Regional Fair in 1974 our produce and animals won all the prizes.

The Farm-School was a Diocesan endeavor managed by La Salettes. We were counting on more men who would come from the United States. But they never came. Lueck and the two Marks were overextending their capacity for work, and we were short on Missionaries for other Parishes.

The Successes and Failures of Our Farm Venture

All Missionaries working in the Diocese came together three times a year – January, May and September. At every meeting we would discuss Betomba. Many were disappointed because there was no financial profit from the farm; the reason being that Lueck would reinvest the profits for new projects that were needed if the farm was to continue.

Bro. Mark Gallant, M.S. working on the farm in Betomba

Discussions were not always honest, nor charitable, with little consideration or sensitivity for the men involved. When stationed in Betomba from 1972–1976, Donald Pelletier was able to witness the work there and saw all the good that was being done and how all the villages along the Tsiribihina River would refer to Betomba for their livelihood.

Harsh reality was facing us and we realized that we did not have the personnel to continue staffing the Betomba Farm. As we were planting cotton and had our own plane, Mark Koenig got involved in spraying and was hired by the National Aerial Treatment Company. Painful as it was, the decision was made to close the farm. Not all the Missionaries appreciated the work done there, nor the efforts of the men involved in making it a worthwhile endeavor. Some blamed them as if the failure had been their fault.

After leaving the farm, Mark Koenig continued aerial treatments as well as piloting the Bishop for his trips in the bush. As there was no one at the mission that had time to listen to his hurt feelings, when the work was discontinued, he found a young woman, Liza, who showed compassion and understanding.

Having made a serious retreat of discernment, Mark asked for a dispensation from his vows, married Liza, and returned to the United States where they live very happily, greatly involved in their local Parish. Mark Koenig had been extremely happy and up to all the challenges of life in the bush. What a joy it had been for him to walk in the cotton fields and the bean plantations in Betomba where everything grew.

A Change in Ministry

Leuk preparing his Sunday homily

Lueck's life in Betomba had not been all farm work. He cared for a vibrant Catholic Community there. Having the Catechetical School there for years was a great help for him and for them. They could put into practice what they learned in class.

After the farm was closed in 1977, Lueck went on to serve across the river in Berevo while Mark Gallant went on to serve in Morondava. Betomba is now a mostly abandoned village along the river. The Main House where the Fathers and Brothers had lived was struck by lightning and burned.

The Catholic Community in Betomba remains very fervent and they have used the foundations of the burnt mission residence (struck by lightening) to build a new Church. Soil erosion is all too evident as the yearly flooding of the river continues to carry uncared-for fertile soil and land out into the ocean. Much of the forest around Betomba has been cut; green hills and forests have been burnt, and are now barren. There is presently a very good Catholic School with over 150 students acknowledging that Betomba owes much to the efforts of Lueck and the two Marks.

Lueck and Mark would be very sad and shed tears were they to see the very sad condition of Betomba and the environment. Unfortunately, though we gave land to the people, they are continually fighting over who owns what parcels of land. Others are selling plots for exorbitant gains although we had given them that land.

Lueck was still very much in his environment when he crossed the river to take charge of the District of Berevo. There again, his construction talents were put to good use. He built a beautiful Convent in which to install a Community of Sisters – the Franciscan Missionaries of Mary. I have spoken of his construction skills that were very helpful in Betomba and would serve him well in Berevo.

An Accident Involving Lueck

In January of 1984, with thick dark clouds in the distance announcing heavy downpour, Lueck sacrificed his siesta to protect the walls and finish roofing of the Father's House. Under the hot sun and early afternoon heat on the roof, he either slipped or passed out and was found unconscious on the cement terrace. With no idea just what happened, it took the sisters over half an hour to revive him.

Residence of Franciscan Missionaries of Mary (F.M.M.) in Berevo, build by Leuk

There were no medical facilities in Berevo, and no doctor. The State Police sent urgent messages to Morondava and Belo. Father Marian Sajdak, M.S. (1943-), Pastor in Belo, was at home, and he had a rapid motor barge. He left immediately for Berevo.

Sister enjoys a refreshing walk through a stream before reaching Berevo

Donald and one of the nurses from the hospital in Morondava, organized a provisional ambulance and drove to the riverbank, almost 100 kilometers (62 miles) to the north. Pushing the motor to the max, Father Marian arrived in Berevo late the afternoon. He has to spend the night there because he could not navigate the river in the dark.

Early in the morning, with Lueck somewhat comfortable in the barge, Marian moved into the river current for the trip down to Belo sur Tsiribihina. For our part, we had waited patiently all night long by the river, and were greatly relieved when we heard a motor in the distance. The message we had received the day before spoke of a very serious accident so you can imagine our anxiety as we waited all night long. A nurse, who came with us, gave him a few injections as we made him comfortable for the long, bumpy and slushy drive in the improvised ambulance.

It was a stroke of God's grace that there was an Amoco Oil Exploration Camp near Mahabo, and it was equipped with a modern Field Hospital. An Irish doctor staffed it. We drove there directly. X-rays and tests revealed two broken wrists, seven broken ribs and a perforated lung.

An Airplane's Mission of Mercy

While Lueck was waiting for the doctor in the air-conditioned Field Hospital, he was enjoying ice cream, so we knew he would be alright. Amoco graciously helped out. Their plane flew Lueck to Tananarive where he was cared for until he was able to return to the United States. Once in Tananarive, the doctors did their best to set bones, bandage wounds and make him comfortable. The first occasion possible, he was evacuated to the U.S.

From St. Louis Back to Berevo

Back in St. Louis, physical therapists did what they could to help him. Lueck cooperated thoroughly, exercising hour after hour as he constantly walked the corridors of the St. Louis house to keep himself "in healing mode." Therapy became a way of life, exercising on the way to prayer and meals.

His desire to return to Berevo was so great that no pain was too strong to stop him from recovery. He recovered quickly. Once back in Madagascar, as Lueck was never one to complain, we did not pay much attention to the residual effects of that accident. It was the origin of health issues that would continue to weaken him in the upcoming years.

Chapter 29 – Fr. Normand Mailloux, M.S., A Visionary

Fr. Normand Mailoux, M.S.

The year 1966 saw the arrival of three Missionaries: Brother Mark Koenig and Fathers Norman Mailloux (1930-2010) and me, Jack Nuelle (1937-). The contribution of Mark, especially at the Farm School in Betomba, was beyond measure. Norm and Jack are two men who would leave a lasting and even decisive imprint on the Mission.

Christ had advised his apostles and future Missionaries to travel light and not overburden themselves. Over the centuries, most Missionaries fail to heed the advice Christ gave his disciples, bringing equipment and tons of supplies to the Missions. Norman Mailloux probably broke all records.

Four Million S&H Green Stamps Paid for a New Airplane

As a Missionary, Normand Mailloux brought a plane and a piano. While preparing to come to Madagascar, he had learned two things among many others. One was that during the rainy season travel by road was impossible; and second, that, in the area of the Morondava mission, there were many landing strips, beaches and open fields where a small plane could land. He was convinced that a small Piper plane would solve our transportation problems to the bush.

He also had the genial idea that the only way he could finance the purchase of a plane would be through the collection of S&H Green Stamps from the Sperry & Hutchinson Company. It was, most likely, the largest number of green stamps ever collected and it was done exclusively to purchase a plane. The Green Stamp campaign covered the entire United States and four million stamps would be needed.

Norm was from Danielson, Connecticut and the collecting began in that city. Parishioners and friends in all our U.S. parishes participated. Four men,

Christened "La Salette," the airplane helped save many lives in emergencies

Mark Koenig, Joe Shea, Norm and I, Jack, obtained our pilot's license and the plane named "La Salette" became a very practical means of evangelization.

We were also the sensation of Madagascar as everyone admired American Missionaries using modern means of transportation to reach distant and isolated villages. This was quite a leap – from filanjana, to oxcart, to Jeep and now to an airplane. With special balloon tires the plane could land on roads, beaches, football fields, and dry rice fields. I don't say that there weren't any risky take-offs or landings and that more than once our passengers closed their eyes and prayed, but there were never any serious accidents.

A Few Close Calls and Government Fears

Donald can't forget about one day flying out of Ankavandra with Mark Koenig, they "kissed" the top of bushes as plane surged and cleared the branches. More the once I landed on the sandy beach for the day to minister to the Catholics on the coastal village of Bossy. Joe Shea would swoop down to get a good look at the Rose Flamingos. We all did medical evacuations, saving lives by landing on beaches, open fields, roads and air strips.

Sadly, the existence of airplanes capable of flying anywhere on the island – and even ultimately outside the country – posed a security problem for a paranoiac government that felt strictly obliged to control every aspect of national life. Our plane fell into that category. By the late 1970s, passengers were strictly controlled. Fuel was rationed. Finally, all flights were forbidden, and we were forced to sell the plane. It was purchased by the aero club of the national airline company, Air Madagascar. As far as I know, it is still in use today.

Norm Mailloux, despite his health problems, would bring much to the Mission while serving as Regional Superior during some decisive years of the mission. From the beginning of the Mission in Morondava and well into the time of Bishop Girouard, it was normal that all monies –whether from France, Rome, the United States, or other charitable organizations – would be sent to the Diocese because the Diocese was the only legal entity we had at that time.

The La Salette Region became a "Juridical Person"

Norm therefore set up the La Salette Region to be a juridical person. After that, we would receive all funds from the St. Louis Office while making sure needs of the Diocese would be met. Back in 1931 Fathers Breault and Le Blanc had purchased a large tract of land (almost thirty-five acres or fourteen hectares) in Namahora some two miles east of Morondava. That land was acknowledged to belong to the Congregation. By happenstance, that property was bought on the 17th of June, 1931 day, the day I, Donald, was born. Coincidence?? Maybe, but I do claim a certain affinity to that piece of land.

It is known as Villa La Salette and remained rather abandoned through the years while the Mission developed in Morondava where, besides the Church of Our Lady of La Salette, there were some large spacious buildings belonging to the Diocese. Bishop Girouard had already negotiated from the Congregation seven acres of that land to build the Boys School that would become College of Saint Paul.

Norm at the time had the intuition that it would be good to trade the Namahora Property, ceding it to the Bishop in exchange for the entire Morondava compound. Bishop Bernard seemed to approve while Donald was totally opposed to such a trade, feeling the Bishop was being cheated, getting the poor end of the deal. The dispute was so violent that when the understanding was signed, Donald resigned as Vicar General.

Time, however, proved it to be the most beneficial and providential decision ever made by Bishop Bernard. I, Donald, thank Normand for his vision and insights. Today the Namahora Property is vibrant and active. It has become the popular center of the Diocese. All Diocesan services and offices are there, including the Bishop's residence and offices, the Minor Seminary, and residences for five Religious Communities. It also contains a Diocesan Development Project – the largest farm in Africa to produce spirulina – an all-in-one source of nutrients including protein levels comparable to eggs but with a bitter taste.

Thank you, Norm. You certainly rendered a tremendous service to the Local Church with your far-reaching vision of the future. I thank God every day that I was wrong and that we did not follow my advice.

Norm worked in Miandrivazo with Joe Shea, then went on to Belo where he was director of the district and local pastor, and subsequently on to Morondava as Superior of the Mission.

Workers harvesting Spirulina, a dietary supplement

A Time of Socialist Revolution

This was the time of the Socialist revolution. While Norm had been pastor in both Miandrivazo and Belo, the economy of the country was floundering. Parents could not even pay the small tuition needed to keep our parish schools alive. Lacking enough money to pay the teachers, Norm closed schools both in Miandrivazo and Belo. He would be amazed to see today the thousands of students attending both schools which re-opened a few years later under the direction of Religious Sisters.

Severe health problems prevented Norm from going out into the bush but he did serve well in the centers where he was also available for masses and confessions. For recreation and therapy, he had his piano wherein he found relaxation and comfort. Wherever he went in the Mission his piano would accompany him. Realizing that the central Morondava residence needed more comfortable rooms, he financed the construction of an additional 12 comfortable rooms that serve well unto this day. Norm was most influential in setting up the financial policies that would guide the mission. You can be sure that during his tenure accounts were well balanced. A good confrere, he was most understanding and comforting when we were faced with personal problems. Norm would pace the spacious verandas walking very slowly while reciting his rosary and through his prayers he was probably doing more than the healthy and active missionaries.

Norm was not the most fluent in the Malagasy language but his care and love of the people made up for the deficiencies of communication. Before venturing to Madagascar, Norm had successfully undergone one of the first triple coronary artery by-pass grafts to his heart in the United States. Regrettably,

Normand's piano found a permanent home in the La Salette Scholasticate in Antanarivo

Norm's health was not improving and we were all concerned that his heart would fail. We all agreed that, when the Cardiologist in Tananarive could in no way monitor his heart condition, it was time for him to return to North America.

We were all very sorry to see him leave and surely missed the harmonious sounds of his piano that could be heard throughout the house. His therapy was to sit at his piano and allow his fingers to dance over the keys. Before leaving he indicated that the piano should go to our Scholasticate in Tananarive. It is still being used there. I wonder how many students know where the piano came from? Norm died in United States on November 14, 2010. I was there to preside and preach at his funeral. Upon his request he is buried in Danielson, Connecticut in a plot that belonged to his family.

Chapter 30 – Valued Missionary Brothers

We have already spoken about Brother Larry and his contribution to the mission. As mentioned above, there were two other Brothers, both named Mark, who contributed much to the evangelization efforts and setting up of our mission. They easily moved from place to place, wherever their expertise was required.

After Larry returned to the United States, it was Mark Gallant who finished the church in Mandabe. In 1975 when Martial Law was declared over the entire island Mark Gallant (1941-2020) was again alone in Betomba. Cut off from help, he was understandably anxious, not knowing just how to cope in such an unexpected situation. The government declared that all guns had to be handed over to the National Police. Since we had no permits for some of them, he threw all unregistered rifles and shotguns into the river and sent the declared rifles to the National Police. It wasn't the best time to be alone in Betomba but he managed well and we lost nothing.

(from left) La Salette confreres, Fr. Donald Pelletier meets with Bro. Larry Deschenes, a gifted builder

After Brother Steve, who served from 1928 to 1936, we had two other American Brothers who served with distinction from 1960 until 1986, giving total satisfaction in their work while leaving a wonderful impression with the people. Both Marks did well in the Malagasy language and were able to establish friendships that endure to this day.

After he left Betomba, Mark Gallant came to Morondava where he spoiled everyone as Local Treasurer. An outstanding cook, he managed the kitchen very well and made sure there were ample food and supplies for hungry missionaries. Our men in the distant bush had to do with a very simple diet and, when they came to Morondava, Mark made sure they were generously served with tasty food and a varied menu. He was well known at the local open-air market and food vendors of fish, chicken and goat meat were constantly at his door, sure he would buy something. We had a large freezer and Mark made sure there was food for any unexpected guest.

(from left) Other La Salette confreres: Brothers Mark Koenig, with his wild boar; Stephen Levickas, a master builder; and Mark Gallant, organizer, accountant and all-around helper

The residence was kept spotless and rooms ready for any arrival. Priests and Brothers of Madagascar were well aware of Morondava's hospitality. Needless to say, we had frequent visitors who came to Morondava for rest and recreation. Mark was the man behind the scenes who made of our residence a home ready to welcome visitors who needed rest, good food and friendly hospitality. Mark was not only an expert in the kitchen but how he mastered the sewing machine making curtains, sheets and other necessities for the house. Many of the articles he made are still used to this day. The ceiling-to-floor stage curtain for our parish hall that he sewed in 1986 is still in use.

Chapter 31 – Anxieties in Times of Revolution

The socialist revolution promised an end to poverty; it didn't happen

When Pete Kohler and Mark Gallant arrived in 1971, we were at our peak with fourteen active Americans in Morondava. That would not last very long. In 1972, Mac died and Brother Larry left. As new missionaries came and others left, our numbers became insufficient to adequately cover the extension of our territory.

The Outbreak of Civil Turmoil

The year Pete and Mark arrived there were already signs of civil unrest and dissatisfaction. That exploded in May of 1972. We would kid Pete telling him he was the trouble-maker that had brought the first violent signs of civil turmoil to the country. We were not about to get involved in local politics but could not ignore what was going on the country nor ignore the fears and anxieties of the people.

A big turning point was the Socialist Revolution of 1975 that would be the beginning of a slow but constant downfall of national, social and economic structures. The year 1975 brought many unfortunate changes in the country. The new socialist government nationalized banks, insurance companies, import, export, electricity and water, oil companies and any other important industry. They stopped short of taking over private schools. The model given was that of the North Korean government of Kim Il-sung, with the promise there would be no poverty in Madagascar. Regrettably, the degradation begun in 1975 continues to this day. We wonder just when our people will have their day in the sun.

During those years not only the remaining French expatriates, but also many foreign missionaries left the country. It was not that the people showed animosity toward them, but many missionaries no longer felt comfortable in the new social climate. Later I met some people who told me that they were sorry that they made the decision to leave.

Declaration of Martial Law

It is to our credit that none of our men ever left for political reasons or for fear of danger. We were often hampered in our ministry. Declaration of Martial Law often sequestered us in our towns and cities for months at a time. Curfews sometimes kept us in our houses from sunset to sunrise. On three occasions we were notified by the American Embassy that they could not assure our safety and it would be better for us to leave the country. On one occasion the U.S. Marines, stationed at the American Embassy in Tananarive, even came to all mission posts where U.S. citizens were stationed in order to check our airfields should there ever be an emergency where they would want to evacuate us.

In 2002, with our security endangered, the Mormon Missionaries and Peace Corps volunteers returned to the United States; but we could never leave our flock in the face of danger. Not that we are better than others but in no way could we flee in the face of danger, in no way could we abandon our flock in a difficult situation. We were never really threatened even though we had to live through some very sad and painful situations.

The endemic national animal is the mischievous ringtail lemur, the oldest primate

Dangers and Close Calls

It did happen on many occasions that the State Police would warn us not to set out on visits to isolated areas where they could not assure our safety. How many of us came across bandits (known as dahalos, a Malagasy name that still instills fear) but were never harmed, nor our residences attacked! I, Jack, had four different encounters. Once I drove through a barrier blocking the middle of a bridge; twice in the bush, my Land Rover outran the spears thrown at me; and once I was stopped on the main highway by a group of bandits dressed like State Police who demanded that I give them a ride. I told them, "Sorry. If I put you all in my Land Rover, we would then be too numerous, and I would no longer be covered by insurance!" As they tried to figure out that dilemma, he stepped on the gas pedal, and took off.

The national tree is the Baobob; the National flower is the bright red poinciana

Serving the mountainous terrane of Ankavandra, Jeremy encountered many bandits and knew all their hideouts. Kiddingly, we were going to name him "Chaplain of Bandits." Once I, Donald, was with him in a very isolated area of Ankavandra and we had stopped for lunch at noon, when we were ambushed by a group of bandits. Three of them came at us from the South — two from the North. Then one of them noticed my cross (I was Bishop at the time) and cried out, "Leave them alone. He is a Priest." We nevertheless jumped in the Land Cruiser and sped out of there.

Chapter 32 –
Fr. Peter Kohler, M.S.,
A Missionary Anywhere in the World

The seventies were the good years despite the socialist revolution. Ushering them in was the arrival of Father Peter D. Kohler (1941-2014), M.S. Pete, as we called him, was born in St. Louis, Missouri on June 2, 1941. He came into the world during World War II, and into Madagascar at the beginning of the socialist revolution.

Ordained in 1968, Pete had a great desire to serve in Madagascar, and volunteered. Three years later, his dream came true. However, like so many others who came to Morondava from North America, he was hampered by not knowing French. Repchick, Silva, Bernier and Shea had stopped over in Rome for a few months to live in and study in a somewhat French environment at our International Scholasticate in Rome, Italy. Pete, however, hoped to overcome that hurdle in a new way. Before embarking for Madagascar, he requested and was granted a year of studies at a French Language School in Lyon, France. Just as those first four American missionaries of the second wave experienced more intercultural training in Rome from sightseeing than from studying, Pete probably learned more French by asking how to get from one from city or monument to another than from the hours spent in the classroom.

Fr. Peter Kohler, M.S.

Similar to all the others, he arrived with a heart filled with dreams and determination. Once in Madagascar, he attended the Language School for newly arrived missionaries in Ambositra. Eight months later, he reached Morondava to begin his missionary life. Collaborating first with me, Jack, and then with Joe Shea, he felt at home out in the bush.

God will Provide

Pete was not one to get weighed down with material things. He felt secure following the Lord's command (Matthew 6:31-34) not to worry about what to eat or drink or wear. His task was to proclaim the Gospel and God would provide for all he needed. At times it was comical to watch him prepare to leave for the bush. Regardless of whether he was to be away for a few days or 2 weeks, whether he was going by car, oxcart, out-rigger canoe, riding a bike, or walking, he would weigh his knapsack to assure that he had no more than twenty-five pounds to carry – and that included his clothing, bedding, mosquito net, and Mass kit!

Notwithstanding certain restrictions, Pete fit right into our team of American Missionaries who worked well, even though we were challenged by the fallacies of Marxist ideology. We were always

Peter riding in a local pouse-pouse carriage

happy to be together. After four years in Berevo, I, Donald, went to Mahabo where I was entrusted to training our lay catechists. Le Blanc, Bernier and Silva were in the Parish. Norm Mailloux was in Morondava with Joe Shea, Lueck and two Marks were on the Tsiribihina, Jack was in Malaimbandy, and John was in Mandabe. There was a great sense of solidarity and together we were happy despite the privations and difficulties.

Pete Kohler served in the bush of Morondava from 1971 to 1976 and his sense of humor, flexibility and positive attitude were a boost to all of us. He arrived at the end of the First Republic and was there for the birth of the Socialist Revolution. He saw immediately the fallacy of this ideology and knew nothing good would come from this adventure into socialism.

His Good Sense of Humor Lessened the Tension

When Pete shared his experiences in the bush, we could not help but laugh with him, and always felt better knowing how Pete would roll with the punches. Nothing seemed to bother him. He always saw the good side of everything. He was a very generous missionary and served very well, touching people with understanding and compassion, helping the poor and sick. However, much like Bernier and Jake, he felt that the language was a bigger barrier than he was prepared for. It prevented him from being effective as a missionary.

Moving On

After five years of very productive work as a missionary, Pete felt that he could serve the mission better as Procurator of the St. Louis Mission Office. He was the only one who could laugh at the fallacies and idiocies of the socialist revolution. He was one of the first to try the bicycle for his visits to the bush until he found out that he carried the bike more often than the bike carried him. Pete loved the mission, loved the work, and loved the people. We all enjoyed his presence here with us. One of the qualities needed to survive in the missions is a sense of humor. It was clear that Pete had a great sense

Saklava mother and child

of humor and could always see the funny side of any situation.

He was taking care of the bush churches in the district attached to the Parish of Our Lady of La Salette. Where at that time he journeyed and served alone, there are today seven priests for the thirty chapels that he covered during his five years. During his time here he survived a cyclone that greatly damaged the church in Belo sur Mer. He was able to find funds and repaired the church that would unfortunately be hit by future cyclones.

As the Mission Procurator in St. Louis, Missouri, Pete's mission energy was indefatigable. He increased the revenue for Madagascar coming from mission appeals. No parish in the United States was too far for him to drive and visit, always speaking to the people from personal experience. He could be funny, and kids loved him. His monthly mission letters – yes, continuing those letters starter by Jake in 1958 – were factual as well as witty and personal, based on his many unique adventures. He served in this capacity as Mission Procurator for over fifteen years.

Logo for Unbound

With all those years of missionary experience, of preaching to bring awareness to the needs of our brothers and sisters in mission countries, he went on to dedicate his energies to raising funds for the CFCA (now called Unbound). His preaching was very effective, and countless underprivileged children in many poor countries benefited from his love and dedication. Pete died one Saturday morning in June, 2014 as he was preparing to leave for another weekend of preaching Jesus' Gospel.

Chapter 33 – Brother Mark Gallant, M.S., A Multi-Gifted Brother

Brother Mark Gallant, M.S.

As stated above, I mentioned that this Missionary Brother, Mark Gallant, was from the Hartford Province. He was born on April 14, 1941 in Ipswich, Massachusetts. After the total destruction of the Major La Salette Seminary in Altamont, New York by a tragic fire, the Major Seminary for the Hartford Province had been transferred to a newly purchased property in Ipswich, Massachusetts, and Mark's mother ended up working there.

When arriving in Morondava in 1971, Mark had already been a Religious for eight years, serving in a variety of ministries. One special quality displayed by all the Brothers who served in the Morondava mission – and that is especially true for Mark – was their adaptability. When there was a job to be done, they were always ready for the challenge. Unfortunately, today there are few vocations for the brotherhood and we have to rely on salaried personnel who in no way can replace the work and dedication of our Brothers.

Mark remained in the Morondava mission until 1986, serving for more than fifteen years. We have already spoken (in Chapter 30) of the role he fulfilled in the very difficult history of Betomba. As already mentioned above, when speaking of the mission post of Betomba, he was able to serve and accept many and varied responsibilities. At one time or another, he took on the responsibility of treasurer, maintenance person, cook, and builder. Mark served in Betomba and then went on to Morondava to serve as treasurer, showing generous hospitality to all fathers coming from the bush and to our many visitors.

Welcoming Visitors

During those years, the Morondava residence was the only lodging available for visitors coming to Morondava. You can be sure the spacious rooms were clean and comfortable, while meals were delicious and appreciated by everyone. Daily he went to the marketplace. He

Fresh tuna would be brought to Mark by wives of local fishermen

became well-known, and soon the merchants got to know his tastes. They would often come directly to the mission house before setting up their stand for the day at the market, offering him choice food. It was not unusual to see a woman walking into the mission compound carrying on her head three or four large tuna fish or a man coming to sell a large slab of goat meat. Mark was a very good manager, an excellent cook, a friendly host and we were sad to see him leave.

Mark was born, the second of fourteen children, into a Franco-American family. French was no problem for him, and he became very active with the French community in Morondava, always available when the parish required his services. Mark had an excellent singing voice, and participated well in liturgies in both French and Malagasy. Very personable, he had many friends with whom he has remained loyal through the years.

A Sad Farewell

Known and loved by everyone Mark was given a very sincere and emotional farewell by the Morondava Parish Community. Back in the United States, Mark would be one of the co-founders with me, Jack, of the new North American La Salette Mission Center (LSMC), where he worked for four years. From there he worked at the Provincial Administrative Office. When health issues forced his retirement, he still went on to perform many other tasks for the community. He died of the Coronavirus on May 13, 2020.

Logo for La Salette Misssion Center in St. Louis, Missouri

Chapter 34 –
Fr. Gerald (Gerry) Biron, M.S. and Fr. Ernest Corriveau, M.S., Missionaries with a World Outlook

We are only too happy to underline the fine contribution furnished by Father Gerald (Gerry) Biron, M.S. (1934-2018) who, in his double tour of duty, worked first in Antsirabe and then Morondava. Gerry was well known in the Congregation; not only did he work in Rome but was a very active Missionary in the Philippines, Spain, and Argentina, and of course his double venture in Madagascar.

He first came to Antsirabe in the 1960s where, under the guidance of Bishop Claude Rolland, M.S. (1910-1973), he learned the Malagasy language and was assigned to Betafo, with pastoral care of Ambolotara, an isolated center that rested on a nearby mountain. One of his bush churches was perched on the summit of the mountain, almost 7,000 feet above sea level. While studying Malagasy in Ambositra, I, Jack, spent a short period of time with Gerry for a "pastoral experience" and went to stay at that 7,000 foot church in the beginning of winter. Quite a cold shock!

Fr. Gerry Biron, M.S., was a world missionary

Building a Road

The major problem with , Ambolotara was the lack of a road, a challenge only Gerry would dare tackle. It was the time when Catholic Relief Services was new to Madagascar and was trying to finance social projects that would benefit farmers. Gerry did not hesitate to present the project of the road that could be built. It was one of the first "Food for Work" projects sponsored by CRS. He had local engineers map out the projected road.

For months hundreds of men, armed with pickaxes, shovels and wheelbarrows moved thousands of cubic meters of dirt and stone to build a road. Timber was felled to provide material for building multiple small bridges. There were many sceptics, but Gerry overcame this through personal witness. He personally was part of that work force, pitching in every day, helping, encouraging, giving good example.

The people were fed once every day with food from CRS. Justifiably, Gerry got national recognition when the road finally opened up the village to vehicles. It also gave local farmers a means of getting their produce to the large market in Betafo.

Gerry was the only American working with our French and Malagasy missionaries in the Diocese of Antsirabe at that time. He was a good provider and it was greatly appreciated when, after a vacation in the United States, he brought in two new jeeps for the diocese. He helped many poor families and encouraged vocations which he has continued to support throughout the years.

Off to Our Other Missions and Then...

When he left Antsirabe, it was to serve in La Salette missions in other parts of the world: Spain and Argentina. After a serious accident in Argentina which nearly took off his leg, he returned to the U.S. His knowledge of Spanish was invaluable in Hispanic ministry.

But Gerry was a missionary at heart and would eventually come back to work in Madagascar, this time to serve with us in Morondava. At that time our numbers had greatly diminished and we were very happy to welcome Gerry, especially that he was already fluent in the Malagasy language. With his legendary generosity and tenacity Gerry moved into Mahabo with Fathers Jean de la Croix Rakotoarimanana, Le Blanc and Jack.

As usual, he brought with him many new ideas on how to help the poor while finding new ways to evangelize. There were two projects that not only kept him very busy but witnessed to his great desire to help people. Gerry saw the fertile soil of Mahabo and decided that he would have a large vegetable garden so as to furnish fresh vegetables for the religious of Morondava and to sell to local hotels and restaurants. He was very successful and twice a week would drive to Morondava with his Renault 4L – it was always a wonder how he fitted into that small car – loaded with fresh vegetables and, of course, we marveled on the size and quality of his tomatoes, lettuce and other vegetables. He did prove to everyone that with work and determination it is possible to grow vegetables in the Morondava area.

In an altogether different and more delicate area, Gerry moved in to help the poor, mostly elderly Malagasy peasants who could barely eek out an existence. On every street corner and in every little village in the bush there is a general store where everyone can get daily supplies, such as oil, sugar, coffee, salt, candles, matches, condensed milk, rice, and so many basic items. These little merchants buy their supplies in Mahabo from a middle-man who bought wholesale in Morondava. As is too often the case, the middle-man makes all the profit exploiting these poor retailers.

I Can Get it for You Wholesale

To help poor families make a better living, Gerry started a quasi-charitable wholesale business for all these basic products. Gerry would often go to Morondava on other business – for example, to deliver vegetables – and for his return trip, would fill his car with merchandise purchased at a wholesale price. He was satisfied to cover transportation cost, and small village vendors were so very happy to get their small supplies at cost price – no middleman taking a profit. This brought many poor to the mission of Mahabo, and especially gave them a means of subsistence since they could now sell these items at the regular price and still make a profit. Needless to say, he made enemies among the richer merchants.

This became a major project, as Gerry would buy tons of supplies. It was a huge enterprise that took much energy and time from Gerry. He proved that it was possible to help the small local merchants. Sadly though, since there was no one to

Frequent open food markets in Madagascar

Fr. Ernest Corriveau, M.S.

take over the project when Gerry had to leave, today the middle-man continues to make the most profit.

On weekends and even weekdays Gerry was always ready and willing to serve the nearby bush churches while helping with ministry in Mahabo. Gerry had a great many stories, and it pleased Le Blanc to sit on the breezy veranda and listen and chuckle at his stories while smoking his pipe.

Gerry loved to serve, making trips to minister in Ankilizato, a thirty-mile dirt road that would require a few hours, especially during the rainy season. Unfortunately, he had serious health problems with his foot that were the result of his accident in Argentina. This ultimately led to his leaving Mahabo in 1985 and returning to the states for urgent medical care. It became a very debilitating illness that, after years of constant care, would lead to amputation. So after just 2 more years of generous service, Gerry returned to the United States. It was a loss for the mission but there was no way our local doctors could treat his infected foot. After a long illness he died in Hartford in February, 2018.

Fr. Ernie Corriveau, M.S., Truly Gifted

Another gifted missionary who deserves gratitude is Father Ernest Corriveau, M.S. (1937-) who volunteered to serve in Madagascar. He has a docile fatherly temperament that served him well when he taught in the La Salette Seminary in Enfield, New Hampshire. Combine this with the measured and firm leadership qualities he displayed as Provincial when he led the Province of the Immaculate Heart of Mary through some turbulent times, Ernie's presence was truly a gift to the mission. Together, they revealed excellent missionary capabilities.

Despite serious health problems he wanted to work and serve the poor in a mission country. He was fluent in French and, true to his generous and determined nature, Ernie made a valiant effort to learn the Malagasy language. After a few months to get accustomed to the climate, he went to Ambositra for the language course. It was there that constant dysentery and stomach problems convinced him that God was calling him elsewhere.

Mary's message, "When people are converted" applies to every culture

I, Jack, was Regional Superior at the time and had the woeful task of convincing Ernie that his health concerns would not allow for him to stay. We had had great hopes for Ernie who could have served well for religious formation of our young religious but God had other plans. I don't have to relate how Ernie, a staunch walker and expert swimmer, was very comfortable in Morondava where he could not only walk the endless miles of pristine beaches but also take these thousand strokes in the clear waters of the Mozambique Channel. Ernie would go on a few years later to serve the entire La Salette Congregation as Superior General (1988-1994).

Chapter 35 – "Déjà Vu" Politics, On a Local Level

Despite all the political corruption and various crises, the Church was making constant progress and remained a strong pillar in society. Church leaders enjoyed great credibility. During the crucial moments of civil unrest, they were key figures leading to the reconciliation of political factions, helping the whole country to move on. Despite some reluctance from the Vatican, priests and nuns were always very visible during demonstrations, street protests, popular gatherings to show discontent. Nevertheless, politically the country went from one deception to another.

Soldiers enforced martial law in the cities during the Malagasy cultural revolution

There was much hope and assurance of a better future in 1960, again in 1975, in 1991, and again in 2002. But at every turn, people were manipulated and greatly deceived by their political leaders. Democracy is not an easy or ready-made reality in a poor country. The government elected in 2013, after five years of an illegal transitional government (2009-2013), continued to deceive and people could only continue to wait for a better future.

Morondava had fared very well in the First Republic. There were two influential ministers who did much to favor our city and surrounding rural area. As the saying goes, after the feast comes famine! From 21972 onward, our region was not only politically neglected but abandoned. So many projects, so many major investments had been started, and all were abandoned after corruption and faulty management caused failure.

If they were operational today, Morondava would be a model of economic development. We could establish a full-blown cemetery with all the dead projects: orange grove, cotton fields, sugar-cane plantation, shrimp farm, slaughter-house, and so on; all are memories and all failed because of corrupt politicians.

Progress Comes Ever So Slowly

We can be grateful to the benefactors who have enabled the Catholic Mission to assure social growth and progress. In 1958 when I, Donald, arrived in Morondava we had only four schools and some four hundred students. Today we have not only Primary Grades, but Secondary Schools, Junior Colleges and a Catholic University.

We are assuring education for almost 24,000 students on various levels. All the progress seen through the years is due to help and support from our families, friends and the St. Louis province. We have eight Catholic Medical Centers, and one Catholic Hospital in Belo Tsiribihina where we care for thousands of sick patients.

Malagasy School in Marofototra

Chapter 36 – More Personal Experiences

I, Donald have already highlighted many of our men and their contribution to the mission but as I look at the sixty years – 1958 to 2021 – I wish to move to some more personal experiences which were very much in communion and interdependent with three other men who were closely bonded with me in deep friendship. Not that I would want to underestimate Joe Silva and John Repchick, but Lueck, Joe Shea, Jack and Donald did share one mind and one heart. As I mentioned earlier, both Joe Silva and John Repchick left in 1982 for health reasons.

The cathedral was served by well-trained altar servers, thanks to Joe Shea. Fr. Pelletier stands

No Man is an Island

No one can work alone. If I, Donald, accomplished anything as a fellow priest and then as bishop, it was with a community of brothers. Though we were not always in the same locale, it seemed we were always replacing one another. Joe Shea replaced Jack and I in 1972 and then I replaced him in 1982. Lueck and Shea replaced me in Antsalova, Lueck, Joe and Jack took on leadership roles... and so it went. We were as one.

These are memories, and each time I unveil them, there are scenes that repeat themselves, and others that shed new light on their importance. When I arrived in 1958, I studied Malagasy in Morondava and then was stationed there for the next fourteen years. Many and varied responsibilities, first as a docile Assistant to Franco, then as Pastor, Superior, Diocesan Vicar General, Vicar Capitular, Treasurer and Bishop.

(from left) Art Lueckenotto explains something to visiting La Salettes, Bishop Donald Pelletier and Fr. Mémé Rakotondraibe, present Secretary General

Constant Health Issues

They were good years. We were young and healthy. Joe Shea had gone from Mandabe to Antsalova while Lueck would arrive in 1964, Jack, Norm and Mark Koenig in 1966, and Pete Kohler and Mark Gallant in 1972. A constant fear for missionaries is the health issue, and we all had to cope with various tropical deceases. No one was exempt from bouts of malaria. We had been told to take preventative medications but our malaria carriers – those pesky female anopheles mosquitos – were immune to quinine and we all had to submit to the discomforts and dangers of malaria. When we read the annals of our first missionaries, starting in 1921 in Betafo and Antsirabe, and on to the first sustained missionary efforts in Morondava from 1928, we read how they were frequently afflicted with malaria at a time when medications were not available.

After years of taking various forms of quinine and other medications we experienced hearing and sight problems and were told to stop taking certain types of medication, which we joyfully did. There was yellow fever, black-water fever, typhoid, hepatitis, amoebic dysentery, tuberculosis, and even cholera.

Despite the numerous and varied bugs and many tropical deceases, we managed to stay quite healthy. I think most of us paid our dues and spent some time at the Medical Clinic in Tananarive. It was Joe Shea who gave us the first serious fear in 1961 with a ruptured appendix. About the same time, Father Bernier had a serious urinary infection.

Jack Nuelle visiting elderly woman in her home

Health issues did not dampen our zeal or generosity for ministry and most of us have survived rather well. While in Morondava, Lueck and Joe Shea both served with me, while Jack would be my assistant for seven years. Joe Shea would replace me in 1972 while I would take over from him again in 1982. Our Lady of La Salette Parish, the oldest parish in the diocese – consisted of five distinct areas: Morondava "ville" (known as Andriaka), to the north (Avaradrova), to the south (Bethania), to the east (Namahora), and to the southeast (Antanambao). It would be the model and an example for all other parishes.

We always had good lay leadership while parish associations and groups were very active. Joe got the altar servers organized, as well as a choir and we could be proud of the parish. Both the altar boys and choir are active to this day grateful to Joe Shea.

At that time the parish covered the entire city and rural areas of Morondava, and we all hold a special place in our hearts for those days when there was such good communion for the entire area. Today there are six parishes in the city of Morondava, and, in the original parish of Our Lady of La Salette there are still four well-attended Masses each weekend.

Our Younger Years

From 1966 to 1972 Jack and I, who staffed La Salette of Morondava, were not always the most prudent in our ventures. There was never a "day off" in our calendars, but they were good years, filled with creativity and daring. We were still in the First Republic. Our roads, though only dirt, were in good condition most of the year, and we were young and fool-hearty. Jack would spend two weeks in the bush, then head back home where we would spend a few days together, Then I would head out for two more weeks, and the cycle would continue. We alternated between the bush and the home parish.

Jack's mother would send tons of toys, school supplies, clothing and together we ran some of the most successful Parish Fairs ever held in Morondava. We were able to open some fourteen schools with over thirty-five bush chapels to visit. It seemed there was nothing to prevent us from evangelizing everyone. In 1968, to commemorate the 40th anniversary of the arrival of the first missionaries in 1928, we had a "pilgrim virgin" statue that we took to visit every single village of the district. This brought many blessings to the people.

When together at home after a long hard day's work, after the evening meal, the two of us would walk to the beach and, while sitting on the sand dunes, enjoy the cool ocean breeze, listening to the surf and admiring the moon's reflection over the water. We would share how God was working in our lives and for the churches in Morondava. It was a wonderful way to end a busy day of missionary activity.

Meanwhile, Lueck was busy at the farm. Joe Shea with Norm Mailloux worked well in Miandrivazo. Joe Silva, in Malaimbandy with Brother Celse Scotton, was busy building the sisters' convent and spacious school. At first, missionaries would be allowed to go home every five to seven years but as air travel developed very quickly, we were allowed three months every three years.

The Blessing of Growth

Outrigger canoe traditionally used in fishing and also brought missionaries to coastal villages

In 1967 the Sacred Heart Brothers arrived to take over our Boy's School in Namahora. Under the Brothers' direction, school enrollment increased rapidly. We would come once a month from La Salette in Morondava to say Masses for the students. It wasn't until 1978 that Bishop Bernard decided to create a second parish for the city, this one in Namahora. It would be known Mary Queen. I had celebrated the first Christmas Mass in Namahora in 1971 and thus with the opening of a second parish in Morondava we witnessed growth and progress for the Catholic Mission.

There is no doubt that during all those years and all the years of working here in Morondava, there was one constant reality and that was growth. In fact, we could not keep up with growth. Throughout the sixties and seventies, we were baptizing 1,500 babies and 500 adults while in the eighties and nineties it was closer to 2,000 babies and 1,000 adults. With such figures you can understand why we speak of growth. True – we did lose some on the way but then we had to build or extend churches so these people could worship.

You would think that with so many baptisms we would be moving ahead on general average, but as population grew and people moved into the area the Catholic population never went above 8%. Population was growing as fast, if not faster than our statistics would want to indicate.

My journey throughout these many years has been rather simple. After my first fourteen years in Morondava I had a ten-year tour in other districts of the diocese: four years in Berevo, another four in Mahabo at our training center for catechists, followed by two years in the Northern districts of Ankavandra and Antsalova. Then in 1982 I returned to Morondava, as pastor of Our Lady of La Salette, and Mary Queen, and finally was ordained Bishop in the year 2,000. Except for the ten years in the bush I al-

With years of experience to guide him, Donald, Director of the Normal School from 1976-1980, prepareshis classes at the catechetical school

ways ministered in Morondava and the surrounding villages. If much of the attention and progress seems to be concentrated in and around Morondava, we nevertheless did our best to reach out to the extreme and distant districts of Ankavandra and Antsalova. I was there only two years but then Joe Shea, Lueck and especially Jeremy did much to evangelize those two districts. The area is vast – some 8,000 square miles – sparsely populated, just 100,000 people, with no roads in the district of Ankavandra, and only one road in Antsalova from south to north, open only eight months of the year. Stationed there as a young 50-year-old, I did all my visits on foot averaging 100 miles a month. I was in great shape and should have stayed there!

Walking Everywhere

Joe Shea and Lueck took Antsalova and Ankavandra over after me and did much to organize the centers and bush churches. Sparsely populated, there are more oxen than people! That is why cattle rustlers have their day in the sun. In my two years, I walked four times the 90 miles that separate Ankavandra from Antsalova. I would stop half-way in the town of Tsiandro where I would spend one week giving the sacraments to the Christians who lived there. Tsiandro was a beautiful village that set on what is known as the Bemaraha plateau and, as it sets 2,200 ft. above sea level, it enjoys a cooler climate than other areas. Coffee and vegetables grow well there, contrary to any possibilities in Ankavandra and Antsalova.

Difficult as were those years, being alone with few visitors, I was nevertheless very happy serving the people of both Ankavandra and Anstalova. It was during my stay in Antsolova that I received the one and only family visit from my nephew Mike Poirier who was serving as a Peace Corps volunteer in Kenya.

Native Malgash Bishop Bernard Ratsimamotoana, M.S., bishop of Morondava from 1964-1998

In 1982, when Joe Shea was pastor in Morondava, there had been a serious accident at the Annual Parish Fair, where over twenty children were seriously injured and hospitalized. Some had to be evacuated to Tananarive. The accident caused great grief and anxiety to Joe. He was so shaken that it was judged that he needed rest in the United States. Bishop Bernard made a special trip to Antsalova, begging me to return to Morondava to fill in for Joe.

It was with great regret that I left the North where I already had plans for new projects. In Antsalova, there lives a diocesan local priest who, after ten years of ministry alone in that district, left the priesthood and married a Sakalava woman. I realize now that we were all responsible for his departure. We left him there alone showing little or no support. It is no wonder that he faltered.

Our Need for Personal Support

These isolated districts require strong men and no man should be left there alone. Fortunately, God's grace was watching over me and I only remained two years in the North. With time and growth, we were able to separate the two districts of Antsalova and Ankavandra, but the three of us, and later Jeremy, left much of our sweat and tears in those districts.

The Crowned Fisher Eagle

Two elegant Madagascar Crowned Fish Eagles perched high above

Antsalova, west of Ankavandra, is in the coastal plain and still has considerable forest with much game and many lakes rich in fish. In Antsalova can be found an endangered species of a beautiful, proud Crowned Fisher Eagle known as Ankoay. This beautiful eagle is all but extinct. Antsalova is the last region of Madagascar where some thirty of them are trying to survive. There is an NGO that works exclusively to protect this eagle and also to assure its reproduction. The female hatches but two eggs a year and often, once the first has hatched, she then kills the second.

Not always easy to understand how so much money can be spent to protect animals when people in the area do not have the basic necessities. They, like the eagles, like the lemurs of the region, make for a tasty meal! We try to explain to the people how necessary it is that this beautiful eagle survives as part of our national heritage. Tourists will be attracted to come just to admire this remarkable eagle. That could potentially be a source of economic growth.

North Koreans Arrive

In the late seventies and early eighties, during the socialist revolution, President Didier Ratsiraka frequently invited North Koreans to visit and inspect many areas of Madagascar. Some of them lived in the northern area where I was stationed, surveying and studying the possibilities of development with the hopes of importing the North Korean economic and political model to Madagascar. They told the people that prayer was a waste of time as there was no God and only the President of Madagascar would feed them and look out for their welfare. Providentially they all left our area after three years.

The Tsingy Forests

Antsalova now boasts of what will someday become the most popular and fascinating National Park in Madagascar. The Bemaraha Tsingy is a UNESCO World Heritage site. This combination of three Tsingy Forests in the Bemaraha area is the largest Tsingy Forest site on earth, covering 675,000 acres. It is a forest of razor-sharp limestone needles, some of them soaring to 250 feet in height. Despite impossible roads, the Bemaraha Tsingy already draws thousands of visitors every year. When we worked there, walking through the area that we could admire, we never imagined that someday it would attract so many tourists.

God's Gifts of Nature

Wandering through the wilderness of Madagascar – and I, Donald, can speak personally of the western coastal regions of the island – can be frightening and exhilarating. One is surrounded with God's gifts. They come in all colors, sizes, shapes and tastes. Take for example an orange. Many oranges grow wild in the area. They can become a very precious gift. After you have walked for three or four hours in the hot sun and you reach a village tired and thirsty, what could be more inviting than a basket filled with juicy, sweet oranges waiting to quench your thirst. It is like a miracle and a real source of lifting up your heart, mind and body to praise God for His gifts.

The Bible speaks of "a land flowing with milk and honey" (Exodus 3:17). Once with the catechist, I had left a village (Bemonto) very early in the morning (4:00 am) without breakfast or coffee and after three hours when the sun was already up in the sky my stomach not only growled but my body weakened and I could no longer go on. The catechist had me sit in the shade of a Tamarin tree and, leaving me alone, went on his own, quite assured that I would not move. No more than ten minutes later he returned with two large honeycombs oozing with golden honey in the glare of the morning sun. I gulped the thick honey, spitting out the wax, and after thirty minutes, I had the energy to move on, not only nourished and strengthened but with a grateful heart for God's gift of nature.

I enjoyed my two years in Ankavandra-Antsalova and was very sad to leave but rejoiced when Joe Shea and eventually Lueck were sent there to continue the work. One day in August 1982 Bishop Bernard Ratsimamotoana, M.S. (1925-2005), drove to Antsalova to ask me if I would consider returning to assume pastoral care of the Morondava Parish. Joe Shea needed a good vacation in the United States and it seemed it was time for me to return to Morondava. As mentioned earlier, during the annual Parish Fair there had been a serious tragic accident when the upper veranda of school collapsed under the weight of too many people. It was a miracle that nobody died, but there were many serious injuries which required extensive medical attention. Encouraged by lawyers, many victims decided to file court charges demanding considerable indemnity and penalties. Joe Shea, already shaken by the accident itself, was all the more upset with the court cases. This unrest and anxiety prompted the Bishop to recall me to replace him at the parish. As it turned out all victims recovered very well while we were able to settle all cases out of court. For that satisfying outcome, we thank the Lord and Our Lady.

Chapter 37 – Lay Catechists, Men and Women Witnessing to God

Catechists from Morondava with Frs. Władyskaw Czosnek, M.S. (front row, third from left) and Jack and Donald seen on far ends of back row

It is maybe time to say a word about our closest collaborators in our Mission work, the catechists. Pastoral methods, very particular to Africa (and here we include Madagascar) and very evangelical in nature, were the work of the Holy Spirit as a response to the needs of Africa. Lay catechists have always been of particular importance in mission countries, where priests were only able to visit different parts of their mission periodically, sometimes once or twice a year.

In the beginning of this mission narrative, when McDonald and Le Blanc arrived, Breault left for three months to visit Catholic communities which had been established by laypersons in the vast area that, today, composes three dioceses. There would have been no progress in evangelization without the vital contribution of lay catechists who fulfill the task of leaders and ministers of small rural communities.

Lay Catechists – Keeping Faith Alive

Missionaries were never numerous and had to cover vast rural areas where people lived in small villages of 500 to 1,000 people. These were fragile Catholic communities that could only be visited by a priest once or twice a year. A fundamental concern was how to keep the faith alive and growing for communities that were deprived of the priest, and must therefore live their faith without the Eucharist. As such, these lay catechists need to be recognized and given a particular place of honor within the history of the mission.

When the first priest, who in 1926 made the trip from Miarinarivo to Maintirano, arrived there, he was greatly surprised to find six active Catholic communities. Six churches caring for large communities that were founded in the early 1920s before any missionary priest came into the area. They were established by dedicated faith-filled lay leaders who served as catechists. Without a priest, but inspired and guided by the Holy Spirit, the lay catechist took on the role of being the main teacher of the faith in that church. The La Salettes in the Diocese of Antsirabe uniquely furthered the efforts of evangelization throughout the Island more than thirty years before Vatican II. They published a book, "Sunday Worship Without a Priest," that helped catechists to nourish their people every week through the scriptures. It was used by catechists across the entire Island.

The Catechist's Ministry

Today, the missionary, together with community leaders, will discern and usually name a man (we do have women catechists also) to assume that important role. Although the catechist ministers mostly on Saturday and Sunday, his mission as Church leader is a full-time job. On weekends he teaches catechism classes, prepares the Sunday Liturgy, plus his homily, and makes sure the chapel is clean and ready for Sunday worship. He does not necessarily need to do all those activities himself but he is responsible for working with and guiding others to assure that Sunday will be a day appropriately dedicated to worship.

During the week he visits the sick, presides funerals, while always being attentive to the needs of the Catholics who are usually a minority in the village. When the missionary visits, he opens his house for the priest, or assures that there is a decent place for him to stay. His wife will help in preparing meals and organizing other church-related activities. The catechist will not only give a report of activities but present various groups preparing for Sacraments: Baptism, First Communion, Confirmation and eventually Marriage.

Some of our older catechists were truly outstanding men who served with great faith and generosity. It seems that during the first generation of neophytes, God does shower some extraordinary graces on both individuals and on the community as a whole; this is the reason why we were all greatly influenced by these elderly men who had given their lives for the Church. We have already spoken about Victor Maheny in Belo sur Mer and his extraordinary contribution to the local church. Others were:

- Antoine, for example, served for over fifty years in Berevo, the geographical center of the Morondava mission.

- Ignace was extraordinarily devoted to Father Fr. Władysław Czosnek, M.S., in Betomba and Malaimbandy for thirty years, many of them spent helping to train younger men.

- Jean Marie was among the first to come down the Tsiribihina River into the Sakalava region. He also served the church for over fifty years.

- Alphonse faithfully served in Antsalova, in the northern sector of the mission; and there were so many others.

Lay Catechists Support Their Priests

Here, we wish only to underscore that we, as priests and foreigners, could not help but be impressed, touched, and greatly enriched by the faith of these catechists. If some of us were able to survive alone in the isolated bush, it was because we enjoyed the support, friendship, comprehension, understanding, and above all forgiveness of these men of God.

We are all better priests, better missionaries for having known and worked with these lay leaders so vital and necessary for the growth of the Church. We see how God will always provide for the care of his flock and, where there are no priests, he will call men and women to serve and minister to the needs of the community. True, a community needs the Eucharist but, when not available, Faith can grow and survive through the Living Word.

In the Missions we often find ourselves very close to the reality lived in the Acts of the Apostles as we truly experience many lay people who journeyed and assisted Paul and Peter. All of us realized how much we owed for the service of our catechists.

Catechist, Germain Visiteur, received a meritorious reward; he served in the northernmost area of the diocese

Chapter 38 – The Beautiful Gate

I, Donald, wish to share with you one of my faith experiences and how we can come to realize that we are but poor instruments in the hands of our Father. It was in 1982. I was back in Morondava to replace Joe Shea as Pastor of Our Lady of La Salette. Because I had been away for ten years, I was doing the parish visit to renew relations with those I knew, and make contact with the new generation. It became my custom to go out every evening from 5pm to 8pm when people were usually back home after day's work.

It happened one night...

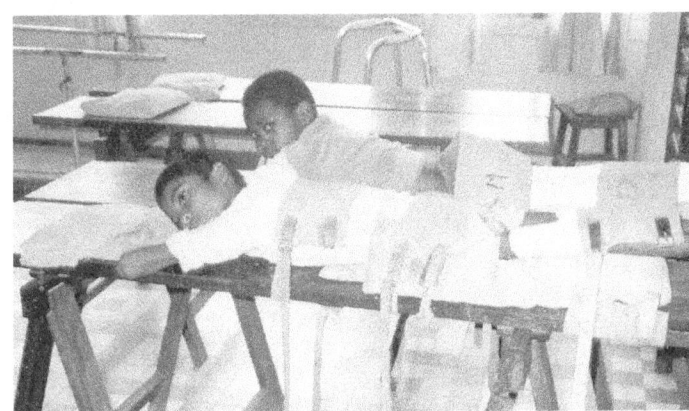

Supervised by medical personnel, children receive physical therapy at the "Beautiful Gate" Center

That night I was visiting the northern sector of Avaradrova. It was already dark and there was little moonlight. The path was very narrow and, though walking cautiously, I tripped and fell headlong into the sand. It wasn't a stone that I had tripped on, nor a log, nor an animal, but a young boy, curled up in the middle of the narrow path. My pride having been hurt, my first reaction was anger. "What is the idea of blocking the path? Couldn't you see me coming?" And I went on with my tirade. Then, as he did not answer, I looked a little closer and I realized he was crippled. Both legs were shriveled, and he could not walk. I had a quick change of heart. I apologized, asked his forgiveness, and then accompanied him to his home which was not far away.

He was living with his grandmother, as neither his mother or father would have anything to do with such a crippled child. His physical handicap was considered a curse. Let grandma care for him! During the day he would stay home, out of sight, and only venture out at night, going to the beach. He was on his way back from the beach when I tripped over him.

Ashamed at my anger, I spoke with the grandmother and offered to see if we could not at least get him – Letiana was his name – into school. The sisters accepted, and, having purchased a wheelchair, I assured that Letiana would be able to attend classes at Immaculate Conception School. The school was not equipped with ramps for handicap access, and it was a joy to see how other students helped Letiana get up the stairs to the classrooms.

One day someone told me that, with the help

Teacher's first day of class for the mentally handicapped in Morondava; they learn to connect sound and symbols

of operations, orthopedic shoes, and braces, Letiana should one day be able to walk. With his grandmother's approval I took him up to Antsirabe where the large Polio Center of Madagascar is located. It was not easy to arrange. The Center already had too many patients, and I knew nothing about Polio or about the after-effects of this paralyzing sickness. I had to learn the inner workings of this child's situation, and all that would be needed for patients.

Letiana stayed at the Polio Center for two years. After numerous operations, he was fitted with braces, shoes and given two canes, resulting, almost miraculously, in his being able to stand up straight and walk. When he returned to Morondava he made quite a sensation. Many people considered this a minor miracle.

It didn't take very long before other distraught parents came to me with their child suffering from the effects of Polio. I soon found myself on the road to Antsirabe with three more victims of Polio; and the next time there were ten, and it seemed there was no end. It was never easy, neither for me nor for the children who had to leave home, go to live in a different (colder) climate, and undergo operations. I was often tempted to put an end to bringing more and more patients to Antsirabe.

It was there also that I was introduced to a School for the Deaf and Mute, and also for the Blind. Both schools were operated by the Lutheran Church and it was much easier working with them, knowing that we were both faith-based organizations.

Having been rehabilitated, he works at the cobbler shop of the Center

The Foundation of the Center called the Beautiful Gate

It didn't take long before the deaf, the mute, and the Polio victims had grown to such numbers that special schools for them were established in Morondava. The Lutheran Church opened a school for the deaf and mute while we opened our Center for the Physically Disabled. Based on the Biblical episode in Acts 3:2-8, it is known as *The Beautiful Gate*. At one time in the entire area of Morondava we had identified seven hundred children who suffered from effects of Polio and 100 of them could not walk or stand straight without braces and orthopedic shoes.

What began as an accident, turned out to be a major project; today five sisters work full time at our center for handicapped persons. This requires specialized training and extraordinary love, patience, and understanding. They teach, direct, nurse, and cook for these children. We are now able to serve both the physically and mentally challenged at the Center.

I can but praise the dedication and generosity of the Lutheran staff at schools in Morondava and Antsirabe. It is not easy in a poor country to deal with persons challenged by these disabilities, and I can but praise the patience and love shown by our Catholic sisters who manage the

The Beautiful Gate Center, making specialized shoes for local lepers.

Handicap Center. It is a continual struggle to find adequate funds to keep the Center's activities going.

Discovering their Talents and Place in Malagasy Society

Some of our patients have not made much progress while others remain my pride and joy. One major challenge for the sisters is to help the children discover their talents and place in society. A good example is Martial. He was born with no arms or hands. He now earns his living, and is married and has four children. God alone knows the hours and time I spent trying to heal his physical and emotional wounds that would eventually be healed when God sent him a woman who would love him, marry him and with him raise a family.

Going to the beach or a swim or a strenuous walk in the sand always brought joy

Another example is young man named "Brillant." He was too crippled to do anything, but went with others to Antsirabe for treatment. Once returned to Morondava after the operations, he showed aptitudes that enables him to become a cobbler, setting up shop in the Handicap Center. He learned to fashion custom-made shoes and braces for fellow polio victims. His creativity brought him also to make custom shoes for lepers in the nearby Leprosarium.

While most, if not all of these children, were at one time or the other rejected, considered useless, shamed, a curse to be excluded from society, they suffered pain and were wounded in their hearts. It was not only a question of physical rehabilitation; they needed to know they were loved, valued, and had an important role to play in society. Was it their fault that they were born or contracted this disease early in life?

I had the support of our Bishop, priests, brothers and other religious for this project. The project of *The Beautiful Gate*, and those working there continue to be witnesses. Their love and lives say to all physically or mentally handicapped persons: "In the name of Jesus Christ, get up and walk" (see Matthew 9:5). Beyond physical rehabilitation, they all needed compassion and love to help them realize that they were loved and had worth in the eyes of society.

There remains much to be done in Madagascar so that physically challenged people may enjoy the rights of ordinary citizens. We are most grateful that in Morondava, the Lutheran and Catholic Churches are doing much to help those needy little ones.

Chapter 39 – Fr. Arthur Lueckenotto, M.S., The Perfectionist

If you are looking for a perfectionist, a very meticulous and orderly person, you would not have to search any further than Analaiva, a small village 22 kilometers (13.5 miles) east of Morondava. Father Lueck was perfection personified, and if you are going to do anything, doing it "well" was not good enough. It had to be perfect. Very few men have this very deep innate need for perfection – and he coveted it in all aspects of his life: religious life, priestly ministry, manual work, and personal relationships.

Like all of us, his missionary journey began in Morondava. From there he went on to Betomba, then to Berevo, Antsalova, Malaimbandy and finally to Analaiva. Never one to love the city, Lueck was most comfortable serving in isolated bush districts. He would come to Morondava, shop for the materials he needed, and head back to his mission post. Many people living in Morondava had never seen Lueck, or knew very little of him until he came to Analaiva.

Fr. Arthur Lueckenotto, M.S., easily spread joy

Lueck's mission journey in the Diocese of Morondava spanned fifty years, and his final assignment was to Analaiva. His legacy in that mission district can be easily discovered in two beautifully built churches and three school buildings. They bring to light through Lueck's life the words of Psalm 90:17, "May the favor of the Lord our God be ours. Prosper the work of our hands!"

Lueck welcomes the Franciscan Missionaries of Mary to the isolated mission district of Berevo

There is no question that the diocese will ever resume activity in Betomba where Lueck had organized and run the "farm school" for many years. Lueck's building expertise was not only with materials. He built up fervent Christian communities wherever he was stationed. And when the farm school closed in Betomba, the Christian community was strong and is still alive there, with a chapel that stands on the foundations of what had been the Fathers house. Struck by lightning, the house burnt to the ground. But from its ashes a church has been built.

In Berevo, the Sisters' convent and the priest's rectory both speak well of Lueck's need for perfection. A remote and isolated village, both the sisters and priests are most comfortable in residences he built there. In his method of building, Lueck was not only a perfectionist, but also a very creative one.

The Gift of Creativity

A good example was the way he built the convent in Berevo. In an area of the country where the dry season is long and clean water is scarce, he incorporated into the design a reservoir under the entire building. It holds thousands upon thousands of liters of rain water. As soon as the rains begin, and the conduits are cleaned, all water from the roof is tunneled down into the reservoir which is otherwise sealed. At the lowest point of the reservoir which is under the kitchen sink, he installed a small hand pump to bring up water for cooking and cleaning. The water lasts for most of the year.

Lueckenotto digging a most-needed well

Then he dug a deep well, giving much needed water for a garden. At certain times of the day, villagers could come and pump water, costing about two cents a bucket (as a village participation for repairing the pump after a breakdown). Everyone profited from his creativity. The parish rectory could well serve as a model for other districts. Despite its modest appearance, it is very practical, spacious and could lodge three men very comfortably.

During his tenure in Antsalova, Lueck enlarged the rectory and set up a workshop that would serve for future constructions. He hoped that one day a group of religious sisters would come. He began working on the foundations for a convent, until he gave up hope that sisters would ever accept to work in such an isolated place. In 2004 sisters finally arrived. A comfortable convent was built upon foundations that Lueck left there.

Lueck spent only a few years in Malaimbandy. Back in the 1980s when I, Jack, was in charge of the district, I built a beautiful but small church in Ambatolahy in memory of my parents who had recently died. It was my final accomplishment before leaving for Rome. It was sufficient at that time for the needs of the parish.

At the inauguration of the church, I had said that my fervent prayer was that the Christian witness of its members would be so great that one day church would become too small for the needs of the community. And that is what happened.

By the time Lueck took charge of the church, it was too small. Lueck greatly enlarged church, built a spacious convent for the sisters, enlarged the rectory, and began on the foundation for the new school. Jeremy would finish his work.

Lueck's final residence would be in Analaiva. While, as was his custom, Lueck remained and was extremely active in the ministry of the church and school there, he also began construction of a new church in Betsipotika. Despite his health problems, at the age of seventy-five he would jump on his motorcycle, and head to Morondava, either for La Salette community meetings or to buy and collect supplies. He became a familiar sight in the streets of Morondava.

His Motorcycle

Actually, it would be his motorcycle that would be the cause of his return to the United States. Every evening, for security reasons, he would push the motorcycle into the rectory over a rather make-shift and somewhat unsteady ramp. One evening pushing a little too fast, the motorcycle slipped, fell on his leg, and caused serious fractures of the bone. It took many operations and interminable months for healing to begin. Then new complications occurred with his heart, and he left for North America with the firm conviction that he would return.

Despite his age, Lueck remained very alert and confident, visiting his churches on the motorcycle in all kinds of weather. Always one to save money he would prefer the motorcycle to the Land Cruiser because it was cheaper to run. Although in his many assignments he was often alone, he remained a great conversationalist, never at a lost to speak and share his experiences. If you were to stop in for a visit with him, you made sure you had plenty of time as he would have so much to share with you.

Although a great talker, he did not use up many reams of paper for his correspondence. With a very small handwriting, we often said that Lueck could write a whole letter on the back of a postage stamp!

The Great Person who came from Meta, Missouri

The small church in Ambatolahy was enlarged by Lueck

We cannot marvel at and admire the work and missionary spirit of Lueck without mentioning his family and his small town of Meta, Missouri. Of all of us, I don't think anyone experienced greater support than Lueck from his family and indeed from the entire town of Meta. It was a farming community and people were used to "hauling together" when there was a need.

They were truly unique in their support for their hometown and favorite missionary. There was no end to the generosity and support that he received through the years. The church in Betsipotika and the third school building were funded entirely by his family and the people of Meta.

I am sure Lueck desired to give his life entirely to the mission of Morondava, ending his days while ministering to the people of Madagascar, and leaving his bones in the mission cemetery with Bishop Girouard, and Leblanc and McDonald. However, the two debilitating accidents – in Berevo and then in Analaiva – took their toll on the health of this man of extraordinary virtue, strength and talent. Despite their best plans, both Joe Shea and Art Lueckenotto were called home to heaven from the United States.

The church in Analaiva is a monument to Lueck's ingenuity

Chapter 40 –
Fr. Joe Shea's Leadership Role

Fr. Joe Shea, M.S. kept his youthful spirit alive during his fifty years in Morondava

While I was busy with the handicapped children, Jack was working in his shop in Malaimbandy and with Marriage Encounter, Joe Shea, as pastor of the Cathedral in Morondava, had another vital and crucial responsibility: he was Vicar General of the Diocese. Bishop Bernard, at just thirty-nine years of age, was very young when he was named Bishop and then was appointed to serve in his hometown Diocese where he had a large family with many nephews and nieces.

Family Ties that Bind

Culture was still very powerful in Morondava, and the Bishop would have a very powerful and demanding responsibility to his family. Even Rome was aware that this cultural demand would be a source of problems. Joe, in his own way, was the man to keep the Bishop focused on "higher responsibilities." Yes, the Bishop not only had great respect for Joe but even feared him which was an excellent and providential factor in helping the Bishop assume his leadership while keeping his independence from his family.

There was total trust and mutual respect between Joe and the Bishop and for almost twenty years Joe served as Vicar General helping the Bishop remain free from the pressures of his family. Joe had a wonderful easy way about him, but there were limits to his patience and endurance. The Bishop understood this and they worked well as a team for the greater good of the diocese.

Joe was fluent in the Malagasy language but wasn't always able to translate into the Malagasy language his American logic, his ways of thinking, or his Irish humor. The thoughts which Joe was turning over in his mind in English did not always come out clearly in Malagasy. Many times, with much concern, the people would ask: "What is Joe trying to say?" Even in English, with his mind ahead of his speech, we couldn't always grasp what Joe was trying to explain but we knew that, with his heart of gold, it was always good. He was so good, so devoted to the people and there was no service he would not render them – and do it for twenty-four hours a day! You never had to be afraid of waking Joe up, even in the middle of the night.

In the General Chapter of 1988, two things affected Mo-

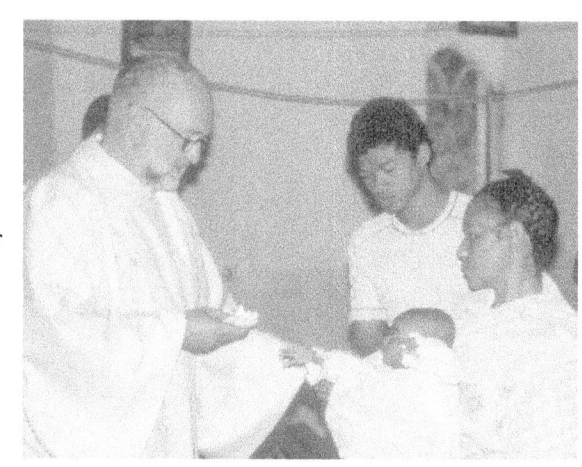

Preaching and Sacraments were at the center of Joe's missionary ministry

rondava: Jack Nuelle was elected to the General Council in Rome, and the status of the Region of Morondava was changed to be linked as a dependent Region to Antsirabe rather than to St. Louis – while still depending financially on St. Louis for three more years.

Joe was elected the last Regional Superior of Morondava. He finalized the transfer of the Region completely to the Province of Madagascar. After years of supporting Bishop Bernard, of working behind the scenes to keep the diocese moving, he was now ready for some extended vacation time.

Joe Returns to the United States

There were two very important reasons for Joe to remain in the United States; the first was his mother's failing health, and the second was the need to staff the Mission Office in St. Louis which had agreed to continue to support the work in Morondava and needed someone to staff it. Joe agreed to stay in the United States and his work in the Mission Office was most important for us who needed financial support for our work. However, Joe's heart remained in and with Morondava. He visited once, and would have liked to just remain here, but he also felt the call to remain in St. Louis to staff the Mission Office.

At the same time, after six years on the General Council in Rome, I, Jack, was forced to remain in the United States for cancer treatment. While still belonging to the Region and hoping to return, I was diagnosed with cancer and could not return Madagascar. I was asked to reorganize all the mission operations of the three Provincial Mission Offices of Hartford, Attleboro and St. Louis. The result was the creation of the *North American La Salette Mission Center*.

A New Mission Center for the U.S.

The interior of St. Joseph's Church in Bemanonga

Now, with the death of Joe's mother, my new ministry as Director of the new La Salette Mission Center assured funds for the mission, Joe returned to Morondava in 2000. He came with the same energy and enthusiasm he had exhibited at the time of his original departure in 1957 as a young missionary. Now heavy set, his presence was positive, powerful and contributed so much to the well-being of our community and mission. I, Donald, always said that, had he remained in Morondava in 1991, he would have been the Bishop to succeed Bishop Bernard.

While stationed in Morondava, Joe was able to purchase land in Bemanonga and set up a new mission plant. Following in Mac's logic, he, too, said that Morondava would someday be swallowed up by the advancing ocean and when that happened, we could move to higher ground. That would be Bemanonga.

In any case, Joe did develop both the Christian Community and Church Compound in Bemanonga and, should that disastrous flood ever come to Morondava, we would have "higher ground" to which we could move – I say higher ground because Bemanonga is only a little more than three feet above Morondava!

New Catechist Family Quarters

Joe, never one to say no when asked to do something, accepted to take over our Training Program for Catechists in Mahabo. Their family quarters in Mahabo had been built in 1956, and were in great need of maintenance and renovation. Joe took on the task.

During the 2002 political crisis, there were four control barriers on the three-mile stretch of the road between Bemanonga and Morondava. Joe would travel the road every day and, yes, he and the car would get checked over four times each way! One day, when his patience was taxed beyond the reasonable limit, Joe got out of the car slammed the door with such energy that he broke the glass in the window. Now that requires quite a strong arm! After that, Joe would usually be let through. After all, some of those who controlled the barrier were Joe's parishioners.

All of us, on many occasions, have been very happy to travel by outrigger canoe (*lakafiara*) to visit communities along the coast. Before gaining the open water of the Indian Ocean from the inlet of Morondava, one has to maneuver through a pass under heavy surf. Most of us have had to pay our dues, and found ourselves either in an overturned pirogue, or soaking wet from salt water. Joe, with his luck, was a frequent victim and would create much laughter walking home soaked to the bones and not too happy with the experience. All of us will have much to share with Sts. Peter and Paul in heaven, sharing our adventures of ocean voyages and frequently overturned vessels. We never learned to walk on water!

Sailing the Ocean Blue

During those ocean voyages, should wind cease and the sail go limp (and this was a frequent occurrence), you would bake under the hot sun for hours praying that at least a slight breeze would come up to fill the sail.

I don't think Joe would ever forget the time when he, hoping to avoid that danger, made the trip South on a motorized launch. However heavy surf swept over the diesel motor, flooding it. For three days he and his companions were adrift in the ocean, running out of food and water. We were also concerned, knowing that they had not reached their destination.

Joe returns from a St. Paul-like journey on the sea

Fortunately, workers from an oil exploration company, prospecting along the coast, picked them up on their radar beam. As only he could, Joe was very vocal when sharing this experience and how he was getting ready to eventually feed the sharks.

As I mentioned earlier, Joe arrived in Morondava in early 1958 immediately after his Priestly Ordination. He also studied the Malagasy language here in Morondava with a Mister Felix who had been called by Mgr. Etienne Garon to open a School for Boys. During his first ministerial assignment, Joe had a rather stormy beginning. He went to Mandabe with Berube. It was no honeymoon, as anyone can imagine who knows Berube's many idiosyncrasies, not to mention his personal problems. Thank God, Joe weathered that storm.

The Challenges and Gifts of Mission Ministry

From Mandabe, Joe was sent to Antsalova, another isolated and difficult mission. There he had to work with Father Joseph Burcklen, M.S. (1913-1998), a Frenchman who had been through World War II, and escaped twice from German Prison Camps. Once again, in his dealings with Burklen, Joe had to be very diplomatic and soft spoken. While there, Joe experienced a ruptured appendix. He could have easily been the first of this new wave of missionaries to pass on to eternal life. Happily, he was able to get to the Sisters Clinic in Tananarive, where he was saved.

From there, Joe became director of the mission post in Berevo (1962-1964), and had three great, exciting, and profitable years. Then he moved on to Miandrivazo where, as always, he won peoples' hearts with his kindness and energetic spirit.

Joe therefore served in most of our Mission Districts and Parish Centers, in the Diocese. Everywhere he left memories of a missionary totally dedicated to the service of his people.

Joe's slow journey across the city on his motorbike allowed him to converse with many people along the way

Chapter 41 –
Fr. John (Jack) Nuelle, M.S.,
A Friend and Life-Long Missionary

Fr. Jack Nuelle, M.S.

In the preceding pages, Donald has often spoken about me, Jack Nuelle. My baptismal name is John, but don't let that secret get out! Although several missionaries from America arrived after me, Donald wanted to wait and tell my story near the end of these memories.

He wanted to keep me for the end, as he and I became the best of friends and that friendship is still very much alive despite living and ministering in distant places over the years. I was born in St. Louis, Missouri in January 1937, the eighth child in a Catholic family of ten. I have always assured people that my vocation began in my family, so much so that I put off my Priestly Ordination for a year so that I could finish my studies in Rome and, only then, return to the U.S. where my family could be present.

Initially Learning Malagasy on the Bus

In 1961, three years prior to Priestly Ordination, I had volunteered for Madagascar and been accepted by the Provincial. I kept that dream foremost in my mind as I studied, taking extra Missiology courses offered at the Gregorian University. One year, while riding in the bus to the University in the morning, I would sit with one of the Malagasy brothers, Jean Marovony, and teach him English. In the afternoon on the way home, he would help me learn about Madagascar – the language, culture, and church.

As I was entering my last year of studies in Rome, there was a new Provincial, and he did not want me to leave for the missions. He assigned me to teach in the Minor Seminary in Jefferson City, Missouri. At the end of my first year, the Superior General, Father Conrad Blanchet, M.S. (1915-1998) intervened, and a year later I was able to leave for Morondava. God works in strange ways, and during those years of teaching, I was able to learn to pilot a plane; and I flew the newly acquired La Salette Super Piper Cub into Danielson, Connecticut for its inaugural flight a few days before my departure for Morondava in August, 1966.

Norm Mailloux had already arrived in Madagascar, and I travelled with Mark Koenig. We were the last to travel by ship from New York. We sailed to Sardinia, then flew to Rome, and by car to La Salette where we placed our missionary spirits at the feet of Mary, Queen of the Missions. From Marseille we continued by ship to Egypt where the Suez Canal was temporarily blocked. So we took a trip to Cairo, to see the Sphinx and the pyramids. With the canal re-opened, we were directed to Suez where we reconnected with the ship. With various stops in the Red Sea, a ceremonial crossing of the equator and into the Indian Ocean, we arrived at Majunga. Fr. Rollo Bernier was there to greet us. "Salama, môpera."

Hello there, Father. After a stop in Tananarive to sign papers for residency and a driver's license, we were off to Morondava.

At Home in a Foreign Land

Norm Mailloux had arrived a few months earlier. Mark Koenig and I had arrived just in time for the September meeting. How blessed we were to see all those venerable La Salette Missionaries we had heard so much about – most with their scraggly beards! Since I had studied in Rome for seven years and worked part of each summer vacation at the La Salette Shrine in France, I had one language in common with all of them. Mark's French was rudimentary but he more than compensated for words by his affable personality. There is, indeed, a language of joy for which words are not necessary. Thus we experienced our first encounter which brought a feeling of being at home in a foreign land.

It was at that time that I had my unforgettable first-missionary experience. Earlier Donald had spoken about our basketball team, the "White Devils." We lost that game by one point in overtime. A casualty of the game was that Jake sprained his ankle so badly that he could not drive his Jeep back to Ankavandra. Although only having arrived in Morondava a week earlier, Bishop Bernard designated me to drive him home in Ankavandra. What an unforgettable initiation into missionary life!

My First Treacherous Trip

At daybreak, with the windshield of the Jeep flat on the hood so Jake could keep his foot elevated on top of a pillow, and accompanied by a young man who had come to Morondava with Jake, we set off. As a young man I had learned to drive in a similar old army Jeep traversing the foothills of the Ozarks. "This trip will be no sweat!" I thought. But nothing had prepared me for the roads and bridges – or lack thereof – that I would experience.

The bridge over the Manombolo River – a precarious crossing

The scariest moment was crossing the temporary wooden bridge over the Manombolo River, north of Ambatolahy. Even Jake decided to be taken across the river in a *pirogue (canoe)* rather than ride over that make-shift bridge than ride with me in the jeep. With the young man slowly walking ahead of me, turning around every few feet to direct me, making sure the tires were still on the flimsy boards, we finally made it across the river. We arrived in Miandrivazo in the evening. Early the next morning, now accompanied by the Bishop who had flown there, we continued on to Ankavandra, often searching for where the road was supposed to be. We made it with few mishaps.

I spent a wonderful week with Jake and Bishop Bernard. We drove to various bush churches. With Mass still in Latin, I could concelebrate with the Bishop and Jake and assist at Baptisms. While studying in Rome with Malagasy La Salette Brothers, I had learned a few expressions in Malagasy: Hello. How are you. I am fine. I am glad to be here. That was about the extent of my Malagasy! But every word brought a smile from the people.

The day we returned to Ankavandra, Joe Silva and Brother Celse Scotton arrived in the Unimog (a German all-wheel drive truck) driven by Joe's trusty chauffeur, François. They brought materials to build a proper water installation and shower/toilet in our residence. After a no-luxury week in the bush, I'm sure Jake would enjoy the new shower and toilet facilities to be built. Since the Bishop needed to return to Miandrivazo, I became the designated driver for the trip back to Minadrivazo in the Jeep. Once there I would await the arrival of Joe Silva in the Unimog for my return to Morondava. Knowing the day of their departure from Ankavandra, Joe Shea and I spent the hot afternoon on the second floor veranda of the mission house. We spotted them as they began the last long descent toward the river.

All for a Cold Beer

Crossing the Mahajilo River with the Unimog required the ferry, which was now on our side of the river. As the ferry started to be polled over, Joe Shea and I walked to the bank waiting. We had brought a cold thermos of beer, knowing that Silva would appreciate it. But with the slow polling of the ferry, Silva could not wait. As we held up the thermos, Silva jumped into the river and began wading over. Seeing that, Shea and I jumped into the river also and began wading toward him. We all met in the middle, the water about waist-high. I never met anyone in my life so grateful for a cold beer as Joe Silva in the middle of that river.

Jack learning to be a bearded Madagascar missionary

Our Travels Home

The next day we began our final – or so I thought – day to Morondava. Difficulty crossing another river by ferry delayed us by ten hours. This was because the day before had been a National Holiday and those who ran the ferry had imbibed too much "toaka," the local home-made rum.

While waiting, I wandered along the river bank and on the way, I walked under a vine that contained itchy micro-fibers which got into all the pores of my face, arms, legs and the fibers of my clothing. Nothing had ever prepared me for such a burning itch. The only remedy we had was to get out of my clothes, rub motor oil over my body, deep into the pores, and wait for the itching to calm down, then to wash myself vigorously – along with my clothes – in the river. The only comfort was that riding in the open-air Unimog in wet clothes was almost like air-conditioning.

We made it to Mahabo late that night, and into Morondava the next morning. A few days later I was off, with Norm and Mark, to study Malagasy in Ambositra. Years of satisfying ministry followed with inexpressible joys and unwanted let-downs. The Lord continued to lead me, to surround me with people – both my La Salette brothers and the people I had come to serve – whom I grew to love and who grew to love me as well.

Celebrating First Communion on his initial ministry to the village of Marofihitse

I left Morondava in 1988 without, however, really leaving the mission. I was elected to the General Council in Rome, which provided me to use my missionary experiences to help other La Salette missions in other parts of the world. After six years on the General Council, I was ready to return to Morondava.

A vacation in the U.S., and medical examinations brought me up short. Just a few days before boarding the return flight to Madagascar, I was diagnosed with cancer. Forced to remain in the U.S. after my operations, yet with my heart and thoughts always centered on mission, I was asked to implement a plan to unite the three Provincial Mission Offices into one streamlined operation.

My Proposal Changed My Own Life

While in Rome, as a member of the General Council, I had proposed a new manner of looking at the way funds were raised and distributed by the American Provinces – but in no way did I intend to be the one to organize it. With personnel diminishing, the four North American Provincials, backed by the Procurators of their Mission Offices, told me to implement the plan in 1996, and designating me to set up a single, Central Mission Bureau for raising mission funds in all of North America – the United States and Canada. This bureau would be named the North American La Salette Mission Center, or LSMC, with offices in Hartford, Connecticut, later moved to St. Louis, Missouri.

I had mentioned above the joy it brought to be with these veteran missionaries and to minister beside them. I always said that Donald was my mentor into missionary life. The mission spirit he helped form in me is alive to this day. From 1966 to 1972, we served together in the main parish in Morondava, with some thirty bush churches. The most precious times were the evening chats with Donald, sitting on the sand dunes, sharing missionary dreams.

When Donald left for vacation in 1971, I was named Administrator of the Morondava parish. Peter Kohler arrived at that time. Of course, Donald would be back. But when I left Morondava in December 1972 on vacation, and Donald had just returned from his, he did not come back to Morondava, but was assigned to Berevo. Upon my return, I had initially been told that I would go to Belo sur Tsiribihina, but before I could leave for the north, the plans changed. I was assigned to Malaimbandy. This limited the times that

A happy little girl

the two of us could return to the beach in the evening, sit on the sand dunes, pray together and share on our lives and ministries. But the years we had spent doing that, and the lessons I learned were never forgotten.

Off to Malaimbandy

During my initial year with Joe Silva in Malaimbandy (the town name means: where one tells no lies), the Sisters of Jeanne Delanoue arrived in Malaimbandy to take direction of the school. That was the first blessing. The second was the well-organized bush ministry of twenty-eight bush churches with catechists, and nine guarderies were functioning. The third was that an agricultural project, sponsored by Switzerland, solidified; two local young men were sent for two years of technical training both in wood and metal. Then Joe Silva was moved to Berevo, and I was alone.

New Approaches to Farming

Upon their return from technical training, I set the two young men up in a large workshop – one side for metalwork and the other for woodwork – to help the farmers in the area of Malaimbandy. In an effort to increase rice production and lessen labor in the scorching sun, local farmers were introduced to new methodology in rice planting, requiring the use of ox-drawn plows, harrows and other small agricultural tools. There was, consequently, a need not only to produce these farm instruments locally but also to repair and maintain them.

Those two young men were trained to work in this shop, and a large, modern workshop was set up in Malaimbandy where all metal components could be repaired, and where sturdy farming tools were produced. At times, thanks to grants from philanthropic organizations, regular and specialized metals were ordered from Europe to make farm equipment. Often scrap metal could be found at large construction sites.

Because many oxcarts, which are still the preferred way to travel in the bush, rolled on metal wheels, there were frequent and daily visitors to the shop requesting welding and repairs. Again, this required not only financial contribution but also educational input so that these poor farmers would learn to use and care for their farming tools. Farmers came from up to fifty miles away to buy a plow, or a harrow, or a cultivator and learned how to use them to better their harvests. Today just about everyone owns and knows how to use these hand plow and other simple equipment. But in the 1980s it was not all that evident.

The shop rendered tremendous services and it was meant to continue with a small profit from the work to pay salaries. However, the price of steel skyrocketed, as did other materials necessary for production. So soon the young men were no longer able to manage the shop. A substantial change came when I was elected to the General Council in Rome, and within a few years the shop closed.

In 1968 when Bishop Bernard sent his annual report and statistics to Rome, it took only two months for him to receive a response from the Holy See stating that there must have been a mistake in the report. Considering Baptisms, First Communions, and Confirmations, it could not be possible that there had been but two marriages in the entire diocese in the course of one year. The Bishop answered that unfortunately there had been no mistake and that we had celebrated just two weddings that year. Things changed and we eventually went to fifty, then to one hundred and even more marriages in a year. We were more and more aware of need to support families and help couples grow in their relationship. This was partly possible because I, Jack, listened to the plea of a young couple in Malaimbandy. They said that the church/parish had organizations concentrated on helping development among elders, children and youth. But sadly there seemed to be nothing that could help couples to understand themselves better, deepen their love among disputes, disagreements, problems with money and children, and so on. They asked me, "Is there something that could help us?" I was just about to leave for a vacation after five years, and told them I would see what I could do. I now realize how those questions from that young couple were words from the Lord.

Marriage Encounter for Malagasy Couples

The couples involved with Jack in the first entirely Malagasy Marriage Encounter Weekend

On the very first day home in the United States, after Mass at the local parish, I was asked by parishioners if there was any way they could help me while I was at home. I told them about the questions which the couple in Malaimbandy had asked me. To my astonishment, they answered: "We have exactly what you need!" That was my introduction to Marriage Encounter.

My entire vacation focused on learning about it, experiencing it, writing talks, giving weekends both in English in the United States and in French in Canada, living a deeper weekend of engagement, and feeling the enthusiasm of couples who were ready to support efforts to bring graces to struggling couples in Madagascar.

Returning to Morondava, I learned that I had been elected to be the Regional Superior and moved to Morondava. It also gave me time to focus on efforts to bring the values of Marriage Encounter to Madagascar. Coordinating with efforts by a few religious sisters in Tananarive who wanted to strengthen family life, it took two years to gain the confidence of couples who were willing to participate in a Marriage Encounter Experience.

The First Entirely Malagasy Marriage Encounter Weekend

Two couples went to France and to Canada for training. Then, with the help of French speaking couples from Montreal, we were able to introduce Marriage Encounter weekends in Madagascar. Although the ideal of Marriage Encounter were not counter-cultural, it was a new way of living a couple-relationship because it was based on solid Christian principles. It was difficult to find a venue where this type of weekend could be held. A major difficulty was to interpret many concepts so easily understood in our English and French mentality into the Malagasy language, while simultaneously adapting them to Malagasy culture.

Marriage Encounter for All of Africa

Again, beginnings were very difficult, and initially it took time to contact parishes and Catholic organizations, to discover couples willing to participate in a Marriage Encounter weekend. I am never one to be discouraged. Working with various couples and priests, I trained them to be leaders in Marriage Encounter – soon known in Malagasy as "Miriazy Mirindra." I was also a member of the Pan-African Board where similar problems of adaptation were ironed out for all of Africa. When I left for Rome in 1988, I had established a good core group of couples who fully understood the benefits of a weekend.

The Marriage Encounter group now has established an important venue here in Tananarive where weekends continue to be organized. Many couples and priests have been trained to give weekends, and the movement has spread into almost all the dioceses of Madagascar. Thousands of Malagasy couples found new life in their marriage through the weekends and all this is thanks to a strong conviction that the ideals for Christian marriage proposed by the Marriage Encounter movement could be lived in Madagascar. The Marriage Encounter movement has been recognized by the Bishops of Madagascar and is considered a member of the National Commission for the family.

In 1986, while working to introduce Marriage Encounter in Madagascar, I moved to Mahabo to oversee the construction of the residence. Once finished, a new community of religious men from Kerala, India, arrived to work in the diocese. I was pastor of Mahabo, and it was decided that these young, enthusiastic C.M.I. Missionaries would be given that parish. It was my privilege to introduce them to the districts of Mahabo and Ankilizato, taking them not only to the main station but to all the bush churches. To this day they are grateful, not only for the time I took to help them but for the timely advice that serves them well to this day. Using the leadership qualities God endowed me with I was elected three times as Regional Superior and called to participate in the Councils of the Congregation.

It was during my tenure as Regional Superior that in 1984 I initiated the long and difficult movement to re-organize La Salette presence in Madagascar. According to Church protocol, mission territories, under the jurisdiction of the Propaganda Fidei in Rome were confided to the care of Religious Missionary Communities which furnished both personnel and financial administration. Thus it was that, in 1898, the Congregation of the Missionaries of La Salette accepted a mandate to serve in Betafo/Antsirabe Madagascar. Missionaries were sent first from France, and later from America. In 1928, as mentioned above, the local Bishops in Madagascar, the Propagation of the Faith in Rome, and our own General Administration gave a favorable nod to establish a separate La Salette Mission on the West Coast of Madagascar, confided to the American La Salettes. Thus, Antsirabe and Morondava both became separate La Salette missionary territories.

When the first American La Salette, Fr. Breault, left Antsirabe to open the mission in Morondava, he was equipped marvelously for certain aspects of missionary

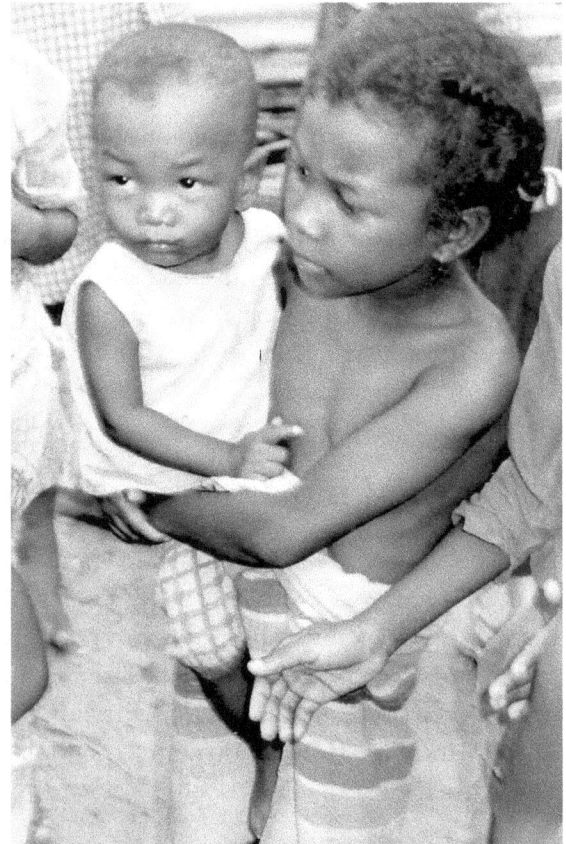

Sakalava children in Morondava

life. They had acquired language skills, and above all, a proficiency in pastoral care. It was natural that they would continue to have ecclesial connections with Antsirabe.

Opening a new mission demanded, however, a readjustment in many ways; some of those changes were territorial (High Plateau versus Costal), others were cultural (Vakinankaratra vs Sakalava), financial (France vs America), ecclesial (established local churches vs sparse nomadic Christian communities), climatic (temperate vs tropical). Adapting to those changes established two La Salette Missions in Madagascar with a slightly different character.

The Vatican's Changes for Those Serving in Mission Countries

In the ensuing years, with the establishment of Prefectures, Vicariates and Dioceses, deeper adjustments were required. With the proclamation of the document by Pope Paul VI in 1978 entitled "Directives For The Mutual Relations Between Bishops And Religious In The Church", the Vatican brought forth new conditions that changed former ways of administering and serving the Church in mission countries. As mentioned earlier, Norm Mailloux facilitated many changes for Morondava.

However, slowly we came to realize that it would no longer be feasible to have two distinct Religious La Salette entities in Madagascar – one in Antsirabe and the other in Morondava. Travel and communication had vastly improved. Personnel in both Morondava and Antsirabe was no longer exclusively La Salette; other Religious communities worked alongside them. And La Salettes worked in at least four different dioceses.

Changing Times Required La Salettes to Change

As Regional Superior of Morondava, and working in conjunction with Father Norbert Ramboasalama, M.S., Provincial of Antsirabe, I initiated a series of questionnaires, meetings, retreats and gatherings which brought together all La Salettes serving in Madagascar. The main reason was to determine if the Province in Antsirabe and the Region in Morondava could be unified into one Malagasy Province. This process would take four years to accomplish.

At the beginning it was evident that there would be much hesitation, and even outright reluctance on the part of Antsirabe. Many Fathers, even in Morondava, were totally against such a merger, saying that there was too much history that reinforced the need for separation. I, however, saw it as the future of the La Salette Mission in Madagascar.

I had a personal vision, and worked to bring others to see it too. I held to my convictions that the charism and spirit of reconciliation, which is at the center of our La Salette existence, would help us recognize that we are religious brothers working for the good of God's mission on this beautiful island nation.

Two La Salette Entities Become One Province

Three years later, decisions were made both in Morondava and Antsirabe during the Chapters of 1987 requesting unification. These received confirmation by both France and the United States, and were accepted and promulgated by the General Chapter of 1988. Morondava was to retain its status as a separate Region for the next three years, while Joe Shea, the new Regional Superior, slowly updated various financial, civil, and religious administrative formalities. During those three years, Morondava would still be dependent on the United States financially but depend administratively on Antsirabe. At the end of those three years, the Region would cease to exist. It was Joe who would usher in the birth of one La Salette Province in Madagascar, unified under the title of "Mary, Mother of the Church."

Water Wells for Women and Schools for Children

While working in the bush of Morondava from 1966 to 1972, I was instrumental in helping many villages set up water wells that would lessen women's heavy chore of daily fetching water, often from polluted and infected water holes. With clean water in those outlying villages, sanitary conditions, especially for children, were improved. A secondary product of having clean water wells in the village, was that children no longer had to accompany their mothers to fetch water, and were able to attend school.

A young girl carrying a bucket

Good done for others often comes back as a blessing. The work I had done to improve water in the villages south of Morondava was most providential. It gave me an incentive to provide a more efficient system for clean water at the mission of Malaimbandy. Brother Celse Scotton had initially dug some thirty feet for water. Tt was sufficient at that time. With the addition of a community of sisters, living on the mission compound, creation of a large garden that literally drank the water in growing crops, I, Jack found it necessary to dig deeper. I also installed a deep submergible pump to furnish a plentiful supply of water. To this day the mission in Malaimbandy relies of that well for its water supply.

New Church Windows for Malaimbandy and Ambatolahy

The Sanctuary of the church in Ambatolahy

Using qualities that God provided, I loved to be creative. In Malaimbandy I built a parish hall and enlarged the school. In both churches, Malaimbandy and Ambatolahy, I designed windows of colored patterns embedded in cement blocks that contribute much to the prayerful atmosphere of those churches. Using the original walls and roof of the "gite d'étap" that had been given to Girouard in 1950, I significantly enlarged the Malaimbandy residence. Yet it was and remains the simplest and certainly smallest rectory in the diocese.

When I lived and ministered there, the 120 miles of road from Malaimbandy to Morondava were a nightmare. During the rainy season – December to April – too often I would have to spend the night, enjoying the stars while sleeping on the side of the road. With my guitar and a good singing voice I had an easy and good relationship with the youth and was often called to work with the youth of the diocese. I already mentioned that I was a pilot. I continued flying even after we sold the La Salette plane, using the plane from the Morondava Aero Club for medical evacuation – especially for medical evacuation.

While on the General Council, and as Director of the LSMC, I was blessed to return to Madagascar many times. I hope that type of blessing will continue.

The sky is the limit of Jack's ministry

Chapter 42 – Nearing Fulfillment of a Mission Mandate

Bishop Donald after Mass with the children of Ambodimanga

We were never very numerous as a group of American La Salette Missionaries in Madagascar. As we were getting older and more men were required to leave, we nevertheless have kept alive the spirit of our founders – Breault, Girouard, Le Blanc and McDonald. I, Donald, think I can justifiably speak for all the American Missionaries when I say that we have been very happy, blessed and excited to have been called to serve here. Even with diminished numbers, we remain eager to respond to the challenges of evangelization despite and the deterioration of the social and economic fabric of the nation.

Usually when missionaries get together and share their experiences, they also speak of the progress going on in the country where they minister. Unfortunately for Madagascar we continue to witness an increasing regression in social and economic areas, while daily frustration remains a constant reality. Our greatest joy is that the faith continues to be lived deeply by our people.

We were Blessed with Dedicated Men

Another important factor in the eighties was that the St. Louis Province would no longer have men to send to Morondava. This was not an isolated reality, unique to the St. Louis Province. The last member of the Attleboro Province to go to the missions in the Philippines was in the 1970s, and from Hartford to Argentina in the early 1980s. Much like St. Louis, those provinces continued to support the missions confided to them. Now all funds for all missions come to them through the *La Salette Mission Center.*

For many years we prayed and discerned what would be the future of this mission that had been founded in 1928 from America. A very important decision had to be taken as regards our priorities. What should be considered as more important, financial support or personnel for the mission? It was not an easy decision and the process took many years before we decided that Morondava should be part of the Province of Madagascar. In 1988 under Jack's and Joe's leadership we kept some autonomy as a Region of Antsirabe and then in 1991 we became an integral part of the Province of Madagascar. With that move, one phase of the beautiful thirty-year relationship between the Region of Morondava and the Province of St. Louis ended. But financial help continued, both directly from the St. Louis Mission Office until 1997 when the *North American La Salette Mission Center* was inaugurated, and it still continues today through that agency.

The decisions made by our missionaries to return home to the U.S. was not just personal. It was part of integral mission reality. Foreign Mission personnel would necessarily be obliged to phase out. Our realistic hope is that the missionary spirit which animated our founding Fathers will endure and grow.

Now Our Vocations in Madagascar are Numerous

Our La Salette Congregation in Madagascar has been blessed with numerous native vocations over the years. In fact, the Madagascar Province is the second largest in the Congregation. There have been 12 La Salette Bishops in Madagascar over the years, and six were indigenous Malagasy, serving both the dioceses of Antsirabe and Morondava and other Catholic dioceses on the island. We can be proud of helping God's graces flourish and touch other parts of the island.

Children from a First Communion class

The majority of native La Salette vocations have come from the High Plateau. Morondava, while still very much a Missionary Church, has recruited young men to join the La Salette Congregation. Through the years seven young men were ordained for the La Salette Congregation and are serving to this day. One was Provincial Superior for six years, another served as Novice Master and a third founded our La Salette Mission in Haiti. I think we can be proud of the vocations that the Morondava Mission has nurtured for the La Salette Community.

Within a few more years, we can foresee that all La Salettes serving in Madagascar will be native Religious – both priests and brothers. We can all justly find fulfillment in the way we have cooperated with the Holy Spirit, and the way we have helped bring the message of Our Lady of La Salette to these shores.

In Morondava the Mary Queen Cathedral stands proud, a permanent memorial to those good years when Missionaries in Morondava and the St. Louis Province worked in tandem for God's mission.

Chapter 43 –
Fr. Jeremy Morais, M.S., Undaunted Champion of the Poor

Fr. Jeremy Morais, M.S.

The initial La Salette Missionary endeavor in Morondava was from North America. The bigger picture shows that other personnel also came from France, Poland, Italy, and Antsirabe, without which we would never have been able to staff such a vast area with our small group of Americans. In 1950 help came with the arrival of the Missionaries of the Holy Family, and the district of Manja-Morombe would eventually become a separate diocese. In 1987 Bishop Bernard was also able to welcome the Carmelites of Mary Immaculate from India.

In 1988, Jack left to serve on the General Council, while remaining part of the Malagasy Region. His definite integration into the St. Louis Province came in 1996. In 1991 Joe Shea returned temporarily to St. Louis, only to return in the year 2,000. Evacuated to the United States because of a serious medical condition in 2006, he died there in 2007. By the time the Morondava Region merged with the Antsirabe Province, we were only five (Joe, Lueck, Jeremy, Jack and I) American Missionaries remaining, and I figured we were writing the last chapter of American La Salettes in Madagascar.

Presently in Morondava, we are two – Jeremy and myself. I pray we will both still be here next year to celebrate the centennial. After one hundred years of American La Salette presence in Madagascar, the two of us are very happy and proud to carry on the torch that was lit in 1921.

Fr. Jeremy Morais, M.S., Arrives

Our very last and best La Salette recruit arrived in 1987 in the jolly and energetic person of Father Jeremy Morais M.S. (1953-). Jeremy, born in Sterling, Nova Scotia, Canada and grew up in Red Lake, a small city in northern Ontario. It was a mining area. He is proud to be a Canadian citizen but recognizes that all his training to be a La Salette was done in the United States.

He belonged to the American Province of Mary, Queen of Peace, based originally in Olivet, Illinois, and later in Milwaukee, Wisconsin. He has no regrets about now being a member of the Malagasy Province where he once served on the Provincial Council. We, the last two Americans living in Morondava, are now members of the Province of Madagascar while not losing our ties with America.

Here We Go Again...

Jeremy, when hampered by a leg wound, was adopted by the children from the Handicapped

This is a "déjà vu" situation, recalling when in 1936 Le Blanc, Mac and Girouard became members of the French Province in order to remain in Morondava. Our American Province has continued to show much interest and support for our work. If ever, for health issues or any other reason, we would have to return to the United States, we can be assured of the warmth and generosity of our brothers in America. There is still a very strong connection with the American Province while serving here in Madagascar.

When Joe Shea returned to the United States in 2007, he was very much at home with his La Salette Brothers who accompanied him during his terrible suffering, operations and the last months of his life in Hartford. The American Province accepted to help defray the medical bills. Returning also for health reasons, Father Lueckenotto was equally at home as he continued his medical care. His heart was in Madagascar but, after participating in the large Provincial gathering of all members in Orlando, Florida, he returned to St. Louis where he died suddenly.

The Transitions in Our La Salette Missionary Life Continue...

With the creation of a single Malagasy Province in 1991, we transitioned from a Missionary Region, wherein we depended for personnel and finances from elsewhere, to a local self-governing Province. Needless to say, our Malagasy fathers and brothers were elated. For all of us, perhaps especially for those of us coming from the Morondava Region, the changeover wasn't always easy; even if we could deal very well with the new leadership, we also had to accept a change in our lifestyle.

All our La Salette communities follow the same *La Salette Rule of Life* and we were trained to obey our Superiors, so there was no problem for our religious life. Being part of the new Province of Madagascar we now had to accept a simpler lifestyle and had to do without some of the comforts we could afford when St. Louis provided the funds. We knew that would happen when we decided to become part of the Province of Madagascar, and we embraced the change when it came.

Jeremy arrived in 1987 when the move to become one Province was beginning to take shape. He was able to attend the Malagasy language school in Ambositra where he did very well. From the very beginning everyone admired Jeremy's compassion, his love for the children, the handicapped, the poor, the underprivileged, the exploited.

A Voice for Justice and Fairness

Very energetic and determined, there is no compromise for him in the face of an injustice and corruption. He would voice his opinion for everyone to hear and had no tolerance when faced with any kind of discrimination. As he is very vocal in all his reactions, he has been the object of not only criticism but serious life-threatening menaces. He could well be our first martyr if some of his enemies had their way.

His interventions on behalf of the poor and exploited farmers have not fared well with those who feel they can continue to abuse their authority.

On multiple occasions, Jeremy took an unexpected trip to Tananarive to intervene with higher authority, reporting serious abuses of authority in isolated areas of Ankavandra. He had friends who stood by him, and most often he was successful. As could only be expected while defending the rights of the helpless, his actions gained him friends who stood by him, while at the same time creating enemies. They tried to get rid of him, constantly demanding that I, as Bishop, remove him from Ankavandra. I once received a very angry letter from one of Jeremy's enemies who was serving time in jail. He wrote to tell me that when he was released, at the first opportunity he got, he would kill Jeremy.

Spoon in hand, the children easily awaited a meal

When people speak of Jeremy, they think immediately of Ankavandra where he served for many years. However, he spent his first years serving in Morondava with Joe Shea. Jeremy had a youthful personality, and always related well with youth. As a youth himself, he had been very active as a Boy Scout, and loved it.

After his ordination in 1981, as a member of the Province of Mary, Queen of Peace in Milwaukee, Wisconsin, he had asked to serve as a missionary in Morondava. But, as was the case for so many of us, the Provincial asked him to wait – just for five years. The Province needed someone with Jeremy's youthful character and flamboyance for the ministry of Vocational Recruitment. Jeremy had all the qualities. The Provincial assured him that after that, after five years, he would be free to leave for Madagascar.

Jeremy complied, yet always let everyone know that he was destined for Morondava. It was during his first assignment in Morondava that Jeremy was happy to be reconnected with the Scouting movement. His enthusiasm gave new life to the local scout troop.

Building Roads to Somewhere...

Jeremy's ministry would later bring him back to Morondava for a time, but he was happiest serving in Ankavandra. His greatest challenge was the total and complete isolation of Ankavandra. This prompted and inspired him to build and repair roads. There would be no progress, no growth, no development (material, spiritual, social) in Ankavandra without some road to communicate with either Miandrivazo (ninety miles south) or Tsiroanomandidy (ninety miles east). During the Colonial Period the roads were maintained in quite good condition, because every able-bodied man had to give ten days a year to work the roads. But that is no longer the case.

So, every year, at the end of the rainy season, with a team of five to ten strong young men, Jeremy would work for three weeks, opening up a passage through severely damaged areas of the road to Miandrivazo. Even then, in a good four-wheel drive Toyota Land Cruiser, it would take him ten hours to maneuver the ninety miles from Ankavandra to Miandrivazo. If that were not enough Jeremy had to maintain the ferry to cross the very wide Mahajilo River at Miandrivazo. With little or no help from the government but with great determination, and for over a period of ten years, Jeremy kept that road open to four-wheel drive vehicles.

New Roads and New Possibilities

This also opened the way for poor local farmers to sell their crops in the larger cities, and return home with daily necessities. The local merchants, who exploited the people, knew that with Jeremy gone, there would be no road, no way for locals to ship their crops. They would be obliged to sell at a cheaper price to the merchants. That was one reason why the influential merchants and corrupt administrators were asking for his transfer.

The children flocked to Jeremy

Despite all the time, effort, and money Jeremy spent working on the road to Miandrivazo, he knew the future of Ankavandra would ultimately depend on a road, not through Miandrivazo, but through Tsiroanomandidy to the east. This was certainly the most practical, and actually the most natural and rational way to overcome the isolation of Ankavandra. The major obstacle, however, lay in the fact that Ankavandra is located in a valley at the base of a solid 2,000-foot cliff. There is no way to reach Tsiroanomandidy without scaling that steep rocky climb. To cut a road into that cliff would require serious engineering, serious money and tons of dangerous work with dynamite.

No one was quite ready to finance such a project, despite the fact that it would be a financial boost for both the local and national economy. For years Jeremy sought funds and wrote up projects which were accepted and for which financing was assured and even allotted. A road was built on the High Plateau, and reached the top of the cliff, almost in view of Ankavandra; but no one wanted to finish the last ten miles! Finally, the people took the project in hand and cut a road up the mountain. Some cars were able to get down without too much difficulty. But none could get back up! The climb was too steep, and there was little or no traction due to the fine dust on the road.

Gerry Biron, Lueck and Jeremy were all road builders that would enable locals to use their vehicles – oxcarts, cars, pick-up trucks and motorcycles – during the dry season. These served the entire community, not just special interest groups. We know that missionary work is similar to building roads and bridge. Sometimes before building them between heaven and earth, missionaries need to build dirt roads and wooden bridges so that people can travel in their own country – whether to the market or to church. Some roads and bridges were necessarily temporary, lasting only until the first torrential rains.

New Roads to Progress

We had two men in the Region who contributed greatly to keeping roads open – Lueck from Antsalova or Berevo, and Jeremy from Ankavandra. They both deserve much credit. They had to sleep under the stars, camp and

Group of Scouts and Church of the Sacred Heart in Akavandra

cook meals or eat them cold. They worked hard filling holes and leveling off steep drops. It would take Jeremy three weeks to assure that the ninety miles from Ankavandra to Miandrivazo were passable. Lueck would take weeks of back-breaking work to open the roads from either Antsalova or Berevo to Belo. But what joy and pride it brought to reach their destination! Both Jeremy and Lueck used money sent from family and supporters in America to pay and feed the workers while getting little recognition from the government.

Jeremy's name will remain forever in Ankavandra where he left the new spacious church dedicated to the Sacred Heart, a school, and a sisters' convent. Jeremy's spirit of love and concern for children, his concern for the poor, the exploited, the marginalized, and his attention to the needs of young men and women remains alive in Ankavandra.

Scouting Available to Boys and Girls

As mentioned earlier, from his early childhood, Jeremy had been involved with the Boy Scouts of America. His interest never diminished and his great love for scouting serves him well as he conveyed his enthusiasm to many youth – both boys and girls – in Madagascar. He has served many years as scout chaplain on the diocesan level and now also works on the National Level. He is a staunch believer of scouting and certainly has given the best of his talents and energies to promote scouting in Morondava. If scouting is alive and active and in all the parishes of the diocese it is due to Jeremy's great love of scouting.

Thanks to benefactors, Jeremy built in Akavandra this splendid ediface in honor of the Sacred Heart

Arrival of La Salette Sisters

It was only a few years ago that the La Salette Sisters took up residence in Ankavandra. Their ministry is to direct the school. As is the reality in every district when sisters arrive, they become fully engaged in the pastoral ministry of the whole district. When the first La Salette Sisters arrived in Ankavandra, in order to purchase supplies, they would have to walk at least fifty miles – and that includes climbing the 2,000 foot escarpment – before they could get a taxi-brousse to continue their trip to Tsiroanomandidy. Now, at least in the dry season with the road open, they can more easily make the trip to Tsiroanomandidy. Should anyone ever fall sick during the rainy season, however, they can but trust in God's Providence because there is no other way to get them to a medical center.

From Ankavandra Jeremy went to Ambatolahy. It was a small town on the sandstone bluffs of the Manambolo and Sakeny Rivers. In the colonial days it was a center for many tobacco plantations, although tobacco was no longer planted there. When Jack was asked to combine the mission district of Ambatolahy with that of Malaimbandy in 1976 the only worshiping place was a small, narrow tobacco-drying shed that had been converted to serve as the church.

A New Church for the Mission District of Ambatolahy

Jack's parents had just died, and left him some money. Jack decided to use it to build a new church. The mission had some land to the northern outskirts of the town, near to where a new road was being built by the government. He decided that a new church should go there. He wanted it to be "the people's church" with everyone contributing to its construction.

From planning to finished product, with many stops and starts as materials became available and people were finished from their rice planting and harvesting, it would take nearly twelve years to accomplish. Then, with growth occurring because the new road allowed for easy transportation of products, the population increased, as did the Faith.

Years later, Lueck would be stationed in Malaimbandy, and begin enlarging the church – four times larger than the original! Jeremy would follow Lueck and finish the church. By then, Ambatolaly had become once again a flourishing independent mission district. Under Jeremy's direction, a sister's convent was built as well as a School.

The New Church of St. Norbert

Many new churches sprang up in the bush. Among them was the small church of St. Norbert. A man from Our Lady of Sorrows Parish in Hartford, Connecticut asked Jack if a small church could be built in Madagascar for $10,000. Jack said yes and contacted Jeremy. One condition: it must be named St. Norbert. Jeremy agreed and built the church with the help of the new Catholic community. Seeking a picture for the church, Jack contacted the Norbertine Religious Community in the United States. They agreed to help. What they finally sent was the donation of a bronze plaque, 12 x 18 inches of St. Norbert. It now resides in the Church of St. Norbert just a few miles east of Ambatolahy.

The New Church of St. Reginald

Jeremy's next assignment was to Morondava where he served as Pastor of the Cathedral in Namahora as well as diocesan treasurer. One of his last achievements there was starting a new parish in a fishing village north of Morondava. It is home to the nicest, most spacious beach in the Morondava area. It had grown tremendously, and Jeremy saw the need for a parish church there. Today it is a flourishing parish. The Church built in honor of Saint Reginald in memory of his deceased brother.

Presently Jeremy serves in Belo sur Mer. It is one of the most beautiful villages on the West Coast of Madagascar. Fr. Aloysius Spielman had been the first Catholic priest to visit that village in November of 1933. John Brady and Thomas Mansfield visited and founded a Catholic Community in 1934. Mansfield fell in love with the village and would have loved to remain there even though there is little to eat but fish. Jeremy is now very happy as the Catholic Church continues to grow. There is now a school and a medical center under the care of Trinitarian Sisters of Rome.

As always, Jeremy's very energetic and enterprising spirit is reaching out to various villages around Belo sur Mer. There had been small Catholic Communities at one time but most of them were weak and fragile. With frequent visits new life is found in these villages: Marofototra, Ambararata, Ankevo, Antsira, Ankilifolo. Under his dynamic direction Belo sur Mer will become a very promising district.

The new church in Belo sur Mer

Chapter 44 –
Bishop Donald Pelletier,
the Second American Bishop of Morondava

When the La Salette Malagasy Province was united in 1991, we were five Americans belonging to it. After Jack's transfer to St. Louis in 1996 and the deaths of Joe and Lueck, Jeremy and I are now the last two Americans working and very happy in Morondava.

A New Cathedral For Morondava

That same year, in 1991, the construction of the new Cathedral of Mary Queen in Namahora was finished. Since 1955 the original wooden church of Our Lady of La Salette in Morondava had served as Cathedral. On August 15, 1991, in the very midst of a serious political crisis, the new Cathedral was consecrated with three bishops in attendance. With Joe Shea's departure in 1991, Bishop Bernard began showing signs of fatigue after thirty years of leadership. I consequently moved to Namahora and took over from Joe Shea as Vicar General. But in no way could I replace the fear and respect Joe could instill in our fragile Bishop. We did all we could to encourage and support him but outside forces were stronger that we.

Bishop Donald Pelletier, M.S.,
Second American Bishop of Morondava

In February 1996 Bishop Bernard suffered a very serious automobile accident that could have been fatal but left him with a broken arm and collar bone. It took him six months to recuperate in Tananarive and when he returned to Morondava it appeared evident that he was suffering from minor depression and was powerless under pressures of his family and friends. It was a difficult time for all of us and at one of our meetings Lueck very frankly challenged him to resign.

Rome accepted his resignation in August of 1998 with an admonition that he should leave the diocese.

After 34 years it would not be easy to find someone to replace him, especially since the finances of the diocese were in a very bad way. I was elected to serve as Diocesan Administrator during the vacancy and considering my age and fatigue I, Donald, was willing to assure an interim even though the process of finding a new bishop could be a lengthy one.

I Became the Third Bishop of Morondava

The Papal Nuncio worked very diligently on the Diocesan documents, consulted extensively but finally there was no other choice. I could take no pride as Nuncio went to the bottom of the barrel and there was no other solution. I am sure that if Joe Shea or Jack had been here, they would have been first choices but I was the last choice.

There had been an American as first Diocesan Bishop and after Bishop Bernard maybe the Lord figured there should be another American. I was ordained the third Bishop of Morondava on the February 13, 2000, the first ever to be ordained in Morondava. I became a jubilee Bishop when Morondava was plagued with a cholera epidemic and political and civil tensions were elevated because the government had ejected Medecins Sans Frontières (Doctors Without Borders) from the country.

Surrounded by family and friends, Donald's ordination as bishop brought the ends of the world together

People feared the worse from the cholera threat. It was a memorable day as it was the first Episcopal Ordination ever in Morondava, and people were very happy that six members of my family – my Aunt, Brother, Sister, and Cousins – were able to attend. Jack Nuelle was also able to come from the United States for the occasion.

Setting Up the Diocese as Separate from La Salette

The Morondava Minor Seminary, our hope for the future of the Church in Madagascar

Both our Superior General and Nuncio had given me precise instructions on what should or could be my mission as Bishop. Until the year 2000 the Diocese was very much the exclusive responsibility of La Salettes and the Congregation was the only real visible Catholic entity in the Diocese. Bishop Bernard had been only too happy to reside in a La Salette residence and there was no visible structure outside the La Salette Congregation. It was evident this could not last and the Nuncio told me that I would have to assure autonomy and identity of the local Church, that is, the diocese.

Even as Diocesan Administrator I had already moved to Namahora where we set up a Bishop's House with three offices: Education, Finances and a Secretariat. Slowly we built the Minor Seminary and a residence for priests. People began to realize that the Diocese had the basic independent structures.

It was only right that the Bishop should reside next to his Cathedral and I set up a Pastoral Center for the Diocese. A large comfortable residence was built for the Diocesan Priests with large dining area and another large meeting room. Thus, the diocese had a new visibility.

The recruiting and formation of local clergy has always been a crucial question in Africa and Madagascar. We cannot deny or wish to hide that there have been problems. Of the four diocesan priests that were ordained in Morondava (1962-1995), two left the priesthood and a third has had serious medical problems. My priority was the Minor Seminary where we would form holy priests ready to serve with the same zeal and generosity as the Cure d'Ars. The new residence was named after St. Jean Marie Vianney, patron of all priests.

Even though there were many problems, in ten years I was able to ordain four priests who for the moment are doing well in their ministry. With the cooperation from other dioceses, there are now eight diocesan priests and, with twenty young men in the Major Seminary, there is much hope for the future.

How Does it Feel to Be a Bishop?

After forty years of missionary work, people will ask me: "How does it feel to be a Bishop?" I did not consider it as a promotion but a means to serve with greater generosity on a much wider scale, even universal, as Bishops become members of a College that extends to all nations.

On the Shoulders of Giants

I have always been very conscious of the heritage received from our first missionaries and thus felt honored to carry on their work. Though it will never be finished, I help to move it into a new and definite phase. Like John the Baptist, our joy is complete because the bridegroom (the Church) has come of age. A new Religious Congregation, the Friars Minor Capuchins arrived and took over the Belo district. Now they have seven Capuchin priests working in the Diocese. After so many long years of hard labor, finally the diocese of Morondava has come into its own.

Progress and Growth is Happening by the Grace of God

I am sure that all the men and women who have gone ahead of us can but praise God for the marvels that he performed and how the mustard seed has grown into a large Tamarin Tree where the people of God can find rest and comfort under its shade. Progress continues in all the districts and parishes, building on the foundations that were first laid one hundred years ago by our founding La Salette Missionaries. At that time our chapels were of mud with thatched roofs. Today most of the bush chapels

**Bishop Donald on his fiftieth of Priestly Ordination during Mass
with Joe Shea and Jack Nuelle in St. Theresa's Church in Blackstone, Massachusetts**

are of cement with sheet-metal roofs, and as such require less maintenance and are more comfortable. All churches in the main center have had to be enlarged or doubled in size to accommodate the growing communities. Today, Mahabo, Miandrivazo, Belo, Ambatolahy, are all in urgent need of a second parish.

The New Church of Sts. Joachim and Anne, Spouses

In 1987 Jack inaugurated a new church in Ambatolahy, a church dedicated to Saints Joachim and Anne, Spouses, a church built in memory of his parents. Ten years later in 1998 we had to enlarge the church, not just doubling but more than tripling its size. Now, in 2014, church attendance has made even this too small. Enlarging it again would be difficult, and so land had been purchased on the eastern side of the village, along the main road where a second church will be built.

Chapter 45 – A Memorable Visit and Relics of a Saint

A very memorable event in my episcopal ministry was the visit of the relics of St. Theresa of the Child Jesus to Morondava in 2003. She is the universal patroness of the Missions. I was baptized in the Parish Church dedicated to St. Theresa in Blackstone, Massachusetts. As a child growing up, I was introduced to Little Theresa, and consequently I have a great devotion to this very popular Saint. I visited Lisieux on my way to Madagascar in 1958 and thus had felt her protection throughout my missionary life. I had built a church in her honor in Befasy and thus was very happy when I learned that the relic would be coming to Madagascar.

It took much time to coordinate the visit of her relics. I was the first bishop to ask that they be brought to the Diocese. I begged that we be given a visit. And even if it would mean only a fifteen-minute stopover at the airport, I would be most grateful. I was hoping that St. Theresa would not come to Madagascar without a visit to Morondava. When the final itinerary was published Morondava was on the list for a twenty-four-hour visit. Praise the Lord!

St. Therese of the Child Jesus (1873-1897)

The Relics of St. Theresa in Morondava

The visit would be in February which is the rainy season. It was under heavy clouds that we welcomed the two helicopters carrying the relics. Not long after it landed, we were in a major storm, with heavy rains pounding Morondava. Monday morning the relics were scheduled to fly to Tulear, but with low visibility – barely a few meters – and heavy cloud cover, the rain kept falling. It was impossible for the helicopters to take off. As a result, the relics of St. Theresa remaining in Morondava for forty-eight hours.

Those forty-eight hours were a time of extraordinary grace. People continued not only to pray but to approach the Sacrament of Reconciliation. We attribute many miracles and cures to that visit, not least of which is the new, beautiful church in honor of St. Theresa that now adorns the village of Antsakoameloka near the Morondava Airport. I had asked for fifteen minutes and St. Theresa had given us forty-eight hours. Talk about getting more than you ask for!

The relics of St. Therese of the Child Jesus carried by the Boy Scouts up to the Morondava Cathedral in 2003

Chapter 46 – Missionaries Pay a Personal Price

Many have asked us what could be the most difficult and painful thing for a missionary in a foreign country. Loneliness, of course, can be a very frequent occurrence for a missionary alone in the bush. When you come back home, exhausted, dirty, and perhaps frustrated after ten days or two weeks in the bush and you return to a dusty, musty rectory with no one with whom to share your experiences, there can be a sense of loneliness that can bring about some discouragement and even revolt against God.

Why am I alone here in the bush? What news awaits me? Good news; but no one to share it with. Or perhaps news of a loved one's death, which always causes pain and a sense of loneliness. Most of us, if not all of us, have had to grieve the death of a parent while far away from family and friends. It is a cause of great sorrow, and one of the heavy prices we accept to pay when we volunteer for a missionary vocation. We have all had to pay our dues at one time or the other.

A faithful missionary, the Malagasy people simply called him "Ray-aman-dreny Mala-la," meaning "Beloved Mother-Father"

A Parent Dies while We are in Mission

Jack was alone on a difficult two-week visit to churches in the bush of Malaimbandy in 1974. A telegram had arrived in Morondava announcing the death of his mother. A copy was later relayed by the State Police to Malaimbandy. When the local postmaster received a copy, he sent someone out to the bush to find Jack. When Jack finally received the news, he was devastated. Not only had there been no warning that his mother was dangerously ill but his mother had been dead for almost month before he got the news. He celebrated a Mass for her at the next bush church he reached. Needless to say, only Christ could know the pain that was his at that time.

Lueck was getting ready for Mass when I brought him news of his father's death. It was all part of the missionary's sacrifice. There was no question of flying half-way around the world to reach home for the funeral. The Lord was our comfort as we grieve

One Hundred Years of Service in Madagascar

This year, the years of total active service from the arrival in 1921 in Betafo, to 2021 spent in Morondava by the two remaining Americans – Jeremy and myself – add up to one hundred years. What a coincidence! Both of us desire the grace of leaving our bones here while awaiting the final resurrection. Today there are fewer and fewer missionaries in foreign fields, and often we hear the term "reverse mission." This occurs when returning missionaries can bring their experiences, joys, difficulties, hope and enthusiasm to the Catholic Communities they now serve in North America.

Besides our indigenous Malagasy La Salette Priests and Brothers serving in the Diocese of Morondava, there are presently two missionaries from France, two from America and four from Poland. And except for the Polish and Jeremy, we are all over retirement age.

This has been a long, extraordinary saga of La Salette North American Missionaries. As we write, it spreads out over one hundred years, mostly here on the West Coast of Madagascar. One way or another, there will be a Centennial Celebration in this year of Our Lord 2021, to thank God for all the graces granted through the years.

La Salette Shrine in Miandrivazo, Madagascar overlooking the Betsiriry Valley

There have been thirty-seven North Americans serving God's Church here during that century, all contributing to the growth of the Catholic Church and the spread of the Jesus' Gospel in Madagascar. The French Jesuits, who were the first Catholic Missionaries to explore the West Coast of Madagascar, really wanted to keep this area as part of their mission. God had other plans and reserved this Mission for humbler, poorer men from North America. American Lutherans have long worked in the southeastern part of Madagascar in and around Fort Dauphin, and it was only right that North American Catholics would evangelize the West Coast of Madagascar.

"You will make this known to all my people."

As we survey the whole island of Madagascar, and count over five million baptized Catholics, thousands of religious Brothers, Sisters and Priests – both Diocesan and Religious – who have zealously served God here in the Malagasy Church, we realize the contribution of the North American La Salettes will appear to be rather small.

The La Salette charism is one of poverty, simplicity, and humility, and our zealous efforts were in keeping with Mary's visit to Maximin and Melanie – two small illiterate children to whom she confided a monumental mission. From the French Alps to the West Coast of Madagascar, Mary sent her children to "...make [her] message known to all [her] people." If for no other reason, their names should never be forgotten. The fact that two La Salettes served as Bishops is an indication that Rome recognized the sacrifices and generosity of the American Provinces.

Chapter 47 – Sent on Mission and Now Passing on the Torch

On May 13, 2010 the fourth Bishop of Morondava was ordained, the first who was not a La Salette. A new chapter in the history of the Mission was beginning wherein American La Salettes would decrease and Faith in Jesus would increase. A young, dynamic Bishop, Marie Fabien Randrialamboniaina, O.C.D., from the East Coast of Madagascar is building on the foundations that we have solidly dug, and the Diocese of Morondava has become one of the most active and hopeful dioceses on this Great Red Island.

He repeats very frequently that we sowed the seed, and he is now harvesting. New men and women Religious Congregations have moved in, bringing additional new life, new hope and a powerful surge in evangelization. People marvel at the progress of these last years, as new schools are being built every year, with new parishes and churches organized to meet their needs.

It is almost unbelievable to see all that Bishop Marie Fabien has been able to accomplish with the arrival of new Religious Congregations. Not only the Hospital in Belo, but we now have a Catholic University – a long step from the first Catholic School that was started in Belo in 1932. The Morondava Diocese is about to become a pilot, model diocese for Madagascar. Every post is growing beyond all our expectations, while the Bishop has new plans every day for the development of the Diocese.

Emeritus and Titular Bishops Joseph Donald Pelletier, M.S. and Marie Fabien

In 2015 we finally had the installation of the first Contemplative Convent when the Carmelite Sisters moved into their new monastery in Marofototra. With the arrival of a contemplative order in the diocese we can say that the church is fully established and we can all say: A job well done!

The Holy Spirit is Still Moving Among Us

We began these memories by saying that we need to open our minds to greater realities when we think of Morondava, Madagascar, to move beyond lemurs and baobab trees. As the Diocese of Morondava moves beyond anything our founders could have dreamt of, the North American La Salette presence is about to come to an end. From preaching the Word of God to the Sakalava people, forming fledgling Catholic communities, helping young boys to discern their vocation to the Priesthood and Religious Life, Morondava is now an established Church, even sending its native sons to other dioceses on the island, to the French island La Réunion, and to Haiti. The new Bishop has a missionary vision, accepting the challenge of sending diocesan priests to other dioceses, and indeed, to other parts of the world.

And so, we are approaching the end or at least the very last chapter of the presence of North American La Salettes in Madagascar. In the United States we have three survivors who are part of the Morondava history:

- Jack Nuelle who, at eighty-four, is still very active in La Salette ministries at the National Shrine in Attleboro, Massachusetts, and still very dedicated to the missionary spirit that led him to Madagascar. That same spirit spurs him to accompany the Malagasy La Salette Missionaries serving in Haiti.

- Joseph Silva who, at 91, is retired in Burlington, Vermont.

- And Mark Koenig, at seventy-nine keeps busy in his retirement in Plover, Wisconsin.

Carmelite spirituality has been in the diocese since the very beginning

As I, Donald, write these final words on May 13, 2020, we just received word of the death of Brother Mark Gallant. For fifteen years he was such a vibrant part of our mission in Morondava. He died from the Coronavirus which is devastating so much of the world. Fr. Joseph Shea died in 2007 and Father Arthur Lueckenotto in 2016.

Coat of Arms of Bishop Donald Pelletier, M.S.
"I have come to Love and to Serve"

That leaves me as the sole remaining survivor here in the mission territory that can go back to when all the Founding Fathers were alive. That is the main reason why I saw an urgent need to collaborate with Jack Nuelle to have a written memorial of this outstanding 100-year history.

If today the mustard seed has grown beyond the boundaries of the Menabe Kingdom; if today the Morondava Mission is sending missionaries to other areas of the island and beyond the Indian Ocean, it is because the seed that was planted fell in fertile ground. The original seed came from Hartford, Connecticut which remains the Mother House of the Congregation in the United States. As numbers keep diminishing in North America, we can be grateful for many indigenous vocations in Madagascar.

This was not meant to be simply a history of our men in Madagascar but rather of what God and his merciful Mother, Our Lady of La Salette, have accomplished with and through these men.

"When you have done all you have been commanded to do, say: 'We are simple servants. We have done no more than our duty'" (Luke 17:10).

Majestic Baobob trees at sunset in Madagascar

www.ingramcontent.com/pod-product-compliance
Lightning Source LLC
Chambersburg PA
CBHW081848170426
43199CB00018B/2842